Study Guide

to Accompany

The Legal Environment Today

Business in Its Ethical, Regulatory, E-Commerce, and International Settings

Fifth Edition

ROGER LeROY MILLER
Institute for University Studies
Arlington, Texas

FRANK B. CROSS
Herbert D. Kelleher
Centennial Professor in Business Law
University of Texas at Austin

Prepared by

Roger LeRoy Miller
Institute for University Studies
Arlington, Texas

William Eric Hollowell
Member of
U.S. Supreme Court Bar
Minnesota State Bar
Florida State Bar

THOMSON
★ ™
SOUTH-WESTERN
WEST

Australia · Canada · Mexico · Singapore · Spain · United Kingdom · United States

THOMSON
SOUTH-WESTERN
WEST

STUDY GUIDE TO ACCOMPANY THE LEGAL ENVIRONMENT TODAY, FIFTH EDITION
BY ROGER LEROY MILLER AND FRANK B. CROSS

Vice President/Editorial Director:
Jack W. Calhoun

Publisher for Business Law & Accounting:
Rob Dewey

Acquisitions Editor:
Steven H. Silverstein, Esq.

Senior Developmental Editor:
Jan Lamar

Executive Marketing Manager:
Lisa Lysne

Production Editor:
Anne Sheroff

Technology Project Editor:
Christine Wittmer

Manufacturing Coordinator:
Charlene Taylor

Printer:
West Printing Company

For permission to use material from this text or product, contact us by

Tel (800) 730-2214
Fax (800) 730-2215

http://www.thomsonrights.com

✳ Highlights ✳
of this
Study Guide

✳ Each Chapter of this **Study Guide** includes—

  ✳ Chapter **Introduction**

  ✳ Easy to Read & Understand, Comprehensive **Outline**

  ✳ **True-False** Questions

  ✳ **Fill-In** Questions

  ✳ **Multiple-Choice** Questions

  ✳ **Short Essay** Questions

  ✳ **Issue Spotters**—hypothetical fact problems & black letter law questions on key issues

✳ Each Unit of this **Study Guide** ends with a **Cumulative Hypothetical** and corresponding **Multiple-Choice** Questions

✳ This **Study Guide** also contains an **Answer Appendix** with answers to all of the Questions & explanations of the Answers

Table of Contents

To the Student

This *Study Guide* is designed to help you read and understand *The Legal Environment Today,* **Fifth Edition**.

How the *Study Guide* Can Help You

This *Study Guide* can help you maximize your learning, subject to the constraints and the amount of time you can allot to this course. There are at least six specific ways in which you can benefit from using this guide.

1. The *Study Guide* can help you decide which topics are the most important. Because there are so many topics analyzed in each chapter, many students become confused about what is essential and what is not. You cannot, of course, learn everything; this *Study Guide* can help you concentrate on the crucial topics in each chapter.

2. If you are forced to miss a class, you can use this *Study Guide* to help you learn the material discussed in your absence.

3. There is a possibility that the questions that you are required to answer in this *Study Guide* are representative of the types of questions that you will be asked during examinations.

4. You can use this *Study Guide* to help you review for examinations.

5. This *Study Guide* can help you decide whether you really understand the material. Don't wait until examination time to find out!

6. Finally, the questions in this *Study Guide* will help you develop critical thinking skills that you can use in other classes and throughout your career.

The Contents of the *Study Guide*

The legal environment sometimes is considered a difficult subject because it uses a specialized vocabulary and also takes most people much time and effort to learn. Those who work with and teach the legal environment believe that the subject matter is exciting and definitely worthy of your efforts. Your text, *The Legal Environment Today,* **Fifth Edition**, and this student learning guide have been written for the precise purpose of helping you learn the most important aspects of the legal environment. We always try to keep you, the student, in mind.

Every chapter includes the following sections:

1. What This Chapter Is About: You are introduced to the main subject matter of each chapter in this section.

2. Chapter Outline: Using an outline format, the salient points in each chapter are presented.

3. True-False Questions: Ten true-false questions are included for each chapter. Generally, these questions test knowledge of terminology and principles. The answers are given at the back of the book. Whenever an answer is false, the reasons why it is false are presented at the back of the book also.

4. Fill-in Questions: Here you are asked to choose between two alternatives for each space that needs to be filled in. Answers are included at the back of the book.

5. Multiple-Choice Questions: Ten multiple-choice questions are given for each chapter. The answers, along with an explanation, are included at the back of this book.

6. Short Essay Questions: Two essay questions are presented for each chapter.

7. Issue Spotters: These questions alert you to certain principles within the chapter. Brief answers to these questions are included at the end of this text.

How to Use this Study Guide

What follows is a recommended strategy for improving your grade in your legal environment class. It may seem like a lot of work, but the payoffs will be high. Try the entire program for the first three or four chapters. If you then feel you can skip some steps safely, try doing so and see what happens.

For each chapter we recommend you follow the sequence of steps below:

1. Read the What This Chapter Is About and Chapter Outline.

2. Read any of the Concept Summaries that may be included in the chapter you are studying in *The Legal Environment Today*, **Fifth Edition**.

3. Read about half the textbook chapter (unless it is very long), being sure to underline only the most important topics (which you should be able to recognize after having read no more than two chapter outlines in this *Study Guide*). Put a check mark by the material that you do not understand.

4. If you find the textbook's chapter easy to understand, you might want to finish reading it. Otherwise, rest for a sufficient period before you read the second half of the chapter. Again, be sure to underline only the most important points and to put a check mark by the material you find difficult to understand.

5. After you have completed the entire textbook chapter, take a break. Then read only what you have underlined throughout the entire chapter.

6. Now concentrate on the difficult material, for which you have left check marks. Reread this material and *think about it*; you will find that it is very exciting to figure out difficult material on your own.

7. Now do the True-False Questions, Fill-In Questions, and Multiple-Choice Questions. Compare your answers with those at the back of this book. Make a note of the questions you have missed and find the pages in your textbook upon which these questions are based. If you still don't understand, ask your instructor.

8. If you still have time, do one or both of the essay questions.

9. Before your examination, study your class notes. Then review the chapter outline in the text. Reread the Chapter Outline in this *Study Guide*, then redo all of the questions within each chapter. Compare your answers with the answers at the back of this *Study Guide*. Identify your problem areas and reread the relevant pages in *The Legal Environment Today*, **Fifth Edition**. Think through the answers on your own.

If you have followed the strategy outlined above, you should feel sufficiently confident and be relaxed enough to do well on your exam.

Study Skills for *The Legal Environment Today*, **Fifth Edition**

Every student has a different way to study. We give several study hints below that we think will help any student to master the textbook *The Legal Environment Today*, **Fifth Edition**. These skills involve outlining, marking, taking notes, and summarizing. You may not need to use all these skills. Nonetheless, if you do improve your ability to use them, you will be able to understand more easily the information in *The Legal Environment Today*, **Fifth Edition**.

MAKING AN OUTLINE

An outline is simply a method for organizing information. The reason an outline can be helpful is that it shows how concepts relate to each other. Outlining can be done as part of your reading or at the end of your reading, or as a rereading of each section within a chapter before you go on to the next section. Even if you do not believe that you need to outline, our experience has been that the act of *physically* writing an outline for a chapter helps most students to improve greatly their ability to retain the material in *The Legal Environment Today*, **Fifth Edition** and master it, thereby obtaining a higher grade in the class, with less effort.

To make an effective outline you have to be selective. Outlines that contain all the information in the text are not very useful. Your objective in outlining is to identify main concepts and to subordinate details to those main concepts. Therefore, your first goal is to *identify the main concepts in each section*. Often the large, first-level headings within your textbook are sufficient as identifiers of the major concepts within each section. You may decide, however, that you want to phrase an identifier in a way that is more meaningful to you. In any event, your outline should consist of several levels written in a standard outline format. The most important concepts are assigned a roman numeral; the second most important a capital letter; the third most important, numbers; and the fourth most important, lower-case letters. Even if you make an outline that is no more than the headings in the text, you will be studying more efficiently than you would be otherwise. As we stated above, the process of physically writing the words will help you master the material.

MARKING A TEXT

From kindergarten through high school you typically did not own your own textbooks. They were made available by the school system. You were told not to mark in them. Now that you own your own text for a course, your learning can be greatly improved by marking your text. There is a trade-off here. The more you mark up your textbook, the less you will receive from your bookstore when you sell it back at the end of the semester. The benefit is a better understanding of the subject matter, and the cost is the reduction in the price you receive for the resale of the text. Additionally, if you want a text that you can mark with your own notations, you necessarily have to buy a new one or a used one that has no markings. Both carry a higher price tag than a used textbook with markings. Again there is a trade-off.

Different Ways of Marking The most commonly used form of marking is to underline important points. The second most commonly used method is to use a felt-tipped highlighter, or marker, in yellow or some other transparent color. Marking also includes circling, numbering, using arrows, brief notes, or any other method that allows you to remember things when you go back to skim the pages in your textbook prior to an exam.

Why Marking Is Important Marking is important for the same reason that outlining is—it helps you to organize the information in the text. It allows you to become an *active* participant in the mastery of the material. Researchers have shown that the physical act of marking, just like the physical act of outlining, helps you better retain the material. The better the material is organized in your mind, the more you will remember. There are two types of readers—passive and active. The active reader outlines or marks. Active readers typically do better on exams. Perhaps one of the reasons that active readers retain more is because the physical act of outlining and/or marking requires greater concentration. It is through greater concentration that more is remembered.

Points to Remember When Marking

1. Read one section at a time before you do any extensive marking. You can't mark a section until you know what is important and you can't know what is important until you read the whole section.

2. Don't over mark. Just as an outline cannot contain everything that is in a text (or in a lecture), marking can't be of the whole book. Don't fool yourself into thinking you've done a good job just because each page is filled up with arrows, asterisks, circles, and underlines. When you go back to review the material you won't remember what was important. The key is *selective* activity. Mark each page in a way that allows you to see the most important points at a glance. You can follow up your marking by writing out more in your subject outline.

HOW TO STUDY AND TAKE EXAMS

There is basically one reason why you have purchased the *Study Guide*—to improve your exam grade. By using this *Study Guide* assiduously, you will have the confidence to take your mid-terms and final examinations and to do well. The *Study Guide*, however, should not just be used a day before each exam. Rather, the guide is most helpful if you use it at the time that you read the chapter. That is to say, after you read a chapter in **The Legal Environment Today, Fifth Edition** you should directly go to the appropriate chapter in the *Study Guide*. This systematic review technique is the most effective study technique you can use.

Besides learning the concepts in each chapter as well as possible, there are additional strategies for taking exams. You need to know in advance what type of exam you are going to take—essay or objective or both. You need to know which reading materials and lectures will be covered. For both objective and essay exams (but more importantly for the former) you need to know if there is a penalty for guessing incorrectly. If there is, your strategy will be different: you will usually only mark what you are certain of. Finally, you need to know how much time will be allowed for the exam.

FOLLOWING DIRECTIONS

Students are often in a hurry to start an exam so they take little time to read the instructions. The instructions can be critical, however. In a multiple-choice exam, for example, if there is no indication that there is a penalty for guessing, then you should never leave a question unanswered. Even if there only remains a few minutes at the end of the exam, you should guess for those questions about which you are uncertain.

Additionally, you need to know the weight given to each section of an exam. In a typical multiple-choice exam, all questions have equal weight. In some exams, particularly those involving essay questions, different parts of the exam carry different weights. You should use these weights to apportion your time accordingly. If an essay part of an exam accounts for only 20 percent of the total points on the exam, you should not spend 60 percent of your time on the essay.

You need to make sure you are answering the question correctly. Some exams require a No. 2 lead pencil to fill in the dots on a machine-graded answer sheet. Other exams require underlining or circling. In short, you have to look at the instructions carefully.

Lastly, check to make sure that you have all the pages of the examination. If you are uncertain, ask the instructor or the exam proctor. It is hard to justify not having done your exam correctly because you failed to answer all the questions. Simply stating that you did not have them will pose a problem for both you and your instructor. Don't take a chance. Double check to make sure.

TAKING OBJECTIVE EXAMINATIONS

The most important point to discover initially with any objective test is if there is a penalty for guessing. If there is none, you have nothing to lose by guessing. In contrast, if a half-point is subtracted for each incorrect answer, then you probably should not answer any question for which you are purely guessing.

Students usually commit one of two errors when they read objective-exam questions: (1) they read things into the questions that don't exist, or (2) they skip over words or phrases.

Most test questions include key words such as:

• all
• always
• never
• only

If you miss these key words you will be missing the "trick" part of the question. Also, you must look for questions that are only *partly* correct, particularly if you are answering true/false questions.

Never answer a question without reading all of the alternatives. More than one of them may be correct. If more than one of them seems correct, make sure you select the answer that seems the most correct.

Whenever the answer to an objective question is not obvious, start with the process of elimination. Throw out the answers that are clearly incorrect. Even with objective exams in which there is a penalty for guessing, if you can throw out several obviously incorrect answers, then you may wish to guess among the remaining ones because your probability of choosing the correct answer is high.

Typically, the easiest way to eliminate incorrect answers is to look for those that are meaningless, illogical, or inconsistent. Often test authors put in choices that make perfect sense and are indeed true, but they are not the answer to the question under study.

Acknowledgments

We wish to thank Suzanne Jasin of K & M Consulting for her expert design and composition of this guide.

We welcome comments and criticisms to help us make this guide even more useful. All errors are our sole responsibility.

Roger LeRoy Miller
Eric Hollowell

Chapter 1:
The Legal and International Foundations

WHAT THIS CHAPTER IS ABOUT

The first chapters in Unit 1 provide the background for the entire course. Chapter 1 sets the stage. From this chapter, you must understand that (1) the law is a set of general rules, (2) in applying these general rules, a judge cannot fit a case to suit a rule, but must fit (or find) a rule to suit the case, and (3) in fitting (or finding) a rule, a judge must also supply reasons for the decision.

CHAPTER OUTLINE

I. THE NATURE OF LAW
Law consists of enforceable rules governing relationships among individuals and between individuals and their society.

A. THE NATURAL LAW TRADITION
Natural law is a system of moral and ethical principles that are believed to be inherent in human nature and discoverable by humans through the use of their natural intelligence.

B. LEGAL POSITIVISM
Legal positivists believe that there is no higher law than a nation's positive law (the law created by a particular society at a particular point in time). The law is the law and must be obeyed.

C. THE HISTORICAL SCHOOL
The historical school looks to the past to discover what the principles of contemporary law should be. Adherents strictly follow past decisions.

D. LEGAL REALISM
Legal realists believe that in making decisions, judges are influenced by their own beliefs, the application of principles should be tempered by each case's circumstances, and extra-legal sources should be consulted.

II. BUSINESS ACTIVITIES AND THE LEGAL ENVIRONMENT
The law is split into different topics to make it easier to study, but more than one of those areas of the law can affect individual business decisions. Whether an activity is ethical is an important part of deciding whether to engage in it, but simply complying with the law may not meet all ethical obligations.

III. SOURCES OF AMERICAN LAW

A. CONSTITUTIONAL LAW
The U.S. Constitution distributes power among the branches of government. It is the supreme law of the land. Any law that conflicts with it is invalid. The states also have constitutions, but the federal constitution prevails if their provisions conflict.

B. STATUTORY LAW
Statutes and ordinances are enacted by Congress and by state and local legislative bodies. Uniform laws and model codes are created by panels of experts and scholars and adopted at the option of each state's legislature.

C. **ADMINISTRATIVE LAW**

Administrative law consists of the rules and regulations issued by administrative agencies, which derive their authority from the legislative and executive branches of government.

D. **CASE LAW AND COMMON LAW DOCTRINES**

Case law includes courts' interpretations of constitutional provisions, statutes, and administrative rules. Because statutes often codify common law rules, courts often rely on the common law as a guide to the intent and purpose of a statute. Case law governs all areas not covered by statutes.

IV.   THE COMMON LAW TRADITION

A. **COMMON LAW**

The American legal system is a **common law** system.

B. *STARE DECISIS*

The use of precedent in a common law system is known as the doctrine of ***stare decisis***. *Stare decisis* makes the legal system more efficient, just, uniform, stable, and predictable. When there is no precedent, a court may look at other legal principles and policies, social values, or scientific data.

C. **EQUITABLE REMEDIES**

As a rule, courts grant an equitable remedy only when the remedy at law is inadequate.

1. **Remedies at Law**

Remedies at law include awards of land, money, and items of value. A jury trial is available only in an action at law.

2. **Remedies in Equity**

Remedies in equity include decrees of specific performance, injunctions, and rescission. Decisions to award equitable remedies are guided by equitable maxims.

V.   CLASSIFICATIONS OF LAW

A. **SUBSTANTIVE AND PROCEDURAL LAW**

Substantive law includes laws that define, describe, regulate, and create rights and duties. *Procedural law* includes rules for enforcing those rights.

B. **CRIMINAL AND CIVIL LAW**

Criminal law regulates relationships between individuals and society. *Civil law* regulates relationships between individuals.

C. **NATIONAL AND INTERNATIONAL LAW**

1. **National Law**

National law is the law of a particular nation. Laws vary from country to country, but generally each nation has either a common law or civil law system. A common law system, like ours, is based on case law. A civil law system is based on codified law (statutes).

2. **International Law**

International law consists of written and unwritten laws observed by independent nations and governing the acts of individuals and governments. Sources include treaties and international organizations.

D. **CYBERLAW**

Cyberlaw is the emerging body of law (court decisions, new and amended statutes, etc.) that governs Internet transactions.

VI.   FINDING THE LAW

A. FINDING STATUTORY AND ADMINISTRATIVE LAW

1. Publication of Statutes
Federal statutes are arranged by date of enactment in *United States Statutes at Large*. State statutes are collected in similar state publications. Statutes are also published in codified form (the form in which they appear in the federal and state codes) in other publications.

2. Finding a Statute in a Publication
Statutes are usually referred to in their codified form. In the codes, laws are compiled by subject. For example, the *United States Code* (U.S.C.) arranges by subject most federal laws. Each subject is assigned a title number and each statute a section number within a title.

3. Publication of Administrative Rules
Rules and regulations adopted by federal administrative agencies are published initially in the *Federal Register*. They are also compiled by subject in the *Code of Federal Regulations* (C.F.R.).

4. Finding an Administrative Rule in a Publication
In the C.F.R., administrative rules are arranged by subject. Each subject is assigned a title number and each rule a section number within a title.

B. FINDING CASE LAW

1. Publication of Court Opinions
State appellate court opinions are often published by the state in consecutively numbered volumes. They may also be published in units of the *National Reporter System*, by West Publishing Company. Federal court opinions appear in other West publications.

2. Finding a Court Opinion in a Publication
After a decision is published, it can be referred to by the name of the case and the volume, name, and page number of one or more reporters. This information is called the **citation**.

C. READING AND UNDERSTANDING CASE LAW

1. Plaintiffs and Defendants
In the title of a case (*Adams v. Jones*), the *v.* means **versus** (against). Adams is the **plaintiff** (the person who filed the suit) and Jones the **defendant** (the person against whom the suit was brought). An appellate court may place the name of the appellant first (*Jones v. Adams.*).

2. Appellants and Appellees
An **appellant** (or **petitioner**) is the party who appeals a case to another court or jurisdiction from the one in which the case was brought. An **appellee** (or **respondent**) is the party against whom an appeal is taken.

3. Judges and Justices
These terms are designations given to judges in different courts.

4. Decisions and Opinions
An opinion contains a court's reasons for its decision, the rules of law that apply, and the judgment.

TRUE-FALSE QUESTIONS

(Answers at the Back of the Book)

__*T*__ 1. Law is a body of enforceable rules governing relationships among individuals and between individuals and their society.

__*F*__ 2. Legal positivists believe that law should reflect universal moral and ethical principles that are part of human nature.

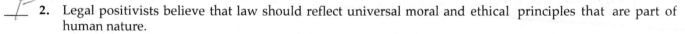

T 3. The doctrine of *stare decisis* obligates judges to follow precedents established within their jurisdictions.

T 4. Common law develops at least in part from rules of law announced in court decisions.

T 5. Statutory law is legislation.

F 6. The U.S. Constitution takes precedence over a conflicting provision in a state constitution.

F 7. Congress enacted the Uniform Commercial Code for adoption by the states.

F 8. Criminal law covers disputes between persons, and between persons and their governments.

T 9. In most states, the same courts can grant legal or equitable remedies.

F 10. A citation includes the name of the judge who decided the case.

FILL-IN QUESTIONS

(Answers at the Back of the Book)

The common law system, on which the American legal system is based, involves the application of principles applied in earlier cases _____ (with similar facts/whether or not the facts are similar). This use of previous case law, or _____ (precedent/preeminent), is known as the doctrine of *stare decisis*, and _____ _____ (emphasizes a flexible/permits a predictable) resolution of cases.

MULTIPLE-CHOICE QUESTIONS

(Answers at the Back of the Book)

D 1. Adam is a legal positivist. Adam believes that

   a. the law should be applied the same in all cases in all circumstances.
   b. the law should reflect universal principles that are part of human nature.
   c. the law should strictly follow decisions made in past cases.
   d. the written law of a society at a particular time is most significant.

B 2. In a suit between Best Products, Inc., and Central Sales Corporation, the court applies the doctrine of *stare decisis*. This means that the court follows rules of law established by

   a. all courts.
   b. courts of higher rank only.
   c. courts of lower rank only.
   d. no courts.

D 3. In a given case, most courts may grant

   a. equitable remedies only.
   b. legal remedies only.
   c. equitable or legal remedies, but not both.
   d. equitable remedies, legal remedies, or both.

C 4. The U.S. Constitution takes precedence over

   a. a provision in a state constitution or statute only.
   b. a state supreme court decision only.
   c. a state constitution, statute, and court decision.
   d. none of the above.

5. In a suit between Delta Data Company and Eagle Information, Inc., the court applies the doctrine of *stare decisis*. This requires the court to find cases that, compared to the case before it, has

   a. entirely different facts.
   b. no facts, only conclusions of law.
   c. precisely identical facts.
   d. similar facts.

6. In a suit between Fine Manufacturing Company and Great Goods, Inc., the court orders a rescission. This is

   a. an action to cancel a contract and return the parties to the positions they held before the contract's formation.
   b. an award of damages.
   c. an order to do or refrain from doing a particular act.
   d. an order to perform what was promised.

7. Case law includes interpretations of federal and state

   a. administrative rules and statutes only.
   b. constitutions only.
   c. administrative rules, statutes, and constitutions.
   d. none of the above.

8. Civil law concerns

   a. disputes between persons, and between persons and their governments.
   b. only laws that define, describe, regulate, and create rights and duties.
   c. only laws that establish methods for enforcing rights.
   d. wrongs committed against society for which society demands redress.

9. The sources of international law include

   a. customs that have evolved among nations in their relations only.
   b. international organizations and treaties only.
   c. laws of individual nations only.
   d. international customs, organizations, and treaties, and national law.

10. A concurring opinion, written by one of the judges who decides a case before a multi-judge panel, is

    a. an opinion that is written for the entire court.
    b. an opinion that outlines only the views of the majority.
    c. a separate opinion that agrees with the court's ruling but for different reasons.
    d. a separate opinion that does not agree with court's ruling.

SHORT ESSAY QUESTIONS

1. What is the primary function of law, and how does the law accomplish it?

2. What is *stare decisis*? Why is it important?

ISSUE SPOTTERS

(Answers at the Back of the Book)

1.   Under what circumstance might a judge rely on case law to determine the intent and purpose of a statute?

2.   The First Amendment provides protection for the free exercise of religion. A state legislature enacts a law that outlaws all religions that do not derive from the Judeo-Christian tradition. Is this law valid within that state? Why or why not?

3.   Apples & Oranges Corporation learns that a federal administrative agency is considering a rule that will have a negative impact on the firm's ability to do business. Does the firm have any opportunity to express its opinion about the pending rule?

Chapter 2:
Ethics and Professional Responsibility

WHAT THIS CHAPTER IS ABOUT

The concepts set out in this chapter include the nature of business ethics and the relationship between ethics and business. Ultimately, the goal of this chapter is to provide you with basic tools for analyzing ethical issues in a business context.

CHAPTER OUTLINE

I. BUSINESS ETHICS
Ethics is the study of what constitutes right and wrong behavior. Ethics focuses on morality and the application of moral principles in everyday life.

A. WHAT IS BUSINESS ETHICS?
Business ethics focuses on what constitutes ethical behavior in the world of business. Business ethics is *not* a separate kind of ethics.

B. WHY IS BUSINESS ETHICS IMPORTANT?
An understanding of business ethics is important to the long-run viability of a business, the well being of its officers and directors, and the welfare of its employees.

II. SETTING THE RIGHT ETHICAL TONE
Some unethical conduct is founded on the lack of sanctions.

A. THE IMPORTANCE OF ETHICAL LEADERSHIP
Management must set and apply ethical standards to which they are committed. Employees will likely follow their example. Ethical conduct can be furthered by not tolerating unethical behavior, setting realistic employee goals, and periodic employee review.

B. CREATING ETHICAL CODES OF CONDUCT
Most large corporations have codes of conduct that indicate the firm's commitment to legal compliance and to the welfare of those who are affected by corporate decisions and practices. Large firms may also emphasize ethics in other ways (for example, with training programs).

C. CORPORATE COMPLIANCE PROGRAMS
Components of a comprehensive corporate ethical-compliance program include an ethical code of conduct, an ethics committee, training programs, and internal audits to monitor compliance. These components should be integrated. The Sarbanes-Oxley Act of 2002 requires firms to set up confidential systems for employees to report suspected illegal or unethical financial practices.

D. CONFLICTS AND TRADE-OFFS
A firm's duty to its shareholders should be weighed against duties to others who may have a greater stake in a particular decision. For example, an employer should consider whether it has an ethical duty to loyal, long-term employees not to replace them with workers who will accept lower pay and whether this duty prevails over a duty to improve profitability by restructuring.

III. BUSINESS ETHICS AND THE LAW
The minimal acceptable standard for ethical business behavior is compliance with the law. Ethical standards, such as those in a company's policies or codes of ethics, must also guide decisions.

A. LAWS REGULATING BUSINESS
Because there are many laws regulating business, it is possible to violate one without realizing it. Ignorance of the law is no excuse.

B. "GRAY AREAS" IN THE LAW
There are many "gray areas" in which it is difficult to predict how a court will rule. The best course is to act responsibly and in good faith.

C. TECHNOLOGICAL DEVELOPMENTS AND LEGAL UNCERTAINTIES
How laws apply in the context of cyberspace is not certain.

IV. APPROACHES TO ETHICAL REASONING
Ethical reasoning is the process by which an individual examines a situation according to his or her moral convictions or ethical standards. Fundamental ethical reasoning approaches include the following.

A. DUTY-BASED ETHICS

1. Religious Ethical Standards
Religious standards provide that when an act is prohibited by religious teachings, it is unethical and should not be undertaken, regardless of the consequences. Religious standards also involve compassion.

2. Kantian Ethics
Immanual Kant believed that people should be respected because they are qualitatively different from other physical objects. Kant's *categorical imperative* is that individuals should evaluate their actions in light of what would happen if everyone acted the same way.

3. The Principle of Rights
According to the principle that persons have rights (to life and liberty, for example), a key factor in determining whether a business decision is ethical is how that decision affects the rights of others, including employees, customers and society.

B. OUTCOME-BASED ETHICS: UTILITARIANISM
Utilitarianism is a belief that an action is ethical if it produces the greatest good for the greatest number. This approach is often criticized, because it tends to reduce the welfare of people to plus and minus signs on a cost-benefit worksheet.

V. PROFESSIONAL RESPONSIBILITY
Professionals must exercise the standard of care, knowledge, and judgment generally accepted by members of their professional group.

A. ACCOUNTANT'S DUTY OF CARE

1. Standard of Care
Accountants must comply with generally accepted accounting principles (GAAP) and generally accepted auditing standards (GAAS) (though compliance does not guarantee relief from liability). If an accountant conforms to GAAP and acts in good faith, he or she will not be liable to a client for incorrect judgment.

2. Violations of GAAP and GAAS
A violation of GAAP and GAAS is considered *prima facie* evidence of negligence. Compliance, however, does not necessarily relieve an accountant of liability: an accountant may be held to a higher standard established by state statute and by judicial decisions.

B. ATTORNEY'S DUTY OF CARE

1. **Standard of Care**
   All attorneys owe a duty to provide competent and diligent representation. The standard is that of a reasonably competent general practitioner of ordinary skill, experience, and capacity.

2. **Liability for Malpractice**
   Failing to exercise reasonable care and professional judgment breaches the duty of care.

C. STATUTORY DUTIES OF ACCOUNTANTS

1. **The Duty of Accountants under Securities Laws**
   An accountant may be liable to anyone who buys a security for misstatements and omissions of material facts in its registration statement (which they often prepare for filing with the Securities and Exchange Commission (SEC) before an offering of securities—see Chapter 31). An accountant must exercise due diligence. Failure to follow GAAP and GAAS is proof of a lack of due diligence. There may also be liability for false statements under the Securities Exchange Act of 1934.

2. **Potential Criminal Liability of Accountants**
   An accountant may be found criminally liable for violations of the Securities Act of 1933, the Securities Exchange Act of 1934, the Internal Revenue Code, and the Sarbanes-Oxley Act of 2002. Under the Sarbanes-Oxley Act, for example, an accountant's false or misleading certified audit statement may result in a fine of up to $5 million and imprisonment of up to twenty years.

VI. COMPANIES THAT DEFY THE RULES

A. ENRON'S GROWTH AND DEMISE
Managers took advantage of accounting standards to overestimate future earnings, which resulted in inflated reports of current earnings. To maintain these exaggerations, the company created subsidiaries to which it could shift unreported losses and assets with inflated values. Many of these shifts occurred outside the U.S. to avoid federal income taxes. When questioned, management refused to investigate and reveal financial improprieties.

B. THE ENRON LEGACY
The unethical conduct resulted in the single largest bankruptcy of a U.S. business firm. This misconduct affected the firm's managers, employees, suppliers, and shareholders, and the community and society in general.

C. MERCK & COMPANY—A BRIEF HISTORY OF VIOXX
The Food and Drug Administration (FDA) gave Vioxx an abbreviated review before allowing Merck to market the drug. Within a few years, studies revealed that the drug was riskier than was previously believed, and Merck voluntarily recalled the product.

D. MERCK'S AWARENESS OF THE RISKS OF VIOXX
Apparently, the FDA and others had alerted Merck Vioxx's possibly dangerous side effects long before the company undertook serious studies of the drug and eventually recalled it. The FDA required Merck to send letters to physicians to correct false or misleading impressions and information.

E. MERCK'S CHOICE
Merck generally continued to maintain that Vioxx as safe until proved otherwise. Company shareholders lost billions in the value of their stock after the product was recalled.

F. THE DEBATE CONTINUES
At what point does a company have an ethical duty to act when presented with evidence that its product may be harmful?

VII. THE SARBANES-OXLEY ACT OF 2002

This act imposes requirements on a public accounting firm that provides auditing services to an *issuer* (a certain company that sells securities to investors).

A. THE PUBLIC COMPANY ACCOUNTING OVERSIGHT BOARD

This board, which reports to the Securities and Exchange Commission, oversees the audit of public companies subject to securities laws to protect public investors and ensure that public accounting firms comply with the provisions of the act.

B. APPLICABILITY TO PUBLIC ACCOUNTING FIRMS

Public accounting firms are firms and associated persons that are "engaged in the practice of public accounting or preparing or issuing audit reports."

1. Nonaudit Services

It is unlawful to perform for an issuer both audit and non-audit services, which include bookkeeping for an audit client, financial systems design and implementation, appraisal services, fairness opinions, management functions, and investment services.

2. Audit Services

A public accounting firm cannot provide audit services to an issuer if the lead audit partner or the reviewing partner provided those services to the issuer in each of the prior five years, or if the issuer's chief executive officer, chief financial officer, chief accounting officer, or controller worked for the auditor and participated in an audit of the issuer within the preceding year.

3. Reports to an Issuer's Audit Committee

These reports must be timely and indicate critical accounting policies and practices, as well as alternatives discussed, and other communications, with the issuer's management.

C. DOCUMENT DESTRUCTION

The act prohibits destroying or falsifying records to obstruct or influence a federal investigation or in relation to a bankruptcy. Penalties include fines and imprisonment up to twenty years.

VIII. BUSINESS ETHICS ON A GLOBAL LEVEL

A. MONITORING THE EMPLOYMENT PRACTICES OF FOREIGN SUPPLIERS

Concerns include the treatment of foreign workers who make goods imported and sold in the United States by U.S. firms. Should a U.S firm refuse to deal with certain suppliers or monitor their workplaces to make sure that the workers are not being mistreated?

B. THE FOREIGN CORRUPT PRACTICES ACT

The Foreign Corrupt Practices Act (FCPA) of 1977 applies to U.S. companies and accountants.

1. U.S. Companies

The FCPA also covers business firms' directors, officers, shareholders, employees, and agents.

a. What Is Prohibited?

The FCPA prohibits the bribery of most foreign government officials to get them to act in their official capacities to provide business opportunities.

b. What Is Permitted?

The FCPA permits payments to (1) minor officials whose duties are ministerial, (2) foreign officials if the payments are lawful in the foreign country, or (3) private foreign companies or other third parties unless the U.S. firm knows payments will be made to a foreign government.

2. Accountants

a. **What Is Required?**
All companies must (1) keep detailed records that "accurately and fairly" reflect the company's financial activities and (2) have an accounting system that provides "reasonable assurance" that all transactions are accounted for and legal.

b. **What Is Prohibited?**
The FCPA prohibits false statements to accountants and false entries in accounts.

3. **Penalties**
Firms: fines up to $2 million. Officers or directors: fines up to $100,000 (cannot be paid by the company); imprisonment up to five years.

4. **Other Nations Denounce Bribery**
A treaty signed by members of the Organization for Economic Cooperation and Development makes the bribery of foreign officials a crime. Other international institutions are also working against bribery.

TRUE-FALSE QUESTIONS

(Answers at the Back of the Book)

_T_ 1. Ethics is the study of what constitutes right and wrong behavior.

_T_ 2. The *minimal* acceptable standard for ethical behavior is compliance with the law.

_F_ 3. According to utilitarianism, it does not matter how many people benefit from an act.

_T_ 4. The best course towards accomplishing legal and ethical behavior is to act responsibly and in good faith.

_F_ 5. The legality of an action is always clear.

_T_ 6. To foster ethical behavior among employees, managers should apply ethical standards to which they are committed.

_F_ 7. If an act is legal, it is ethical.

_T_ 8. Professionals must exercise the standard of care, knowledge, and judgment set by codes of ethics, court decisions, and state statutes.

_F_ 9. Compliance with GAAP and GAAS will relieve an accountant of liability.

_F_ 10. Bribery of public officials is only an ethical issue.

FILL-IN QUESTIONS

(Answers at the Back of the Book)

_____ (Religious standards/ Kantian ethics/ The principle of rights) provide(s) that when an act is prohibited by religious teachings, it is unethical and should not be undertaken, regardless of the consequences. According to _____ (religious standards/ Kantian ethics/ the principle of rights), individuals should evaluate their actions in light of what would happen if everyone acted the same way. According to _____ (religious standards/ Kantian ethics/ the principle of rights), a key factor in determining whether a business decision is ethical is how that decision affects the rights of others.

MULTIPLE-CHOICE QUESTIONS

(Answers at the Back of the Book)

____ 1. Beth is a marketing executive for Consumer Products Company. Compared to Beth's personal actions, her business actions require the application of

    a. more complex ethical standards.
    b. simpler ethical standards.
    c. the same ethical standards.
    d. no ethical standards.

____ 2. Pete, an employee of Quality Sales, Inc., takes a duty-based approach to ethics. Pete believes that he must

    a. achieve the greatest good for the most people.
    b. avoid unethical behavior regardless of the consequences.
    c. conform to society's standards.
    d. place his employer's interest first.

____ 3. Jill, chief financial officer of Kwik Delivery Company, adopts religious ethical standards. These involve an element of

    a. compassion.
    b. cost-benefit analysis.
    c. discretion.
    d. utilitarianism.

____ 4. Eve, an employee of First Federal Bank, takes an outcome-based approach to ethics. Eve believes that she must

    a. achieve the greatest good for the most people.
    b. avoid unethical behavior regardless of the consequences.
    c. conform to society's standards.
    d. place his employer's interest first.

____ 5. Don is a manager with Engineering Aviation Systems. At a company ethics meeting, Don's most effective argument against utilitarianism is that it

    a. gives profits priority over costs. ·
    b. ignores the practical costs of a given set of circumstances.
    c. justifies human costs that many persons find unacceptable.
    d. requires complex cost-benefit analyses of simple situations.

____ 6. Tina, the president of United Sales, Inc., tries to ensure that United's actions are legal and ethical. To ensure this result, the best course of Tina and United is to act in

    a. good faith.
    b. ignorance of the law.
    c. regard for the firm's shareholders only.
    d. their own self interest.

_____ 7. Greg, an accountant, prepares for Fine Distribution, Inc. (FDI), a financial statement that omits a material fact. The statement is included in FDI's registration statement, which Holly reads before buying FDI stock on which she later suffers a loss. Greg may avoid liability to Holly if he

   a. did not have a contract with Holly
   b. did not prepare the registration statement
   c. exercised due diligence in preparing the financial statement.
   d. lacked criminal intent.

_____ 8. Lily is injured in an auto accident, but Mega Insurance Company refuses to pay her claim. She hires Nick, an attorney, who fails to file a suit against Mega before the time for filing runs out. Lily sues Nick. She will

   a. lose, because clients are responsible for their own losses.
   b. lose, because Nick could not reasonably have been expected to file on time.
   c. win, because Mega refused to pay her claim.
   d. win, because Nick committed malpractice.

_____ 9. Alan, an executive with Beta Corporation, follows the "principle of rights" theory, under which an action may be ethical depending on how it affects

   a. the right determination under a cost-benefit analysis.
   b. the right of Alan to maintain his dignity.
   c. the right of Beta to make a profit.
   d. the rights of others.

_____ 10. Gamma, Inc., a U.S. corporation, makes a side payment to the minister of commerce of another country for a favorable business contract. In the United States, this payment would be considered

   a. illegal only.
   b. unethical only.
   c. illegal and unethical.
   d. none of the above.

SHORT ESSAY QUESTIONS

1. What is the difference between legal and ethical standards? How are legal standards affected by ethical standards?

2. What is the accountants' duty of care in the context of their role in business financial systems?

ISSUE SPOTTERS

(Answers at the Back of the Book)

1. If, like Robin Hood, a person robs the rich to pay the poor, does his or her benevolent intent make his or her actions ethical?

2. Delta Tools, Inc., markets a product that under some circumstances is capable of seriously injuring consumers. Does Delta owe an ethical duty to remove this product from the market, even if the injuries result only from misuse?

3.   Acme Corporation decides to respond to what it sees as a moral obligation to correct for past discrimination by adjusting pay differences among its employees. Does this raise an ethical conflict between Acme's employees? Between Acme and its employees? Between Acme and its shareholders?

Chapter 3:
Courts and Alternative Dispute Resolution

WHAT THIS CHAPTER IS ABOUT

This chapter explains which courts have power to hear what disputes and when and outlines what happens before, during, and after a civil trial. The chapter also covers alternative dispute resolution and online dispute resolution.

CHAPTER OUTLINE

I. **THE JUDICIARY'S ROLE IN AMERICAN GOVERNMENT**
   The power of **judicial review**: the courts can decide whether the laws or actions of the executive branch and the legislative branch are constitutional.

II. **BASIC JUDICIAL REQUIREMENTS**

   A. **JURISDICTION**
      To hear a case, a court must have jurisdiction over (1) the defendant or the property involved and (2) the subject matter.

      1. **Jurisdiction over Persons or Property**
         A court has *in personam* (personal) jurisdiction over state residents. Long arm statutes permit courts to exercise jurisdiction over nonresidents who have *minimum contacts* with the state (for example, do business there). A court has *in rem* jurisdiction over property within its borders.

      2. **Jurisdiction over Subject Matter**
         A court of **general jurisdiction** can decide virtually any type of case. A court's jurisdiction may be **limited** by the subject of a suit, the amount of money in controversy, or whether a proceeding is a trial or appeal.

      3. **Jurisdiction of the Federal Courts**

         a. **Federal Questions**
            Any suit based on the Constitution, a treaty, or a federal law can originate in a federal court.

         b. **Diversity of Citizenship**
            Federal jurisdiction covers cases involving (1) citizens of different states, (2) a foreign government and citizens of a state or of different states, or (3) citizens of a state and citizens or subjects of a foreign government. The amount in controversy must be more than $75,000.

      4. **Exclusive v. Concurrent Jurisdiction**
         Exclusive: when cases can be tried only in federal courts or only in state courts. Concurrent: When both federal and state courts can hear a case.

   B. **JURISDICTION IN CYBERSPACE**
      Whether a court can compel the appearance of a party *outside* the physical limits of the court's jurisdiction depends on the amount of business the party transacts over the Internet with parties *within* the court's jurisdiction.

C. INTERNATIONAL JURISDICTIONAL ISSUES

The minimum-contact standard can apply in an international context. As in cyberspace, a business should attempt to comply with the laws of any jurisdiction in which it targets customers.

D. VENUE

Venue is concerned with the most appropriate location for a trial.

E. STANDING TO SUE

Standing is the interest (injury or threat) that a plaintiff has in a case. A plaintiff must have standing to bring a suit, and the controversy must be justiciable (real, as opposed to hypothetical or purely academic).

III. THE STATE AND FEDERAL COURT SYSTEMS

A. STATE COURT SYSTEMS

1. Trial Courts

Trial courts are courts in which trials are held and testimony is taken.

2. Appellate, or Reviewing, Courts

Courts that hear appeals from trial courts look at *questions of law* (what law governs a dispute) but not *questions of fact* (what occurred in the dispute), unless a trial court's finding of fact is clearly contrary to the evidence. Decision of a state's highest court on state law is final.

B. THE FEDERAL COURT SYSTEM

1. U.S. District Courts

The federal equivalent of a state trial court of general jurisdiction. There is at least one federal district court in every state. Other federal trial courts include the U.S. Tax Court and the U.S. Bankruptcy Court.

2. U.S. Courts of Appeals

The U.S. (circuit) courts of appeals for twelve of the circuits hear appeals from the federal district courts located within their respective circuits. The court of appeals for the thirteenth circuit (the federal circuit) has national jurisdiction over certain cases.

3. The United States Supreme Court

The Supreme Court, the highest level of the federal court system, can review any case decided by any of the federal courts of appeals, and it has authority over some cases decided in state courts. To appeal a case to the Supreme Court, a party asks for a writ of *certiorari*. Whether the Court issues the writ is within its discretion.

IV. FOLLOWING A STATE COURT CASE

A. THE PLEADINGS

1. The Plaintiff's Complaint

Filed by the plaintiff with the clerk of the trial court. Contains (1) a statement alleging the facts for the court to take jurisdiction, (2) a short statement of the facts necessary to show that the plaintiff is entitled to a remedy, and (3) a statement of the remedy the plaintiff is seeking.

2. The Summons

Served on the defendant, with the complaint. Notifies the defendant to answer the complaint (usually within twenty to thirty days).

3. The Defendant's Response

No response results in a default judgment for the plaintiff.

a. **Answer**

Admits the allegations in the complaint or denies them and sets out any defenses. May include a counterclaim against the plaintiff.

b. **Motion to Dismiss**

The defendant may file a motion to dismiss. If the court denies the motion, the defendant must file an answer. If the court grants the motion, the plaintiff must file an amended complaint.

B. PRETRIAL MOTIONS

1. **Motion to Dismiss**

(See above.) Either party may file a motion to dismiss if they have agreed to settle the case. A court may file such a motion itself.

2. **Motion for Judgment on the Pleadings**

Any party can file this motion (after the pleadings have been filed), when no facts are disputed and only questions of law are at issue. A court may consider only those facts stated in the pleadings.

3. **Motion for Summary Judgment**

Any party can file this motion, if there is no disagreement about the facts and the only question is which laws apply. A court can consider evidence outside the pleadings.

C. DISCOVERY

The process of obtaining information from the opposing party or from witnesses may include depositions; interrogatories; and requests for admissions, documents, objects, entry on land, and physical or mental examinations. Information stored electronically, such as computer data, can be the object of a request. This may include data that was not intentionally saved, such as concealed notes.

D. PRETRIAL CONFERENCE

This is an informal discussion between the judge and the attorneys, after discovery, to identify the issues, consider a settlement, and plan the trial.

E. JURY SELECTION

The process by which a jury is chosen is *voir dire*—the jurors are questioned, and a party may ask that some not be sworn.

F. AT THE TRIAL

First, each side presents opening statements. Second, the plaintiff presents his or her case, offering evidence, including the testimony of witnesses. The defendant can challenge the evidence and cross-examine the witnesses.

1. **Motion for a Directed Verdict**

After the plaintiff's case, the defendant can ask the judge to direct a verdict on the ground the plaintiff presented no evidence to justify relief. If the motion is not granted, the defendant presents his or her case, after which this motion can be filed again.

2. **Jury Verdict**

In a jury trial, the jury decides the facts and the amount of the award, if any, to be paid by the losing party. This is the verdict.

G. POSTTRIAL MOTIONS

1. **Motion for Judgment *N.O.V.***

The defendant can file this motion, if he or she previously moved for a directed verdict. The standards for granting this motion are the same as those for granting a motion to dismiss or for a directed verdict.

2. Motion for a New Trial
This motion is granted if the judge believes that the jury erred but that it is not appropriate to grant a judgment for the other side.

H. THE APPEAL

1. Filing the Appeal
Appellant files a notice of appeal with the clerk of the trial court, and the record on appeal, an abstract, and a brief with the reviewing court. Appellee files an answering brief. The parties can give oral arguments.

2. Appellate Review
Appellate courts do not usually reverse findings of fact unless they are contradicted by the evidence presented at the trial in the lower court.

a. Options of an Appellate Court
(1) Affirm: enforce the lower court's order; (2) reverse (if an error was committed during the trial); or (3) remand: send back to the court that originally heard the case for a new trial.

b. Appeal to a Higher Appellate Court
If the reviewing court is an intermediate appellate court, the case may be appealed to the state's highest court. If a federal question is involved, the case may go to the United States Supreme Court.

I. ENFORCING THE JUDGMENT
A judgment may not be enforceable, particularly if a losing party does not have sufficient assets or insurance to cover it.

V.   THE COURTS ADAPT TO THE ONLINE WORLD

A. Electronic Filing
To save time, storage space, etc., courts are switching from paper to electronic document filing, using the Internet, e-mail, and CD-ROMs.

B. Courts Online
Most courts have Web sites. What is available on the sites varies.

C. Cyber Courts and Proceedings
The future may see the use of virtual courtrooms, in which proceedings take place only on the Internet.

VI. ALTERNATIVE DISPUTE RESOLUTION (ADR)

A. NEGOTIATION
Parties come together informally, with or without attorneys, to try to settle or resolve their differences without involving independent third parties.

B. MEDIATION
Parties come together informally with a mediator, who may propose solutions for the parties. A mediator is often an expert in a particular field.

C. ARBITRATION
An arbitrator—the third party hearing the dispute—decides the dispute. The decision may be legally binding.

1. Arbitration Clauses
Disputes are often arbitrated because of an arbitration clause in a contract entered into before the dispute. Courts enforce such clauses.

2. **Arbitration Statutes**

Most states have statutes under which arbitration clauses are enforced. The Federal Arbitration Act (FAA) enforces arbitration clauses in contracts involving interstate commerce.

3. **The Arbitration Process**

At an arbitration hearing, the parties make their arguments, present evidence, and call and examine witnesses, and the arbitrator makes a decision. The decision is called an award, even if no money is involved.

D. OTHER TYPES OF ADR

1. **Early Neutral Case Evaluation**

Parties select a neutral third party (generally an expert) to evaluate their positions, with no hearing and no discovery. The evaluation is a basis for negotiating a settlement.

2. **Mini-trial**

A private proceeding in which attorneys briefly argue each party's case. A third party indicates how a court would likely decide the issue.

3. **Summary Jury Trial**

Like a mini-trial, but a jury renders a nonbinding verdict. Negotiations follow. If no settlement is reached, either side can seek a full trial.

VII. ONLINE DISPUTE RESOLUTION

Many Web sites offer online dispute resolution (ODR) services to help resolve small- to medium-sized business liability claims.

A. WHAT LAW APPLIES IN AN ODR PROCEEDING?

Most ODR services do not apply the law of a specific jurisdiction. Results are based on general, common legal principles.

B. NEGOTIATION AND MEDIATION SERVICES

1. **Online Negotiation**

A settlement may be negotiated through blind bidding: one party submits an offer to be shown to the other party if it falls within a previously agreed range. There is a limited time to respond.

2. **Mediation Providers—SquareTrade**

SquareTrade resolves disputes involving $100 or more between eBay customers. SquareTrade also resolves other disputes related to online transactions, using software to walk participants through a step-by-step resolution process.

C. ARBITRATION PROGRAMS

1. **Internet Corporation for Assigned Names and Numbers (ICANN)**

The federal government set up ICANN as a nonprofit corporation to oversee the distribution of domain names. ICANN has issued rules and authorized organizations to resolve related disputes.

2. **Resolution Forum, Inc. (RFI)**

RFI, a nonprofit entity associated with the Center for Legal Responsibility at South Texas College of Law, offers arbitration in an online conference room via a standard browser, using a password.

3. **Virtual Magistrate Project (VMAG)**

VMAG resolves disputes involving users of online systems; victims of wrongful messages, postings and files; and system operators subject to complaints or similar demands. Online-related contract, intellectual property, property, and tort disputes. The goal is resolution within seventy-two hours. Appeal of a result may be made to a court.

TRUE-FALSE QUESTIONS

(Answers at the Back of the Book)

____ 1. Under a long arm statute, a state court can obtain jurisdiction over an out-of-state defendant.

____ 2. Doing substantial business in a jurisdiction over the Internet can be enough to support a court's jurisdiction over an out-of-state defendant.

____ 3. The United States Supreme Court is the final authority for any case decided by a state court.

____ 4. Suits involving federal questions originate in federal district courts.

____ 5. An answer may admit or deny the allegations in a complaint.

____ 6. A motion for summary judgment may be supported by sworn statements and other materials.

____ 7. Only a losing party may appeal to a higher court.

____ 8. Most lawsuits go to trial.

____ 9. In mediation, a mediator makes a decision on the matter in dispute.

____ 10. Most states do not enforce arbitration clauses.

FILL-IN QUESTIONS

(Answers at the Back of the Book)

A motion _____ (to dismiss/for summary judgment) alleges that even if the facts in a complaint are true, their legal consequences are such that there is no reason to go on with the suit and no need for the defendant to file an answer. A motion _____ (to dismiss/for judgment on the pleadings) is filed after the complaint, answer, and any counterclaim and reply have been filed, when no facts are disputed and only questions of law are at issue. A motion for _____ (summary judgment/a new trial) is proper if there is no disagreement on the facts and the only question is which laws apply to the facts.

MULTIPLE-CHOICE QUESTIONS

(Answers at the Back of the Book)

____ 1. Ace Corporation, which is based in Texas, advertises on the Web. A court in Illinois would be most likely to exercise jurisdiction over Ace if Ace

a. conducted substantial business with Illinois residents at its site.
b. interacted with any Illinois resident through its Web site.
c. only advertised passively at its Web site.
d. all of the above.

____ 2. Alpha Company files a suit against Beta Corporation. Before the trial, Alpha can obtain from Beta

a. access to related documents in Beta's possession.
b. accurate information about Beta's trade secrets.
c. an admission of the truth of matters not related to the trial.
d. all of the above.

____   3. Eagle Company, which is based in Florida, owns commercial property in Georgia. A dispute arises over the ownership of the property with Holly, a resident of Alabama. Holly files a suit against Eagle in Georgia. In this suit, Georgia has

   a. diversity jurisdiction.
   b. *in personam* jurisdiction.
   c. *in rem* jurisdiction.
   d. no jurisdiction.

____   4. Central Business Corporation was incorporated in Delaware, has its main office in New Jersey, and does business in New York. Central is subject to the jurisdiction of

   a. Delaware, New Jersey, or New York.
   b. Delaware or New Jersey only.
   c. Delaware or New York only.
   d. New Jersey or New York only.

____   5. Standard Marketing, Inc., loses its suit against Top Sales Corporation. Standard's best ground for an appeal is the trial court's interpretation of

   a. the conduct of the witnesses during the trial.
   b. the credibility of the evidence that Top presented.
   c. the dealings between the parties before the suit.
   d. the law that applied to the issues in the case.

____   6. John files a suit against Kay, and loses. John appeals, and loses again. The United States Supreme Court is

   a. required to hear the case if John appeals again.
   b. required to hear the case if John lost in a federal court.
   c. required to hear the case if John lost in a state court.
   d. not required to hear the case.

____   7. Ann serves a complaint on Bob, who files a motion to dismiss. If the motion is denied

   a. Ann will be given time to file an amended complaint.
   b. Ann will have a judgment entered in her favor.
   c. Bob will be given time to file another response.
   d. Bob will have a judgment entered in his favor.

____   8. Carol files a suit against Don. Before going to trial, the parties meet with their attorneys to represent them, to try to resolve the dispute without involving a third party. This is

   a. arbitration.
   b. litigation.
   c. mediation.
   d. negotiation.

____   9. Sam files a suit against Tina. They meet, and their attorneys present the case to a jury. The jury renders a non-binding verdict, after which the parties try to reach an agreement. This is

   a. a mini-trial.
   b. arbitration.
   c. a summary jury trial.
   d. early neutral case evaluation.

____ 10. Jill submits a claim against Ken to LetsSettle.com, an online dispute resolution forum. An appeal of this dispute may be made to a court by

a. Jill only.
b. Ken only.
c. Jill or Ken.
d. none of the above.

SHORT ESSAY QUESTIONS

1. What is jurisdiction? How does jurisdiction over a person or property differ from subject matter jurisdiction? What does a long arm statute do?

2. What are the advantages and disadvantages of alternative dispute resolution?

ISSUE SPOTTERS

(Answers at the Back of the Book)

Sue contracts with Tom to deliver a quantity of computers to Sue's Computer Store. They disagree over the amount, the delivery date, the price, and the quality. Sue files a suit against Tom in a state court.

1. Their state requires that their dispute be submitted to mediation or nonbinding arbitration. If the dispute is not resolved, or if either party disagrees with the decision of the mediator or arbitrator, will a court hear the case?

2. At the trial, after Sue calls her witnesses, offers her evidence, and otherwise presents her side of the case, Tom has at least two choices between courses of actions. Tom can call his first witness. What else might he do?

3. After the trial, the judge issues a judgment that includes a grant of relief for Sue, but the relief is not as much as Sue wanted. Neither Sue nor Tom is satisfied with this result. Who can appeal to a higher court? Between Acme and its employees? Between Acme and its shareholders?

CUMULATIVE HYPOTHETICAL PROBLEM FOR UNIT ONE—INCLUDING CHAPTERS 1–3

(Answers at the Back of the Book)

Computer Data, Inc. (CDI), incorporated and based in California, signs a contract with Digital Products Corporation (DPC), incorporated and based in Arizona, to make and sell customized software for DPC to, in turn, sell to its clients. CDI ships defective software to DPC, which sells it to Eagle Distribution Corporation. The defective software causes losses to Eagle estimated at $100,000.

____ 1. Federal authorities file charges against CDI, alleging that the shipment of defective software violated a federal statute. CDI asks the court to exercise its power of judicial review. This means that the court can review

a. the actions of the federal authorities and declare them excessive.
b. the charges against CDI and declare them unfounded.
c. the statute and declare it unconstitutional.
d. the totality of the situation and declare it unethical.

____   **2.** Eagle and DPC enter into mediation. In mediation, the parties

a. may come to an agreement by mutual consent.
b. must accept a winner-take-all result.
c. settle their dispute without the assistance of a third party.
d. submit their dispute to a mediator for a legally binding decision.

____   **3.** Eagle is located in Tennessee. Eagle could file a suit against DPC in

a. Arizona only.
b. Tennessee only.
c. a federal court only.
d. Arizona, Tennessee, or a federal court.

____   **4.** Eagle files a suit against DPC, seeking the amount of its losses as damages. Damages is a remedy

a. at law.
b. in equity.
c. at law or in equity, depending on how the plaintiff phrases its complaint.
d. at law or in equity, depending on whether there was any actual "damage."

____   **5.** CDI's managers evaluate the shipment of defective software in terms of CDI's ethical obligations, if any. In other words, CDI's managers are considering the firm's

a. legal liability.
b. maximum profitability.
c. optimum profitability.
d. right or wrong behavior.

Chapter 4:
Constitutional Authority to Regulate Business

WHAT THIS CHAPTER IS ABOUT

This chapter emphasizes that the Constitution is the supreme law in this country and discusses some of the constitutional limits on the law. Neither Congress nor any state may pass a law that conflicts with the Constitution. To sustain a federal law or action, a specific federal power must be found in the Constitution. A state has inherent power to enact laws that have a reasonable relationship to the welfare of its citizens.

CHAPTER OUTLINE

I. THE CONSTITUTIONAL POWERS OF GOVERNMENT

A. A FEDERAL FORM OF GOVERNMENT
In a federal form of government (the United States), the states form a union and sovereign power is divided between a central authority and the states.

B. THE SEPARATION OF POWERS
Under the Constitution, the legislative branch makes the laws; the executive branch enforces the laws; and the judicial branch interprets the laws. Each branch has some power to limit the actions of the other two.

C. THE COMMERCE CLAUSE
The Constitution (Article I, Section 8) gives Congress the power to regulate commerce among the states.

    1. The Commerce Power Today
The national government can regulate every commercial enterprise in the United States. The United States Supreme Court has held, however, that this does not justify regulation of areas that have "nothing to do with commerce."

    2. The Regulatory Powers of the States
States possess police powers (the right to regulate private activities to protect or promote the public order, health, safety, morals, and general welfare). Statutes covering almost every aspect of life have been enacted under the police powers.

    3. The "Dormant" Commerce Clause
When state laws impinge on interstate commerce, courts balance the state's interest in regulating a certain matter against the burden on interstate commerce. State laws that *substantially* interfere with interstate commerce violate the commerce clause.

D. THE SUPREMACY CLAUSE
The Constitution (Article IV) provides that the Constitution, laws, and treaties of the United States are the supreme law of the land.

    1. When Federal and State Laws Are in Direct Conflict
The state law is rendered invalid.

2.   **Federal Preemption**
   If Congress chooses to act exclusively in an area in which states have concurrent power, Congress preempts the area (the federal law takes precedence over a state law on the same subject).

E. THE TAXING AND SPENDING POWERS

1.   **The Taxing Power**
   The Constitution (Article I, Section 8) gives Congress the power to levy taxes, but Congress may not tax some states and exempt others. Any tax that is a valid revenue-raising measure will be upheld.

2.   **The Spending Power**
   The Constitution (Article I, Section 8) gives Congress the power to spend the money it raises with its taxing power. This involves policy choices, with which taxpayers may disagree. Congress can spend funds to promote any objective, so long as it does not violate the Bill of Rights.

II.   BUSINESS AND THE BILL OF RIGHTS

The first ten amendments to the Constitution protect individuals and businesses against some interference by the federal government. Under the due process clause of the Fourteenth Amendment, many rights also apply to the states.

A. FREEDOM OF SPEECH

The First Amendment guaranty of freedom of speech applies to the federal and state governments.

1.   **Speech with Limited Protection**

   a.   **Political Speech**
      States can prohibit corporations from using corporate funds for independent expressions of opinion about political candidates.

   b.   **Commercial Speech**
      A state restriction on commercial speech (advertising) is valid as long as it (1) seeks to implement a substantial government interest, (2) directly advances that interest, and (3) goes no further than necessary to accomplish its objective.

2.   **Unprotected Speech**

   a.   **Defamatory Speech**
      Speech that harms the good reputation of another can take the form of libel (if it is in writing) or slander (if it is oral).

   b.   **Lewd and Obscene Speech**
      States can ban child pornography. One court has banned lewd speech and pornographic pinups in the workplace.

   c.   **"Fighting Words"**
      Words that are likely to incite others to violence.

3.   **Online Obscenity**
   Attempts to regulate obscene materials on the Internet have been challenged, and some have been struck, as unconstitutional.

B. FREEDOM OF RELIGION

Under the First Amendment, the government may not establish a religion (the establishment clause) nor prohibit the exercise of religion (the free exercise clause).

1.   **"Sunday Closing Laws"**
   Restrictions on commercial acts on Sunday have been upheld on the ground it is a legitimate government function to provide a day of rest.

2. **Government Accommodation**
This amendment mandates government accommodation of all religions and forbids hostility toward any.

3. **Business Accommodation**
Statutes prohibit employers and unions from discriminating against persons because of their religion. Employers must "reasonably accommodate" the religious practices of their employees.

III. DUE PROCESS AND EQUAL PROTECTION

A. DUE PROCESS
Both the Fifth and the Fourteenth Amendments provide that no person shall be deprived "of life, liberty, or property, without due process of law."

1. **Procedural Due Process**
Procedural due process requires that any government decision to take away the life, liberty, or property of an individual be accompanied by procedural safeguards to ensure fairness.

2. **Substantive Due Process**
Substantive due process focuses on the content (substance) of legislation.

   a. **Compelling Interest Test**
   A statute can restrict an individual's fundamental right (such as all First Amendment rights) only if the statute promotes a compelling or overriding governmental interest (speed limits, for example, protect public safety).

   b. **Rational Basis Test**
   Restrictions on business activities must relate rationally to a legitimate government purpose. Most business regulations qualify.

B. EQUAL PROTECTION
The Fourteenth Amendment prohibits a state from denying any person "the equal protection of the laws." The due process clause of the Fifth Amendment applies the equal protection clause to the federal government.

1. **What Equal Protection Means**
Equal protection means that the government must treat similarly situated individuals in a similar manner. If a law distinguishes among individuals, the basis for the distinction (classification) is examined.

   a. **Minimal Scrutiny**
   In matters of economic or social welfare, the classification will be considered valid if there is any conceivable *rational basis* on which it might relate to any legitimate government interest.

   b. **Intermediate Scrutiny**
   Laws using classifications based on gender or legitimacy must be substantially related to important government objectives.

   c. **Strict Scrutiny**
   A law that inhibits some persons' exercise of a fundamental right or a classification based on a suspect trait must be necessary to promote a compelling government interest.

2. **The Difference between Substantive Due Process and Equal Protection**
A law that limits the liberty of *all* persons to do something may violate substantive due process. A law that limits the liberty of only *some* persons may violate equal protection.

C. PRIVACY RIGHTS

There is no specific guarantee of this right, but it is derived from guarantees in the First, Third, Fourth, Fifth, and Ninth Amendments. There are a number of federal statutes that protect privacy in certain areas.

TRUE-FALSE QUESTIONS

(Answers at the Back of the Book)

_F_   1.   A federal form of government is one in which a central authority holds all power.

_F_   2.   The president can hold acts of Congress and of the courts unconstitutional.

_T_   3.   Congress can regulate any activity that substantially affects commerce.

_T_   4.   A state law that substantially impinges on interstate commerce is unconstitutional.

_F_   5.   When there is a direct conflict between a federal law and a state law, the federal law is invalid.

_T_   6.   If a tax is a reasonable revenue-raising measure, it is within the federal taxing power.

_F_   7.   The Bill of Rights protects individuals against various types of interference by the federal government only.

_F_   8.   Any restriction on commercial speech is unconstitutional.

_F_   9.   Due process and equal protection are different terms for the same thing.

_T_   10.   A right to privacy is not specifically guaranteed in the U.S. Constitution.

FILL-IN QUESTIONS

(Answers at the Back of the Book)

Police power is possessed by the _____states_____ (federal government/states). Police power refers to the right of the _____states_____ (federal government/states) to regulate private activities to protect or promote the public order, health, safety, morals, and general welfare. Building codes, licensing requirements, and many other _____state_____ (federal/state) statutes have been enacted under the police power.

MULTIPLE-CHOICE QUESTIONS

(Answers at the Back of the Book)

_D._   1.   Of the three branches of the federal government provided by the Constitution, the branch that makes the laws is

a.   the administrative branch.
b.   the executive branch.
c.   the judicial branch.
d.   the legislative branch.

A   **2.** Delta Business Corporation markets its products in three states. Under the commerce clause, Congress can regulate

a. any commercial activity in the United States.
b. only commercial activities that are in interstate commerce.
c. only commercial activities that are local.
d. only activities that have nothing to do with commerce.

A   **3.** Eagle Shipping Company challenges a Georgia state statute, claiming that it unlawfully interferes with interstate commerce. A court will likely

a. balance Georgia's interest in regulating the matter against the burden on interstate commerce.
b. balance the burden on Georgia against the merit and purpose of interstate commerce.
c. strike the statute.
d. uphold the statute.

A   **4.** A Nevada state statute bans business entities from making political contributions that individuals can make. A court would likely hold this statute to be

a. an unconstitutional restriction of speech.
b. constitutional under the First Amendment.
c. justified by the need to protect individuals' rights.
d. necessary to protect state interests.

B   **5.** An Illinois state statute bans certain advertising to prevent consumers from being misled. A court would likely hold this statute to be

a. an unconstitutional restriction of speech.
b. constitutional under the First Amendment.
c. justified by the need to protect individuals' rights.
d. necessary to protect state interests.

B   **6.** Procedures used in South Dakota and other states in making decisions to take life, liberty, or property are the focus of constitutional provisions covering

a. equal protection.
b. procedural due process.
c. substantive due process.
d. the right to privacy.

C   **7.** A Connecticut statute that limits the liberty of *all* persons to engage in a certain activity may violate constitutional provisions covering

a. equal protection.
b. procedural due process.
c. substantive due process.
d. the right to privacy.

A   **8.** A River City ordinance that restricts most vendors from doing business in a heavily trafficked area might be upheld under constitutional provisions covering

a. equal protection.
b. procedural due process.
c. substantive due process.
d. the right to privacy.

9. If Montana enacts a statute that directly conflicts with a federal law

   a. both laws are invalid.
   b. both laws govern concurrently.
   c. Montana's statute takes precedence.
   d. the federal law takes precedence.

10. The First Amendment protects Jill and others from

    a. dissemination of obscene materials only.
    b. speech that harms their good reputations or violates state criminal laws only.
    c. dissemination of obscene materials and speech that harms their good reputations or violates state criminal laws.
    d. none of the above.

SHORT ESSAY QUESTIONS

1. What is the effect of the supremacy clause?

2. What is the significance of the commerce clause?

ISSUE SPOTTERS

(Answers at the Back of the Book)

1. Can a state, in the interest of energy conservation, ban all advertising by power utilities if conservation could be accomplished by less restrictive means? Why or why not?

2. Would a state law imposing a fifteen-year term of imprisonment without allowing a trial on all businesspersons who appear in their own television commercials be a violation of substantive due process? Would it violate procedural due process?

3. Would it be a violation of equal protection for a state to impose a higher tax on out-of-state companies doing business in the state than it imposes on in-state companies if the only reason for the tax is to protect the local firms from out-of-state competition?

Chapter 5:
Torts, Cyber Torts, and Product Liability

WHAT THIS CHAPTER IS ABOUT

Torts consist of wrongful conduct by one person that causes injury to another. *Tort* is French for "wrong." For acts that cause physical injury or that interfere with physical security and freedom of movement, tort law provides remedies, typically damages. This chapter outlines intentional torts, negligence, and strict liability. These categories include torts that are specifically related to business and cyber torts.

Manufacturers, processors, and sellers may also be liable to consumers, users, and bystanders for physical harm or property damage caused by defective goods. This is product liability.

CHAPTER OUTLINE

I. THE BASIS OF TORT LAW
Two notions serve as the basis of all torts: wrongs and compensation. Tort law recognizes that some acts are wrong because they cause injuries to others. Most crimes involve torts, but not all torts are crimes. A tort action is a *civil* action in which one person brings a personal suit against another, usually for damages.

II. INTENTIONAL TORTS AGAINST PERSONS
Intentional torts involve acts that were intended or could be expected to bring about consequences that are the basis of the tort. A **tortfeasor** (one committing a tort) must intend to commit an act, the consequences of which interfere with the personal or business interests of another in a way not permitted by law.

A. ASSAULT AND BATTERY

1. Assault
An intentional act that creates in another person a reasonable apprehension or fear of immediate harmful or offensive contact.

2. Battery
An intentional and harmful or offensive physical contact. Physical injury need not occur. Whether the contact is offensive is determined by the reasonable person standard.

3. Compensation
A plaintiff may be compensated for emotional harm or loss of reputation resulting from a battery, as well as for physical harm.

4. Defenses to Assault and Battery

a. Consent
When a person consents to an act that damages him or her, there is generally no liability for the damage.

b. Self-Defense
An individual who is defending his or her life or physical well-being can claim self-defense.

c. Defense of Others
An individual can act in a reasonable manner to protect others who are in real or apparent danger.

d. Defense of Property
Reasonable force may be used in attempting to remove intruders from one's home, although force that is likely to cause death or great bodily injury can never be used just to protect property.

B. FALSE IMPRISONMENT

1. What False Imprisonment Is
The intentional confinement or restraint of another person without justification. The confinement can be accomplished through the use of physical barriers, physical restraint, or threats of physical force.

2. The Defense of Probable Cause
In some states, a merchant is justified in delaying a suspected shoplifter if the merchant has probable cause. The detention must be conducted in a reasonable manner and for only a reasonable length of time.

C. INTENTIONAL INFLICTION OF EMOTIONAL DISTRESS
Intentional infliction of emotional distress is an act that amounts to extreme and outrageous conduct resulting in severe emotional distress to another (a few states require physical symptoms). Stalking is one way to commit it. Repeated annoyance, with threats, is another.

D. DEFAMATION
Defamation is wrongfully hurting another's good reputation through false statements. Doing it orally is **slander**; doing it in writing is **libel**.

1. Types of False Utterances That Are Torts *Per Se*
Proof of injury is not required when one falsely states that another has a loathsome communicable disease, has committed improprieties while engaging in a profession or trade, or has committed or been imprisoned for a serious crime, or that an unmarried woman is unchaste.

2. The Publication Requirement
The statement must be published (communicated to a third party). Anyone who republishes or repeats a defamatory statement is liable.

3. Defenses against Defamation

a. Truth
The statement is true. It must be true in whole, not in part.

b. Privilege
The statement is privileged: absolute (made in a judicial or legislative proceeding) or qualified (for example, made by one corporate director to another about corporate business).

c. Public Figure
The statement is about a public figure, made in a public medium, and related to a matter of general public interest. To recover damages, a public figure must prove a statement was made with **actual malice** (knowledge of its falsity or reckless disregard for the truth).

E. INVASION OF THE RIGHT TO PRIVACY
Four acts qualify as invasions of privacy:

1. The use of a person's name, picture, or other likeness for commercial purposes without permission. (This is **appropriation**—see below.)

2. Intrusion on an individual's affairs or seclusion.

3. Publication of information that places a person in a false light.

4. Public disclosure of private facts about an individual that an ordinary person would find objectionable.

F. APPROPRIATION
The use of one person's name or likeness by another, without permission and for the benefit of the user. An individual's right to privacy includes the right to the exclusive use of his or her identity.

G. MISREPRESENTATION (FRAUD)
Fraud is the use of misrepresentation and deceit for personal gain. Puffery (seller's talk) is not fraud. The elements of fraudulent misrepresentation—

1. **Misrepresentation** of material facts or conditions with knowledge that they are false or with reckless disregard for the truth.

2. **Intent** to induce another to rely on the misrepresentation.

3. **Justifiable reliance** by the deceived party.

4. **Damages** suffered as a result of reliance.

5. **Causal connection** between the misrepresentation and the injury.

H. WRONGFUL INTERFERENCE

1. **Wrongful Interference with a Contractual Relationship**
Occurs when there is a contract between two parties and a third party who knows of the contract intentionally causes either of the two parties to break it.

2. **Wrongful Interference with a Business Relationship**
If there are two yogurt stores in a mall, placing an employee of Store A in front of Store B to divert customers to Store A constitutes the tort of wrongful interference with a business relationship.

3. **Defenses to Wrongful Interference**
A person is not liable if the interference is justified or permissible (such as bona fide competitive behavior).

III. INTENTIONAL TORTS AGAINST PROPERTY

A. TRESPASS TO LAND
Trespass to land occurs if a person, without permission, enters onto, above, or below the surface of land owned by another; causes anything to enter onto the land; or remains on the land or permits anything to remain on it.

1. **Trespass Criteria, Rights, and Duties**
Posted signs *expressly* establish trespass. Entering onto property to commit an illegal act *impliedly* does so. Trespassers are liable for any property damage. Owners may have a duty to post notice of any danger.

2. **Defenses against Trespass to Land**
Defenses against trespass include that the trespass was warranted or that the purported owner had no right to possess the land in question.

B. TRESPASS TO PERSONAL PROPERTY
Occurs when an individual unlawfully harms the personal property of another or interferes with an owner's right to exclusive possession and enjoyment. Defenses include that the interference was warranted.

C. CONVERSION

1. **What Conversion Is**
   An act depriving an owner of personal property without the owner's permission and without just cause. Conversion is the civil side of crimes related to theft. Buying stolen goods is conversion.

2. **Defenses**
   Defenses to conversion include that the purported owner does not own the property or does not have a right to possess it that is superior to the right of the holder. Necessity is also a defense.

D. DISPARAGEMENT OF PROPERTY
Occurs when economically injurious falsehoods are made about another's product or ownership of property. Torts can be specifically referred to as **slander of quality** (product) or **slander of title** (ownership of property).

IV. UNINTENTIONAL TORTS (NEGLIGENCE)

A. THE ELEMENTS OF NEGLIGENCE

1. **What Negligence Is**
   Someone's failure to live up to a required duty of care, causing another to suffer injury. The breach of the duty must create a risk of certain harmful consequences, whether or not that was the intent.

2. **The Elements of Negligence**
   (1) A duty of care, (2) breach of the duty of care, (3) damage or injury as a result of the breach, and (4) the breach causes the damage or injury.

B. THE DUTY OF CARE AND ITS BREACH

1. **The Reasonable Person Standard**
   The duty of care is measured according to the **reasonable person standard** (how a reasonable person would have acted in the same circumstances).

2. **Duty of Landowners**
   Owners are expected to use reasonable care (guard against some risks and warn of others) to protect persons coming onto their property.

3. **Duty of Professionals**
   A professional's duty is consistent with his or her knowledge, skill, and intelligence, including what is reasonable for that professional.

4. **Factors for Determining a Breach of the Duty of Care**
   The nature of the act (whether it is outrageous or commonplace), the manner in which the act is performed (cautiously versus heedlessly), and the nature of the injury (whether it is serious or slight). Note: Failing to rescue a stranger in peril is not a breach of a duty of care.

C. THE INJURY REQUIREMENT AND DAMAGES
To recover damages (receive compensation), the plaintiff must have suffered some loss, harm, wrong, or invasion of a protected interest. Punitive damages (to punish the wrongdoer and deter others) may also be awarded.

D. CAUSATION

1. **Causation in Fact**
   The breach of the duty of care must cause the injury—that is, "but for" the wrongful act, the injury would not have occurred.

2. Proximate Cause
There must be a connection between the act and the injury strong enough to justify imposing liability. Generally, the harm or the victim of the harm must have been foreseeable in light of all of the circumstances.

E. DEFENSES TO NEGLIGENCE

1. Assumption of Risk
One who voluntarily enters a risky situation, knowing the risk, cannot recover. This does not include a risk different from or greater than the risk normally involved in the situation.

2. Superseding Cause
An unforeseeable intervening force breaks the connection between the breach of the duty of care and the injury or damage. Taking a defensive action (such as swerving to avoid an oncoming car) does not break the connection. Nor does someone else's attempt to rescue the injured party.

3. Contributory Negligence
In some states, a plaintiff cannot recover for an injury if he or she was negligent. The last-clear-chance rule allows a negligent plaintiff to recover if the defendant had the last chance to avoid the damage.

4. Comparative Negligence
In most states, the plaintiff's and the defendant's negligence is compared and liability prorated. Some states allow a plaintiff to recover even if his or her fault is greater than the defendant's. In many states, the plaintiff gets nothing if he or she is more than 50 percent at fault.

F. SPECIAL NEGLIGENCE DOCTRINES AND STATUTES

1. *Res Ipsa Loquitur*
If negligence is very difficult to prove, a court may infer it, and the defendant must prove he or she was *not* negligent. This is only if the event causing the harm is one that normally does not occur in the absence of negligence and is caused by something within the defendant's control.

2. Negligence *Per Se*
A person who violates a statute providing for a criminal penalty is liable when the violation causes another to be injured, if (1) the statute sets out a standard of conduct, and when, where, and of whom it is expected; (2) the injured person is in the class protected by the statute; and (3) the statute was designed to prevent the type of injury suffered.

3. "Danger Invites Rescue" Doctrine
A person can be liable to a party who is injured trying to protect another from the consequences of the first person's act.

4. Special Negligence Statutes
Good Samaritan statutes protect those who aid others from being sued for negligence. Dram shop acts impose liability on bar owners for injuries caused by intoxicated persons who are served by those owners. A statute may impose liability on social hosts for acts of their guests.

V. CYBER TORTS

A. DEFAMATION ONLINE
Under the Communications Decency Act of 1996, Internet service providers (ISPs) are not liable for the defamatory remarks of those who use their services.

B. SPAM
Spam is junk e-mail. The federal government and some states regulate its use, which may constitute trespass to personal property. The First Amendment limits what the government can do to restrict it.

VI.   STRICT LIABILITY

Under this doctrine, liability for injury is imposed for reasons other than fault.

A.   ABNORMALLY DANGEROUS OR EXCEPTIONAL ACTIVITIES

The basis for imposing strict liability on an abnormally dangerous activity is that the activity creates an extreme risk. Balancing the risk against the potential for harm, it is fair to ask the person engaged in the activity to pay for injury caused by that activity.

B.   OTHER APPLICATIONS OF STRICT LIABILITY

A person who keeps a dangerous animal is strictly liable for any harm inflicted by the animal. A significant application of strict liability is in the area of product liability (discussed below).

VII.   PRODUCT LIABILITY

A.   PRODUCT LIABILITY BASED ON WARRANTY LAW

The Uniform Commercial Code designates five types of warranties that arise in sales of goods. These include the following express and implied warranties.

1.   Express Warranties

A seller warrants that goods will conform to a label, a contract, an ad, a brochure, promotional material, samples, and models. It must come at such a time that the buyer could rely on it when agreeing to buy. (A salesperson's opinion—"this is a fine car"—is not an express warranty.)

2.   Implied Warranties

An implied warranty of warranty automatically arises in every sale of goods by a merchant who deals in such goods. An implied warranty of fitness for a particular purpose arises when a seller (merchant or nonmerchant) knows or has reason to know the particular purpose for which a buyer will use goods and knows the buyer is relying on the seller to select suitable goods.

3.   Disclaimers

These warranties may all be disclaimed in specific language if this is done in a manner that protects the buyer or lessee from surprise.

B.   PRODUCT LIABILITY BASED ON NEGLIGENCE

If the failure to exercise reasonable care in the making or marketing of a product causes an injury, the basis of liability is negligence.

1.   Privity of Contract between Plaintiff and Defendant Is Not Required

2.   Manufacturer's Duty of Care

Due care must be exercised in designing, assembling, and testing a product; selecting materials; inspecting and testing products bought for use in the final product; and placing warnings on the label to inform users of dangers of which an ordinary person might not be aware.

C.   PRODUCT LIABILITY BASED ON MISREPRESENTATION

If a misrepresentation (such as intentionally concealing product defects) results in an injury, there may liability for fraud.

D.   STRICT PRODUCT LIABILITY

Under the doctrine of strict liability, a defendant may be liable for the result of his or her act regardless of intention or exercise of reasonable care.

1.   Requirements of Strict Product Liability

Requirements for strict product liability under the *Restatement (Second) of Torts*, Section 402A—

a.   The Product Is in a Defective Condition when the Defendant Sells It

b.   The Defendant Is Normally in the Business of Selling the Product

c. **The Defect Makes the Product Unreasonably Dangerous**
A product may be so defective if either—

1) **The Product Is Dangerous beyond the Consumer's Expectation**
There may have been a flaw in the manufacturing process that led to some defective products being marketed, or a perfectly made product may not have had adequate warning on the label.

2) **There Is a Less Dangerous, Economically Feasible Alter-native that the Manufacturer Failed to Use**
A manufacturer may have failed to design a safe product.

d. **The Plaintiff Incurs Harm to Self or Property by Use of the Product**

e. **The Defect Is the Proximate Cause of the Harm**

f. **The Product Was Not Substantially Changed after It Was Sold**

2. **Product Defects—*Restatement (Third) of Torts***
The *Restatement (Third) of Torts: Products Liability* categorizes—

a. **Manufacturing Defects**
These occur when a product departs from its intended design even though all possible care was taken (strict liability).

b. **Design Defects**
These can occur when a product poses a foreseeable risk of harm that could have been reduced by use of a reasonable alternative design and the omission makes the product unreasonably unsafe. A court would consider such factors as consumer expectations and warnings.

c. **Inadequate Warnings**
These exist when a product poses a foreseeable risk of harm that could have been reduced by a reasonable warning and the omission makes the product unreasonably unsafe. Factors include the content and comprehensibility of a warning, and the expected users.

3. **Other Applications of Strict Liability**
Defendants may be liable to injured bystanders. Suppliers of component parts and lessors may be liable for injuries caused by defective products.

4. **Statutes of Repose**
A statute of repose limits the time in which a suit can be filed. It runs from an earlier date and for a longer time than a statute of limitations.

E. **DEFENSES TO PRODUCT LIABILITY**

1. **Assumption of Risk**
In some states, this is a defense if (1) plaintiff knew and appreciated the risk created by the defect and (2) plaintiff voluntarily engaged in the risk, event though it was unreasonable to do so.

2. **Product Misuse**
The use must not be the one for which the product was designed, and the misuse must not be reasonably foreseeable.

3. **Comparative Negligence**
Most states consider a plaintiff's actions in apportioning liability.

4. **Commonly Known Dangers**
Failing to warn against such a danger is not a ground for liability.

TRUE-FALSE QUESTIONS

(Answers at the Back of the Book)

_T_   **1.** To commit an intentional tort, a person must intend the consequences of his or her act or know with substantial certainty that certain consequences will result.

_F_   **2.** Puffery is fraud.

_T_   **3.** Conversion is wrongfully taking or retaining an individual's personal property and placing it in the service of another.

_F_   **4.** An _ordinary_ person standard determines whether allegedly negligent conduct resulted in a breach of a duty of care.

_T_   **5.** Strict liability is liability without fault.

_F_   **6.** Bona fide competitive behavior can constitute wrongful interference with a contractual relationship.

_F_   **7.** One requirement for a product liability suit based on strict liability is a failure to exercise due care.

_T_   **8.** In many states, the plaintiff's negligence is a defense that may be raised in a product liability suit based on strict liability.

_F_   **9.** A manufacturer has a duty to warn about risks that are obvious or commonly known.

_T_   **10.** Assumption of risk can be raised as a defense in a product liability suit.

FILL-IN QUESTIONS

(Answers at the Back of the Book)

1. Basic defenses to _____ _negligence_ _____ (negligence/intentional torts) include comparative negligence, contributory negligence, and assumption of risk.

2. One who voluntarily and knowingly enters into a risky situation normally cannot recover damages. This is the defense of _____ _assumption of risk_ _____ (contributory negligence/ assumption of risk).

3. When both parties' failure to use reasonable care combines to cause injury, in some states the injured party's recovery is prorated according to his or her own negligence. This is _____ _comparative_ _____ (comparative/ contributory) negligence.

MULTIPLE-CHOICE QUESTIONS

(Answers at the Back of the Book)

_A_   **1.** Alan, the owner of Beta Computer Store, detains Cathy, a customer, whom Alan suspects of shoplifting. This is false imprisonment if

    a. Alan detains Cathy for an unreasonably long time.
    b. Cathy did not shoplift.
    c. Cathy has probable cause to suspect Alan of deceit.
    d. Cathy protests her innocence.

2. To protect its customers and other business invitees, Grocers Market must warn them of

a. hidden dangers.
b. obvious dangers.
c. hidden and obvious dangers.
d. none of the above.

3. Lee, a salesperson for Midsize Corporation, causes a car accident while on business. Lee and Midsize are liable to

a. all those who were injured.
b. only those who were uninsured.
c. only those whose injuries could have been reasonably foreseen.
d. only those with whom Lee was doing business.

4. Best Box Company advertises so effectively that Cardboard Products, Inc., stops doing business with Delta Packaging Corporation. Best is liable for

a. appropriation.
b. conversion.
c. wrongful interference with a business relationship.
d. none of the above.

5. Internet Services, Inc. (ISI), is an Internet service provider. ISI does not create, but disseminates, a defamatory statement by Jill, its customer, about Ron. Liability for the remark may be imposed on

a. ISI and Jill.
b. ISI or Jill, but not both.
c. ISI only.
d. Jill only.

6. Superb Auto Sales sells cars, trucks, and other motor vehicles. A Superb salesperson tells potential customers, "This is the finest car ever made." This statement is

a. an express warranty.
b. an implied warranty.
c. a warranty of title.
d. puffing.

7. A bridge's design is defective and soon after completion it begins to sway in the wind. Everyone stays off, except Carl, who wants to show off. Carl falls from the bridge and sues its maker, who can raise the defense of

a. assumption of risk.
b. commonly known danger.
c. product misuse.
d. none of the above.

8. Kitchen Products, Inc. (KPI), makes knifes and other utensils. Jay is injured while using a KPI knife, and sues the maker for product liability based on negligence. KPI could successfully defend against the suit by showing that

a. Jay's injury resulted from a commonly known danger.
b. Jay misused the knife in a foreseeable way.
c. KPI did not sell the knife to Jay.
d. the knife was not altered after KPI sold it.

R   **9.**   Standard Tools, Inc., makes and sells tools. Tina is injured as a result of using a Standard tool. Tina sues Standard for product liability based on strict liability. To succeed, Tina must prove that Standard

   a. was in privity of contract with Tina.
   b. did not use care with respect to the tool.
   c. misrepresented a material fact regarding the tool on which Tina relied.
   d. none of the above.

C   **10.**   Fran is in Green's Grocery Store when a bottle of Hi Cola on a nearby shelf explodes, injuring her. She can recover from the manufacturer of Hi Cola only if she can show that

   a. she did not assume the risk of the explosive bottle of Hi Cola.
   b. she intended to buy the explosive bottle of Hi Cola.
   c. she was injured due to a defect in the product.
   d. the manufacturer failed to use due care in making the bottle of Hi Cola.

SHORT ESSAY QUESTIONS

1.   What are the elements of a cause of action based on negligence?

2.   How defective must a product be to support a cause of action in strict liability in a product liability suit?

ISSUE SPOTTERS

(Answers at the Back of the Book)

1.   If a student takes another student's business law textbook as a practical joke and hides it for several days before the final examination, has a tort been committed?

2.   After less than a year in business, Superior Club surpasses Ordinary Club in number of members. Superior's marketing strategies attract many Ordinary members, who then change clubs. Does Ordinary have any recourse against Superior?

3.   Real Chocolate Company makes a box of candy, which it sells to Sweet Things, Inc., a distributor. Sweet sells the box to a Tasty Candy store, where Jill buys it. Jill gives it to Ken, who breaks a tooth on a stone the same size and color of a piece of the candy. If Real, Sweet, and Tasty were not negligent, can they be liable for the injury?

Chapter 6:
Criminal Law and Cyber Crimes

WHAT THIS CHAPTER IS ABOUT

This chapter defines what makes an act a crime, describes crimes that affect business (including cyber crimes), lists defenses to crimes, and outlines criminal procedure. Sanctions for crimes are different from those for torts or breaches of contract. Another difference between civil and criminal law is that an individual can bring a civil suit, but only the government can prosecute a criminal.

CHAPTER OUTLINE

I.   CIVIL LAW AND CRIMINAL LAW

A. CIVIL LAW
Civil law consists of the duties that exist between persons or between citizens and their governments, excluding the duty not to commit crimes.

B. CRIMINAL LAW
A **crime** is a wrong against society proclaimed in a statute and, if committed, punishable by society through fines, imprisonment, or death. Crimes are offenses against society as a whole and are prosecuted by public officials, not victims.

II.   CLASSIFICATION OF CRIMES
Felonies are serious crimes punishable by death or by imprisonment in a federal or state penitentiary for more than a year. A crime that is not a felony is a **misdemeanor**—punishable by a fine or by confinement (in a local jail) for up to a year. Petty offenses are minor misdemeanors.

III. CRIMINAL LIABILITY
Two elements must exist for a person to be convicted of a crime—

A. CRIMINAL ACT
A criminal statute prohibits certain behavior—an act of commission (doing something) or an act of omission (not doing something that is a legal duty).

B. INTENT TO COMMIT A CRIME
The wrongful mental state required to establish guilt depends on the crime.

IV. CORPORATE CRIMINAL LIABILITY
Corporations are liable for crimes committed by their agents and employees within the course and scope of employment. Directors and officers are personally liable for crimes they commit and may be liable for the actions of employees under their supervision.

V.   TYPES OF CRIMES

A. VIOLENT CRIME
These include murder, rape, assault and battery (see Chapter 5), and robbery (forcefully and unlawfully taking personal property from another). They are classified by degree, depending on intent, weapon, and victim's suffering.

B. PROPERTY CRIME
Robbery could also be in this category.

1. Burglary
Burglary is the unlawful entry into a building with the intent to commit a felony.

2. Larceny
Wrongfully taking and carrying away another's personal property with the intent of depriving the owner permanently of the property (without force or intimidation, which are elements of robbery).

a. Property
The definition of property includes computer programs, computer time, trade secrets, cellular phone numbers, long-distance phone time, and natural gas.

b. Grand Larceny and Petit Larceny
In some states, grand larceny is a felony and petit larceny a misdemeanor. The difference depends on the value of the property taken.

3. Obtaining Goods by False Pretenses
This includes, for example, buying goods with a check written on an account with insufficient funds.

4. Receiving Stolen Goods
The recipient need not know the identity of the true owner of the goods.

5. Arson
Arson is the willful and malicious burning of a building (and in some states, personal property) owned by another. Every state has a statute that covers burning a building to collect insurance.

6. Forgery
Fraudulently making or altering any writing in a way that changes the legal rights and liabilities of another is forgery.

C. PUBLIC ORDER CRIME
Examples: public drunkenness, prostitution, gambling, and illegal drug use.

D. WHITE-COLLAR CRIME

1. Embezzlement
Fraudulently appropriating another's property or money by one who has been entrusted with it (without force or intimidation).

2. Mail and Wire Fraud

a. The Crime
It is a federal crime to (1) mail or cause someone else to mail something written, printed, or photocopied for the purpose of executing (2) a scheme to defraud (even if no one is defrauded). Also a crime to use wire, radio, or television transmissions to defraud.

b. The Punishment
Fine of up to $1,000, imprisonment for up to five years, or both. If a violation affects a financial institution, the fine may be up to $1 million, the imprisonment up to thirty years, or both.

3. **Bribery**

    a. **Bribery of Public Officials**

        This is attempting to influence a public official to act in a way that serves a private interest by offering the official a bribe. The crime is committed when the bribe (anything the recipient considers valuable) is offered.

    b. **Commercial Bribery**

        Attempting, by a bribe, to obtain proprietary information, cover up an inferior product, or secure new business is commercial bribery.

    c. **Bribery of Foreign Officials**

        A crime occurs when attempting to bribe foreign officials to obtain business contracts. The Foreign Corrupt Practices Act of 1977 (see Chapter 2) makes this a crime.

4. **Bankruptcy Fraud**

    Filing a false claim against a debtor; fraudulently transferring assets to favored parties; or fraudulently concealing property before or after a petition for bankruptcy is filed.

5. **The Theft of Trade Secrets**

    Under the Economic Espionage Act of 1996, it is a federal crime to steal trade secrets, or to knowingly buy or possess another's stolen secrets. Penalties include up to ten years' imprisonment, fines up to $500,000 (individual) or $5 million (corporation), and forfeiture of property.

6. **Insider Trading**

    Using inside information (information not available to the general public) about a publicly traded corporation to profit from the purchase or sale of the corporation's securities (see Chapter 21).

E. **ORGANIZED CRIME**

1. **Money Laundering**

    Transferring the proceeds of crime through legitimate businesses is money laundering. Financial institutions must report transactions of more than $10,000.

2. **The Racketeer Influenced and Corrupt Organizations Act**

    Two offenses under the Racketeer Influenced and Corrupt Organizations Act (RICO) of 1970 constitute "racketeering activity."

    a. **Activities Prohibited by RICO**

        (1) Use income from racketeering to buy an interest in an enterprise, (2) acquire or maintain such an interest through racketeering activity' (3) conduct or participate in an enterprise through racketeering activity, or 4) conspire to do any of the above.

    b. **Civil Liability**

        Civil penalties include divestiture of a defendant's interest in a business or dissolution of the business. Private individuals can recover treble damages, plus attorneys' fees.

    c. **Criminal Liability**

        RICO is often used to prosecute white-collar crimes. Penalties include fines of up to $25,000 per violation, imprisonment for up to 20 years, or both.

VI. DEFENSES TO CRIMINAL LIABILITY

A. **INFANCY**

Cases involving persons who have not reached the age of majority are handled in juvenile courts. In some states, a child over a certain age (usually fourteen) charged with a felony may be tried in an adult court.

B. INTOXICATION

Involuntary intoxication is a defense to a crime if it makes a person incapable of understanding that the act committed was wrong or incapable of obeying the law. *Voluntary* intoxication may be a defense if the person was so intoxicated as to lack the required state of mind.

C. INSANITY

1. The Model Penal Code Test

Most federal courts and some states use this test: a person is not responsible for criminal conduct if at the time, as a result of mental disease or defect, the person lacks substantial capacity either to appreciate the wrongfulness of the conduct or to conform his or her conduct to the law.

2. The *M'Naghten* Test

Some states use this test: a person is not responsible if at the time of the offense, he or she did not know the nature and quality of the act or did not know that the act was wrong.

3. The Irresistible Impulse Test

Some states use this test: a person operating under an irresistible impulse may know an act is wrong but cannot refrain from doing it.

D. MISTAKE

1. Mistake of Fact

Defense if it negates the mental state necessary to commit a crime.

2. Mistake of Law

A person not knowing a law was broken may have a defense if (1) the law was not published or reasonably made known to the public or (2) the person relied on an official statement of the law that was wrong.

E. CONSENT

Consent is a defense if it cancels the harm that the law is designed to prevent, unless the law forbids an act without regard to the victim's consent.

F. DURESS

1. What Duress Is

Duress occurs when a person's threat induces another person to do something that he or she would not otherwise do.

2. When Duress Is a Defense

(1) The threat is one of serious bodily harm, (2) the threat is immediate and inescapable, (3) the threatened harm is greater than the harm caused by the crime, and (4) the defendant is involved through no fault of his or her own.

G. JUSTIFIABLE USE OF FORCE

1. Nondeadly Force

People can use as much nondeadly force as seems necessary to protect themselves, their dwellings, or other property or to prevent a crime.

2. Deadly Force

Deadly force can be used in self-defense if there is a reasonable belief that imminent death or serious bodily harm will otherwise result, if the attacker is using unlawful force, and if the defender did not provoke the attack.

H. ENTRAPMENT

This occurs when a law enforcement agent suggests that a crime be committed, pressures or induces an individual to commit it, and arrests the individual for it.

I. **STATUTE OF LIMITATIONS**
A statute of limitation provides that the state has only a certain amount of time to prosecute a crime.

J. **IMMUNITY**
A state can grant immunity from prosecution or agree to prosecute for a less serious offense in exchange for information. This is often part of a plea bargain between the defendant and the prosecutor.

VII. CONSTITUTIONAL SAFEGUARDS AND CRIMINAL PROCEDURES
Most of these safeguards apply not only in federal but also in state courts by virtue of the due process clause of the Fourteenth Amendment.

A. **FOURTH AMENDMENT**
Protection from unreasonable searches and seizures. No warrants for a search or an arrest can be issued without probable cause.

B. **FIFTH AMENDMENT**
No one can be deprived of "life, liberty, or property without due process of law." No one can be tried twice (double jeopardy) for the same offense. No one can be required to incriminate himself or herself.

C. **SIXTH AMENDMENT**
Guarantees a speedy trial, trial by jury, a public trial, the right to confront witnesses, and the right to a lawyer in some proceedings.

D. **EIGHTH AMENDMENT**
Prohibits excessive bail and fines, and cruel and unusual punishment.

E. **EXCLUSIONARY RULE**
Evidence obtained in violation of the Fourth, Fifth, and Sixth Amendments, as well as all "fruit of the poisonous tree" (evidence derived from illegally obtained evidence), must be excluded.

F. *MIRANDA* **RULE**
A person in police custody who is to be interrogated must be informed that he or she has the right to remain silent; anything said can and will be used against him or her in court; he or she has the right to consult with an attorney; and if he or she is indigent, a lawyer will be appointed. Exceptions to this rule include "public safety."

VIII. CRIMINAL PROCESS

A. **ARREST**
Requires a warrant based on probable cause (a substantial likelihood that the person has committed or is about to commit a crime). To make an arrest without a warrant, an officer must also have probable cause.

B. **INDICTMENT OR INFORMATION**
A formal charge is called an **indictment** if issued by a grand jury and an **information** if issued by a government prosecutor.

C. **TRIAL**
Criminal trial procedures are similar to those of a civil trial, but the standard of proof is higher: the prosecutor must establish guilt beyond a reasonable doubt.

D. SENTENCING GUIDELINES

These guidelines cover possible penalties for federal crimes. A sentence is based on a defendant's criminal record, seriousness of the offense, and other factors.

IX.   CYBER CRIME

A. CYBER THEFT

Computers make it possible for employees and others to commit crimes (such as fraud) involving serious financial losses. The Internet has made identity theft and consequent crimes easier.

B. CYBERSTALKING

Harassing a person in cyberspace (such as via e-mail). Prohibited by federal law and most states. Some states require a "credible threat" that puts the person in reasonable fear for his or her safety or the safety of the person's family.

C. HACKING AND CYBERTERRORISM

Using one computer to break into another is hacking. This is often part of cyber theft. Cyberterrorism is exploiting computers for such serious impacts as spreading a virus through a computer network.

D. PROSECUTING CYBER CRIMES

Jurisdictional issues and the anonymous nature of technology can hinder the investigation and prosecution of crimes committed in cyberspace.

1. **The Computer Fraud and Abuse Act**

   The Computer Access Device and Computer Fraud and Abuse Act of 1984 provides for criminal prosecution of a person who accesses a computer online, without authority, to obtain classified, restricted, or protected data (restricted government info, financial records, etc.), or attempts to do. Penalties include fines and up to five years' imprisonment.

2. **Other Federal Statutes**

   Electronic Fund Transfer Act of 1978, Anticounterfeiting Consumer Protection Act of 1996, National Stolen Property Act of 1988, and more.

TRUE-FALSE QUESTIONS

(Answers at the Back of the Book)

_T_   1.   Only the government prosecutes criminal defendants.

_F_   2.   A crime punishable by imprisonment is a felony.

_F_   3.   Burglary involves taking another's personal property from his or her person or immediate presence.

_F_   4.   Embezzlement requires physically taking property for another's possession.

_T_   5.   Stealing a computer program is larceny.

_F_   6.   Offering a bribe is only one element of the crime of bribery.

_F_   7.   Receiving stolen goods is a crime only if the recipient knows the true owner.

_T_   8.   Generally, a person is not responsible for a criminal act if, as a result of a mental defect, he or she lacked substantial capacity to appreciate the wrongfulness of the act.

_I_   9.   A person who accesses a computer online, without authorization, to obtain protected data commits a federal crime.

_I_   10.   RICO is often used to prosecute acts classified as white-collar crimes.

FILL-IN QUESTIONS

(Answers at the Back of the Book)

Specific constitutional safeguards for those accused of crimes apply in all federal courts, and most of them also apply in state courts under the due process clause of the Fourteenth Amendment. The safeguards include (1) the Fourth Amendment protection from _unreasonable_ (unexpected/unreasonable) searches and seizures, (2) the Fourth Amendment requirement that no warrants for a search or an arrest can be issued without _probable_ (probable/possible) cause, (3) the Fifth Amendment requirement that no one can be deprived of "life, liberty, or property without _due process of law_ (consent/due process of law)," (4) the Fifth Amendment prohibition against double _jeopardy_ (immunity/jeopardy), (5) the Sixth Amendment guaranties of a speedy _trial_ (appeal/trial), _trial by_ (appeal to/trial by) a jury, a public trial, the right to confront _witness_ (counsel/witnesses), and the right to legal counsel, and (6) the Eighth Amendment prohibitions against excessive _bail and fines_ (bail/bail and fines) and cruel and unusual punishment.

MULTIPLE-CHOICE QUESTIONS

(Answers at the Back of the Book)

_D_   1.   Carl wrongfully takes a box from a Delta, Inc., shipping container, puts it in his truck, and drives away. This is

a.   burglary.
b.   embezzlement.
c.   forgery.
d.   larceny.

_C_   2.   Nora is charged with the commission of a crime. For a conviction, most crimes require

a.   only a specified state of mind or intent.
b.   only the performance of a prohibited act.
c.   a specified state of mind and performance of a prohibited act.
d.   none of the above.

_C_   3.   Adam signs Beth's name, without her consent, to the back of a check payable to Beth. This is

a.   burglary.
b.   embezzlement.
c.   forgery.
d.   larceny.

_B_   4.   Owen, a bank teller, deposits into his account checks that bank customers give to him to deposit into their accounts. This is

a.   burglary.
b.   embezzlement.
c.   forgery.
d.   larceny.

B   5.   Jay is charged with the commission of a crime. For a conviction, the standard to find Jay guilty is

     a.   beyond all doubt.
     b.   beyond a reasonable doubt.
     c.   clear and convincing evidence.
     d.   a preponderance of the evidence.

C   6.   Nick is charged with the crime of mail fraud. For a conviction, Nick must be found to have

     a.   had a scheme to defraud.
     b.   used the mails.
     c.   had a scheme to defraud and used the mails.
     d.   none of the above.

B   7.   Sue, a government agent, arrests Tim for the commission of a crime. Tim claims that Sue entrapped him. This is a valid defense if Sue

     a.   did not tell Tim that she was a government agent.
     b.   pressured Tim into committing the crime.
     c.   set a trap for Tim, who was looking to commit the crime.
     d.   was predisposed to commit the crime.

C   8.   John is arrested on suspicion of the commission of a crime. Individuals who are arrested must be told of their right to

     a.   confront witnesses.
     b.   protection against unreasonable searches.
     c.   remain silent.
     d.   trial by jury.

C   9.   While away from her business, Kate is arrested on the suspicion of the commission of a crime. At Kate's trial, under the exclusionary rule

     a.   biased individuals must be excluded from the jury.
     b.   business records must be excluded from admission as evidence.
     c.   illegally obtained evidence must be excluded from admission as evidence.
     d.   the arresting officer must be excluded from testifying.

B   10.   Eve is arrested on suspicion of the commission of a crime. A grand jury issues a formal charge against Eve. This is

     a.   an arraignment.
     b.   an indictment.
     c.   an information.
     d.   an inquisition.

SHORT ESSAY QUESTIONS

1.   What are some of the significant differences between criminal law and civil law?

2.   What constitutes civil liability under the Racketeer Influenced and Corrupt Organizations Act (RICO) of 1968 and what are the penalties?

ISSUE SPOTTERS

(Answers at the Back of the Book)

1. Bob drives off in Fred's car mistakenly believing that it is his. Is this theft?

2. Ellen takes her roommate's credit card, intending to charge expenses that she incurs on a vacation. Her first stop is a gas station, where she uses the card to pay for gas. With respect to the gas station, has she committed a crime? If so, what is it?

3. Ben downloads consumer credit files from a computer of Consumer Credit Agency, without permission, over the Internet. Ben sells the data to Donna. Has Ben committed a crime? If so, what is it?

CUMULATIVE HYPOTHETICAL PROBLEM
FOR UNIT TWO—INCLUDING CHAPTERS 4–6

(Answers at the Back of the Book)

GPS, Inc., designs and sells the technology for advanced global positioning systems that can be used to pinpoint the location of virtually any person or object.

_B_ 1. GPS sells defective software to High Tech Devices Corporation, which sells it to a customer, Intel Locate, Inc. The software causes damages that Intel estimates at $500,000. With respect to Intel, GPS has most likely committed

    a. a crime.
    b. a tort.
    c. a violation of Intel's constitutional rights.
    d. no crime, tort, or violation of constitutional rights.

_B_ 2. During an investigation into GPS's activities, the court orders GPS to provide its business records. As a corporation, GPS can

    a. be compelled to provide only records that do _not_ incriminate its officers.
    b. be compelled to provide records that incriminate its officers.
    c. refuse to provide records that incriminate its officers.
    d. refuse to provide _any_ business records.

_A_ 3. After the investigation into GPS's activities, some of its officers are suspected of having committed crimes. As a corporation, GPS can

    a. be fined or denied certain privileges if it is held criminally liable.
    b. be imprisoned if it is held criminally liable.
    c. be fined, denied privileges, or imprisoned if it is held criminally liable.
    d. not be found to be criminally liable.

_C_ 4. GPS's officers order some employees to access a competitor's computers online to obtain its data without permission. This is

    a. embezzlement.
    b. robbery.
    c. theft.
    d. wire fraud.

5. Congress enacts a law that affects GPS, which challenges the law on the basis of equal protection. This means that GPS claims the law

   a. does not include sufficient procedural safeguards.
   b. limits the liberty of *all* persons in a way that is unconstitutional.
   c. limits the liberty of *some* persons in a way that is unconstitutional.
   d. unduly burdens interstate commerce.

Chapter 7:
Intellectual Property

WHAT THIS CHAPTER IS ABOUT

Intellectual property consists of the products of intellectual, creative processes. The law of trademarks, patents, copyrights, and related concepts protect many of these products (such as inventions, books, software, movies, and songs). This chapter outlines these laws, including their application in cyberspace.

CHAPTER OUTLINE

I. TRADEMARKS AND RELATED PROPERTY

A. TRADEMARKS
The Lanham Act protects trademarks at the federal level. Many states also have statutes that protect trademarks.

1. What Is a Trademark?
A distinctive mark, motto, device, or emblem that a manufacturer stamps, prints, or otherwise affixes to the goods it produces to distinguish them from the goods of other manufacturers.

2. The Federal Trademark Dilution Act of 1995
Prohibits dilution (unauthorized use of marks on goods or services, even if they do not compete directly with products whose marks are copied).

3. Trademark Registration
A trademark may be registered with a state or the federal government. Trademarks need not be registered to be protected.

    a. Requirements for Federal Registration
    A trademark may be filed with the U.S. Patent and Trademark Office on the basis of (1) use or (2) the intent to use the mark within six months (which may be extended to thirty months).

    b. Renewal of Federal Registration
    Between the fifth and sixth years and then every ten years (twenty years for marks registered before 1990).

4. Requirements for Trademark Protection
The extent to which the law protects a trademark is normally determined by how distinctive it is.

    a. Strong Marks
    Fanciful, arbitrary, or suggestive marks are considered most distinctive.

    b. Descriptive Terms, Geographic Terms, and Personal Names
    Descriptive terms, geographic terms, and personal names are not inherently distinctive and are not protected until they acquire a secondary meaning (which means that customers associate the mark with the source of a product)

    c. Generic Terms
    Terms such as *bicycle* or *computer* receive no protection, even if they acquire secondary meaning.

    5. Trademark Infringement
    This occurs when a trademark is copied to a substantial degree or used in its entirety by another.

B. SERVICE, CERTIFICATION, AND COLLECTIVE MARKS
Laws that apply to trademarks normally also apply to—

    1. Service Marks
    Used to distinguish the services of one person or company from those of another. Registered in the same manner as trademarks.

    2. Certification Marks
    Used by one or more persons, other than the owner, to certify the region, materials, mode of manufacture, quality, or accuracy of the owner's goods or services.

    3. Collective Marks
    Certification marks used by members of a cooperative, association, or other organization.

C. TRADE NAMES
Used to indicate part or all of a business's name. Trade names cannot be registered with the federal government but may be protected under the common law if they are used as trademarks or service marks.

D. TRADE DRESS
Trade dress is the image and appearance of a product, and is subject to the same protection as trademarks.

II. CYBER MARKS

A. ANTICYBERSQUATTING LEGISLATION
The Anticybersquatting Consumer Reform Act (ACRA) of 1999 amended the Lanham Act to make cybersquatting clearly illegal. Bad faith intent is an element (the ACRA lists "bad faith" factors). Damages may be awarded.

B. META TAGS
Words in a Web site's key-word field that determine the site's appearance in search engine results. Using others' marks as tags without permission constitutes trademark infringement.

C. DILUTION IN THE ONLINE WORLD
Using a mark, without permission, in a way that diminishes its distinctive quality. Tech-related cases have concerned the use of marks as domain names and spamming under another's logo.

D. LICENSING
Licensing is permitting a party to use a mark, copyright, patent, or trade secret for certain purposes. Use for other purposes is a breach of the license agreement.

III. PATENTS

A. WHAT IS A PATENT?
A grant from the federal government that conveys and secures to an inventor the exclusive right to make, use, and sell an invention for a period of 20 years (14 years for a design).

B. REQUIREMENTS FOR A PATENT
An invention, discovery, or design must be genuine, novel, useful, and not obvious in light of the technology of the time. A patent is given to the first person to invent a product, not to the first person to file for a patent.

C. PATENTS FOR SOFTWARE
The basis for software is often a mathematical equation or formula, which is not patentable, but a patent can be obtained for a process that incorporates a computer program.

D. **PATENT INFRINGEMENT**

Making, using, or selling another's patented design, product, or process without the patent owner's permission. The owner may obtain an injunction, damages, destruction of all infringing copies, attorneys' fees, and court costs.

E. **BUSINESS PROCESS PATENTS**

Business processes are patentable (but laws of nature, natural phenomena, and abstract ideas are not).

IV. COPYRIGHTS

A. **WHAT IS A COPYRIGHT?**

An intangible right granted by statute to the author or originator of certain literary or artistic productions. Protection is automatic; registration is not required.

B. **COPYRIGHT PROTECTION**

Protection lasts for the life of the author plus 70 years. Copyrights owned by publishing houses expire 95 years from the date of publication or 120 years from the date of creation, whichever is first. For works by more than one author, copyright expires 70 years after the death of the last surviving author.

C. **WHAT IS PROTECTED EXPRESSION?**

To be protected, a work must meet these requirements—

1. **Fit a Certain Category**

It must be a (1) literary work; (2) musical work; (3) dramatic work; (4) pantomime or choreographic work; (5) pictorial, graphic, or sculptural work; (6) film or other audiovisual work; or (7) a sound recording. The Copyright Act also protects computer software and architectural plans.

2. **Be Fixed in a Durable Medium**

From which it can be perceived, reproduced, or communicated.

3. **Be Original**

A compilation of facts (formed by the collection and assembling of preexisting materials of data) is copyrightable if it is original.

D. **WHAT IS NOT PROTECTED?**

Ideas, facts, and related concepts are not protected. If an idea and an expression cannot be separated, the expression cannot be copyrighted.

E. **COPYRIGHT INFRINGEMENT**

A copyright is infringed if a work is copied without the copyright holder's permission. A copy does not have to be exactly the same as the original—copying a substantial part of the original is enough.

1. **Penalties**

Actual damages (based on the harm to the copyright holder); damages under the Copyright Act, not to exceed $150,000; and criminal proceedings (which may result in fines or imprisonment).

2. **Exception—Fair Use Doctrine**

The Copyright Act permits the fair use of a work for purposes such as criticism, news reporting, teaching (including multiple copies for classroom use), scholarship, or research. Factors in determining whether a use is infringement include the effect of the use on the market for the work.

F. **COPYRIGHT PROTECTION FOR SOFTWARE**

The Computer Software Copyright Act of 1980 provides protection.

1. **What Is Protected?**

The binary object code (the part of a software program readable only by computer); the source code (the part of a program readable by people); and the program structure, sequence, and organization.

2. **What May or May Not Be Protected**
   The "look and feel"—the general appearance, command structure, video images, menus, windows, and other displays—of a program.

G. **COPYRIGHTS IN DIGITAL INFORMATION**
   Copyright law is important in cyberspace in part because the nature of the Internet means that data is "copied" before being transferred online.

   1. **The Copyright Act of 1976**
      Copyright law requires the copyright holder's permission to sell a "copy" of a work. For these purposes, loading a file or program into a computer's random access memory (RAM) is the making of a "copy."

   2. **Further Developments in Copyright Law**

      a. **No Electronic Theft Act of 1997**
         Extends criminal liability to the exchange of pirated, copyrighted materials, even if no profit is realized from the exchange, and to the unauthorized copying of works for personal use.

      b. **Digital Millennium Copyright Act of 1998**
         Imposes penalties on anyone who circumvents encryption software or other technological anti-piracy protection. Also prohibits the manufacture, import, sale, or distribution of devices or services for circumvention. ISP s are not liable for their customers' violations.

      c. **MP3 and File-Sharing Technology**
         MP3 file compression and music file sharing occur over the Internet through peer-to-peer (P2P) networking. Doing this without the permission of the owner of the music's copyright is infringement.

V. **TRADE SECRETS**

   A. **WHAT IS A TRADE SECRET?**
      Customer lists, formulas, plans, research and development, pricing information, marketing techniques, production techniques, and generally anything that provides an opportunity to obtain an advantage over competitors who do not know or use it.

   B. **TRADE SECRET PROTECTION**
      Protection of trade secrets extends both to ideas and their expression. Liability extends to those who misappropriate trade secrets by any means. Trade secret theft is also a federal crime.

   C. **TRADE SECRETS IN CYBERSPACE**
      The nature of technology (especially e-mail) undercuts a firm's ability to protect its confidential information, including trade secrets.

VI. **INTERNATIONAL PROTECTION**

   A. **THE BERNE CONVENTION**
      The Berne Convention is an international copyright treaty.

   1. **For Citizens of Countries That Have Signed the Berne Convention**
      If, for example, an American writes a book, the copyright in the book is recognized by every country that has signed the convention.

   2. **For Citizens of Other Countries**
      If a citizen of a country that has not signed the convention publishes a book first in a country that has signed, all other countries that have signed the convention recognize that author's copyright.

B. THE TRIPS AGREEMENT

Trade-Related Aspects of Intellectual Property Rights (TRIPS) Agreement is part of the agreement creating the World Trade Organization (WTO). Each member nation must not discriminate (in administration, regulation, or adjudication of intellectual property rights) against the rights' owners.

C. WORLD INTELLECTUAL PROPERTY ORGANIZATION (WIPO) COPYRIGHT TREATY

Current international law includes the WIPO Copyright Treaty of 1996, which the United States implemented in the Digital Millennium Copyright Act of 1998.

D. THE MADRID PROTOCOL

Under this treaty, a U.S. company wishing to register its trademark abroad can submit a single application and designate other member countries in which they would like to register the mark.

TRUE-FALSE QUESTIONS

(Answers at the Back of the Book)

____ 1. To obtain a patent, an applicant must show that an invention is genuine, novel, useful, and not obvious in light of current technology.

____ 2. To obtain a copyright, an author must show that a work is genuine, novel, useful, and not a copy of a current copyrighted work.

____ 3. In determining whether the use of a copyrighted work is infringement under the fair use doctrine, one factor is the effect of that use on the market for the work.

____ 4. A personal name is protected under trademark law if it acquires a secondary meaning.

____ 5. A formula for a chemical compound is not a trade secret.

____ 6. A trade name, like a trademark, can be registered with the federal government.

____ 7. A copy must be exactly the same as an original work to infringe on its copyright.

____ 8. Only the *intentional* use of another's trademark can be trademark infringement.

____ 9. Using another's trademark in a domain name without permission violates federal law.

____ 10. Trademark dilution requires proof that consumers are likely to be confused by the unauthorized use of the mark.

FILL-IN QUESTIONS

(Answers at the Back of the Book)

Copyright protection is automatic for the life of the author of a work plus _____ (70/95/120) years. Copyrights owned by publishing houses expire _____ (70/95/120) years from the date of the publication of a work or _____ (70/95/120) years from the date of its creation, whichever is first. For works by more than one author, a copyright expires _____ (70/95/120) years after the death of the last surviving author.

MULTIPLE-CHOICE QUESTIONS

(Answers at the Back of the Book)

____   1.   Alpha, Inc., uses Beta Corporation's patented design in Alpha's plan for a similar product, without Beta's permission. This is

   a.   copyright infringement.
   b.   patent infringement.
   c.   trademark infringement.
   d.   none of the above.

____   2.   Omega, Inc., uses a trademark on its products that no one, including Omega, has registered with the government. Under federal trademark law, Omega

   a.   can register the mark for protection.
   b.   cannot register a mark that has been used in commerce.
   c.   has committed trademark infringement.
   d.   must postpone registration until the mark has been out of use for three years.

____   3.   Ann invents a new type of light bulb and applies for a patent. If Ann is granted a patent, the invention will be protected

   a.   for 10 years.
   b.   for 20 years.
   c.   for the life of the inventor plus 70 years.
   d.   forever.

____   4.   The graphics used in "Grave Robbers," a computer game, are protected by

   a.   copyright law.
   b.   patent law.
   c.   trademark law.
   d.   trade secrets law.

____   5.   Production techniques used to make "Grave Robbers," a computer game, are protected by

   a.   copyright law.
   b.   patent law.
   c.   trademark law.
   d.   trade secrets law.

____   6.   Tech Corporation uses USA, Inc.'s trademark in Tech's ads without USA's permission. This is

   a.   copyright infringement.
   b.   patent infringement.
   c.   trademark infringement.
   d.   none of the above.

____   7.   Clothes made by workers who are members of the Clothes Makers Union are sold with tags that identify this fact. This is

   a.   a certification mark.
   b.   a collective mark.
   c.   a service mark.
   d.   trade dress.

____ 8. Tony owns Antonio's, a pub in a small town in Iowa. Universal Dining, Inc., opens a chain of pizza places in California called "Antonio's" and, without Tony's consent, uses "antoniosincalifornia" as part of the URL for the chain's Web site. This is

   a. copyright infringement.
   b. patent infringement.
   c. trademark dilution.
   d. none of the above.

____ 9. Data Corporation created and sells "Economix," financial computer software. Data's copyright in Economix is best protected under

   a. the Berne Convention.
   b. the Paris Convention.
   c. the TRIPS Agreement.
   d. none of the above.

____ 10. National Media, Inc. (NMI), publishes *Opinion* magazine, which contains an article by Paula. Without her permission, NMI puts the article into an online database. This is

   a. copyright infringement.
   b. patent infringement.
   c. trademark infringement.
   d. none of the above.

SHORT ESSAY QUESTIONS

1. What does a copyright protect?

2. What is a trade secret and how is it protected?

ISSUE SPOTTERS

(Answers at the Back of the Book)

1. Delta Company discovers that it can extract data from the computer of Gamma, Inc., its major competitor, by making a series of phone calls over a high-speed modem. When Delta uses its discovery to extract Gamma's customer list, without permission, what recourse does Gamma have?

2. Global Products develops, patents, and markets software. World Copies, Inc., sells Global's software without the maker's permission. Is this patent infringement? If so, how might Global save the cost of suing World for infringement and at the same time profit from World's sales?

3. Eagle Corporation began marketing software in 1995 under the mark "Eagle." In 2005, Eagle.com, Inc., a different company selling different products, begins to use "eagle" as part of its URL and registers it as a domain name. Can Eagle Corporation stop this use of "eagle"? If so, what must the company show?

Chapter 8:
Contract Formation

WHAT THIS CHAPTER IS ABOUT

Contract law concerns the formation and keeping of promises, the excuses our society accepts for breaking such promises, and what promises are considered contrary to public policy and therefore legally void. This chapter introduces the basic terms and concepts of contract law.

CHAPTER OUTLINE

I. THE FUNCTION AND DEFINITION OF CONTRACTS

A. SOURCES OF CONTRACT LAW
Contract law is common law, which governs all contracts except when statutes or administrative regulations have modified or replaced it. Statutory law—particularly the Uniform Commercial Code (UCC)—governs all contracts for sales of goods.

B. THE FUNCTION OF CONTRACT LAW
Contract law is designed to provide stability and predictability for buyers and sellers. Contract law ensures compliance with a promise and entitles a nonbreaching party to relief when a contract is breached. In determining the existence of a contract, the element of intent is of prime importance (see below).

C. DEFINITION OF A CONTRACT
A **contract** is a promise for the breach of which the law gives a remedy or the performance of which the law recognizes as a duty (that is, an agreement that can be enforced in court). A contract may be formed when two or more parties promise to perform or to refrain from performing some act now or in the future. A party who does not fulfill his or her promise may be subject to sanctions, including damages or, in some circumstances, being required to perform the promise.

D. THE OBJECTIVE THEORY OF CONTRACTS
Intent to enter into a contract is judged by objective (outward) facts as interpreted by a reasonable person, rather than by a party's subjective intent. Objective facts include (1) what a party says when entering into a contract, (2) how a party acts or appears, and (3) circumstances surrounding a deal.

II. ELEMENTS OF A CONTRACT

A. REQUIREMENTS OF A VALID CONTRACT

1. **Agreement**
   This requirement includes an offer and an acceptance. One party must offer to enter into a legal agreement, and another party must accept the offer.

2. **Consideration**
   Promises must be supported by legally sufficient and bargained-for consideration.

3. **Contractual Capacity**
   This includes characteristics that qualify the parties to a contract as competent.

    4. Legality
A contract's purpose must be to accomplish a goal that is not against public policy.

B. DEFENSES TO THE ENFORCEABILITY OF A CONTRACT

    1. Genuineness of Assent
The apparent consent of both parties must be genuine.

    2. Form
A contract must be in whatever form the law requires (some contracts must be in writing).

III. TYPES OF CONTRACTS
Each category signifies a legal distinction regarding a contract's formation, performance, or enforceability.

A. CONTRACT FORMATION

    1. Bilateral versus Unilateral Contracts
Bilateral contract—a promise for a promise (to accept the offer, the offeree need only promise to perform). *Unilateral contract*—a promise for an act (the offeree can accept only by completing performance).

    2. Formal versus Informal Contracts
Formal contract—a special form or method of creation is required for enforcement. *Informal contract*—a contract that is not formal (certain contracts must be in writing, however).

    3. Express versus Implied-in-Fact Contracts
Express contract—the terms of the agreement are fully and explicitly stated in words (oral or written). *Implied contract*—implied from the conduct of the parties.

B. CONTRACT PERFORMANCE
Executed contract—a contract that has been fully performed on both sides. *Executory contract*—a contract that has not been fully performed by one or more of the parties.

C. CONTRACT ENFORCEABILITY
Valid contract—has all elements necessary to entitle at least one party to enforce it. *Void contract*—produces no legal obligations on the part of any of the parties. *Voidable contract*—valid contract that can be avoided by one or more of the parties. *Unenforceable contract*—contract that cannot be enforced because of certain legal defenses.

IV. AGREEMENT

A. REQUIREMENTS OF THE OFFER
An offer is a promise or commitment to do or refrain from doing some specified thing in the future. The elements for an offer to be effective are—

    1. Intention
The offeror must intend to be bound by the offer. Intent is determined by what a reasonable person in the offeree's position would conclude the offeror's words and actions meant. Expressions and statements that are not offers include (1) expressions of opinion, (2) preliminary negotiations, and (3) ads, catalogues, price lists, and circulars.

    2. Definiteness of Terms
All major terms must be stated with reasonable definiteness in the offer (or, if the offeror directs, in the offeree's acceptance). Courts are sometimes willing to supply a missing term when the parties have clearly manifested an intent to form a contract.

    3. Communication of the Offer
The offer must be communicated to the offeree.

B. TERMINATION OF THE OFFER

1. Termination by Action of the Offeror

The offeror can revoke an offer by express repudiation or by performance of acts that are inconsistent with the offer and that are made known to the offeree. A revocation becomes effective when the offeree or offeree's agent actually receives it.

2. Termination by Action of the Offeree

a. Rejection of the Offer by the Offeree

An offer may be rejected by words or conduct evidencing an intent not to accept the offer. Asking about an offer is not rejecting it. Rejection is effective only on its receipt by the offeror or the offeror's agent.

b. Counteroffer by the Offeree

The offeree's attempt to include different terms is a rejection of the original offer and a simultaneous making of a new offer. The *mirror image rule* requires the acceptance to match the offer exactly.

3. Termination by Operation of Law

a. Lapse of Time

An offer terminates automatically when the time specified in the offer has passed. The specified time begins to run when the offeree receives the offer, not when it is sent. If no time is specified, the offer terminates at the end of a reasonable period, as determined by the subject matter of the contract, business and market conditions, and other relevant circumstances.

b. Other Events that Terminate an Offer

The offeree's power to accept can be terminated by destruction of the subject matter of the offer, the death of incompetence of either party (whether or not the other party has notice), or a statute or court decision that makes the offer illegal.

C. ACCEPTANCE

The offeree must accept the offer unequivocally.

1. Communication of Acceptance

A bilateral contract is formed when acceptance is communicated (must be timely). In a unilateral contract, communication is unnecessary, unless the offeror requests notice or has no adequate means of determining if the act has been performed, or the law requires notice.

2. Mode and Timeliness of Acceptance

An acceptance is timely if it is made before the offer is terminated. Acceptance is effective when it is sent by whatever means is authorized by the offeror. This is the **mailbox rule**.

3. Technology and Acceptance Rules

Generally, on the Internet, the mailbox rule is not needed because online acceptances are instantaneous (see Chapter 10).

V. CONSIDERATION

Consideration is the value given in return for a promise.

A. ELEMENTS OF CONSIDERATION

1. A Bargained-for Exchange

The promise must induce the value, and the value must induce the promise. Situations that lack this element include "past" consideration (promises made with respect to events that have already taken place are unenforceable).

2. **Something of Legal Value**
Something of legal value must be given in exchange for a promise. It may be a return promise. If it is performance, it may be (1) an act (other than a promise); (2) a forbearance (refraining from action); or (3) the creation, modification, or destruction of a legal relation.

a. **Adequacy of Consideration**
Generally, a court will not evaluate adequacy (the fairness of a bargain), unless its absence indicates fraud, duress, incapacity, undue influence, or a lack of bargained-for exchange.

b. **Preexisting Duty Rule and Past Consideration**
A promise to do what one already has a legal duty to do does not constitute consideration. A promise made in return for an event that has already occurred also lacks consideration.

c. **Unforeseen Difficulties**
When a party runs into unforeseen difficulties that could not have been anticipated at the time a contract was entered into, the parties may agree to extra compensation. Such difficulties do not include risks ordinarily assumed in business.

B. **PROMISSORY ESTOPPEL**
Under the doctrine of **promissory estoppel** (detrimental reliance), a person who relies on the promise of another may be able to recover in the absence of consideration if—

1. The promise was clear and definite.
2. The reliance is justifiable.
3. The promisor knew or had reason to believe that the promisee would likely rely on the promise, and the reliance induced a change of a substantial and definite character.
4. Justice will be better served by enforcement of the promise.

VI.   CAPACITY

Persons who are minors, intoxicated, or mentally incompetent but not yet adjudicated officially as such, have capacity to enter into a contract; but they can normally avoid liability under the contract.

VII.   LEGALITY

To be enforceable, a contract must not violate any statutes or public policy. A covenant not to compete, for example, to be enforceable, must be no more restrictive than necessary to protect a legitimate business interest.

VIII.   GENUINENESS OF ASSENT

A. **MISTAKES**
It is important to distinguish between mistakes made in judgment as to value or quality and mistakes made as to facts. Only the latter have legal significance.

1. **Bilateral (Mutual) Mistakes**
When both parties make a mistake as to a material fact, either party can rescind the contract. The same rule applies if the parties attach materially different meanings to a word or term in the contract that may be subject to more than one reasonable interpretation.

2. **Unilateral Mistakes of Fact**
A unilateral mistake as to a material fact does not afford a mistaken party relief. Exceptions: include (1) if the other party knows or should know of the mistake or (2) if the mistake is due to a mathematical error and is done inadvertently and without gross negligence.

B. **FRAUDULENT MISREPRESENTATION**
If an innocent party is fraudulently induced to enter into a contract, the contract normally can be avoided. Fraud consists of: (1) misrepresentation of a material fact, (2) an intent to deceive, and (3) the

innocent party's justifiable reliance on the misrepresentation. To collect damages, a party must also have suffered an injury.

C. INNOCENT MISREPRESENTATION
This occurs when a person misrepresents a material fact without an intent to defraud (believes a statement to be true). One relying on the statement to his or her detriment can rescind the contract.

D. UNDUE INFLUENCE
Occurs when a contract enriches a party at the expense of another dominated by the enriched party. The contract is voidable. Essentially, the party taken advantage of does not exercise free will.

E. DURESS
Involves conduct of a coercive nature, such as forcing a party to contract by threatening the party with a wrongful or illegal act. Can be a defense to the enforcement of a contract and a ground for rescission.

F. ADHESION CONTRACTS AND UNCONSCIONABILITY
To avoid a contract, an adhering party must show that the parties had substantially unequal bargaining positions and that enforcement would be unfair or oppressive.

IX.   STATUTE OF FRAUDS
The Statute of Frauds stipulates what types of contracts must be in writing to be enforceable. If a contract is not in writing, it is not void but the Statute of Frauds is a defense to its enforcement.

A. CONTRACTS THAT MUST BE IN WRITING TO BE ENFORCEABLE
Contracts involving interests in land, contracts that cannot be performed within one year of formation, collateral ($5,000 or more under the 2003 amendments to the Uniform Commercial Code—Chapter 10).

B. EXCEPTIONS TO THE STATUTE OF FRAUDS
An oral contract may be enforced if (1) a promisor makes a promise on which the promisee justifiably relies to his or her detriment, (2) the reliance was foreseeable to the promisor, and (3) injustice can be avoided only by enforcing the promise. An oral contract may also be enforced if the party against whom enforcement is sought admits to its existence in court proceedings.

XI.   THIRD PARTY RIGHTS

A. ASSIGNMENTS
The transfer of a contract right to a third person is an assignment.

1. Rights That Cannot Be Assigned
Rights cannot be assigned if a statute prohibits assignment, a contract is personal (unless all that remains is a money payment), the assignment materially increases or alters the risk or duties of the obligor, or the contract provides that it cannot be assigned.

2. Exceptions
A contract cannot prevent an assignment of (1) a right to receive money, (2) rights in real property, (3) rights in negotiable instruments (checks and notes), or (4) a right to receive damages for breach of a sales contract or for payment of an amount owed under the contract (even if the contract prohibits it).

B. DELEGATIONS
Duties are not assigned; they are delegated. A delegation does not relieve the delegator of the obligation to perform if the delegatee fails to perform.

1. Duties That Cannot Be Delegated
Any duty can be delegated unless (1) performance depends on the personal skill or talents of the obligor, (2) special trust has been placed in the obligor, (3) performance by a third party will vary materially from that expected by the obligee, or (4) the contract prohibits it.

2. **Effect of a Delegation**

The obligee must accept performance from the delegatee, unless the duty is one that cannot be delegated. If the delegatee fails to perform, the delegator is still liable.

C. **THIRD PARTY BENEFICIARIES**

There are two types of third party beneficiaries: intended and incidental. An intended beneficiary is one for whose benefit a contract is made; if the contract is breached, he or she can sue the promisor. The benefit that an incidental beneficiary receives from a contract between other parties is unintentional; an incidental beneficiary cannot enforce the contract.

TRUE-FALSE QUESTIONS

(Answers at the Back of the Book)

F   1. All promises are legal contracts.

T   2. An agreement includes an offer and an acceptance.

F   3. All rights under a contract can be assigned.

F   4. A contract providing that one party is to pay another "a fair share of the profits" is enforceable.

T   5. Inadequate consideration may indicate fraud, duress, or undue influence.

T   6. A promise to do what one already has a legal duty to do is not legally sufficient consideration.

T   7. A minor may generally disaffirm a contract entered into with an adult.

T   8. Under a mistake of fact, a contract can sometimes be avoided.

F   9. A contract for a transfer of an interest in land need not be in writing to be enforceable.

T   10. Only an intended beneficiary acquires legal rights in a contract.

FILL-IN QUESTIONS

(Answers at the Back of the Book)

Whether or not a party intended to enter into a contract is determined by the ___objective___ (objective/subjective) theory of contracts. The theory is that a party's intention to enter into a contract is judged by ___objective___ (objective/subjective) facts as they would be interpreted by a reasonable person. Relevant facts include: (1) what the party said; (2) what the party ___did___ (did/secretly believed); and (3) the ___circumstances surrounding___ (circumstances surrounding/party's personal thoughts concerning) the transaction. Generally, courts examine facts in ___a particular transaction___ (a particular transaction/similar transactions) to determine whether the parties made a contract and, if so, what its terms are.

MULTIPLE-CHOICE QUESTIONS

(Answers at the Back of the Book)

D   1. Eve questions whether there is consideration for his contract with Frank. Consideration has two elements—there must be a bargained-for exchange and the value of whatever is exchanged must be

   a. adequately sufficient.
   b. definitely sufficient.
   c. economically sufficient.
   d. legally sufficient.

2. Amy claims that she and Brad entered into a contract. The intent to enter into a contract is determined with reference to

  a. the conscious theory of contracts.
  b. the objective theory of contracts.
  c. the personal theory of contracts.
  d. the subjective theory of contracts.

 3. Before opening her new sports merchandise store, Kay places an ad in the newspaper showing cross-training shoes at certain prices. Within hours of opening for business, the store is sold out of some of the shoes. In this situation

  a. Kay has made an offer to the people reading the ad.
  b. Kay has made a contract with the people reading the ad.
  c. Kay has made an invitation seeking offers.
  d. any customer who demands goods advertised and tenders the money is entitled to them.

 4. Alpha Properties, Inc., makes an offer in a letter to Bob to sell a certain lot for $5,000, with the offer to stay open for thirty days. Bob would prefer to pay $4,000, if Alpha would sell at that price. To leave room for negotiation without rejecting the offer, Bob should reply

  a. "I will not pay $5,000."
  b. "Will you take $4,000?"
  c. "I will pay $4,000."
  d. "I will pay $4,500."

 5. Metro Transport asks for bids on a construction project. Metro estimates that the cost will be $200,000. Most bids are about $200,000, but A&B Construction bids $150,000. In adding a column of figures, A&B mistakenly omitted a $50,000 item. Because Metro had reason to know of the mistake

  a. A&B can avoid the contract because Metro knew of the errors.
  b. A&B can avoid the contract because the errors were the result of negligence.
  c. Metro can enforce the contract because the errors were unilateral.
  d. Metro can enforce the contract because the errors were material.

 6. Jill offers to buy a book owned by Ken for $50. Ken accepts and hands the book to Jill. The transfer and delivery of the book constitute performance. Is this performance consideration for Jill's promise?

  a. Yes, because Jill sought it in exchange for her promise, and Ken gave it in exchange for that promise.
  b. Yes, because performance always constitutes consideration.
  c. No, because Ken already had a duty to hand the book to Jill.
  d. No, because performance never constitutes consideration.

 7. Mary enters into an implied-in-fact contract with Nick. The parties' conduct

  a. defines the contract's terms.
  b. determines the facts.
  c. factors in the implications of the contract.
  d. is irrelevant in terms of the facts.

8. Edie, a sixteen-year-old minor, buys a car from Fine Autos and wrecks it. To disaffirm the contract and satisfy a duty of restitution, Edie must

  a. neither return the car nor pay for the damage.
  b. only return the car.
  c. only pay for the damage.
  d. return the car and pay for the damage.

9. Gamma Company and Omega Corporation enter into an oral contract for the sale of a warehouse. Before Omega takes possession, this contract is enforceable by

  a. Gamma only.
  b. Gamma or Omega.
  c. neither Gamma or Omega.
  d. Omega only.

 10. Joy insures her warehouse under a policy with Kappa Insurance Company. Joy assigns the policy to Lyle, who also owns a warehouse. Kappa's best argument against the assignment of the policy is that

  a. Kappa did not consent to the assignment.
  b. Kappa was not paid for the assignment.
  c. the assignment will materially alter Kappa's risk.
  d. this is a personal service contract.

SHORT ESSAY QUESTIONS

1. What are the basic elements of a contract?

2. What are the elements of fraudulent misrepresentation?

ISSUE SPOTTERS

(Answers at the Back of the Book)

1. Nina signs and returns a letter from Owen, referring to an antique and its price. When Owen delivers the item, Nina sends it back, claiming that they have no contract. Owen claims they do. What standard determines whether these parties have a contract?

2. Mona faxes an offer to Nate, who accepts in a return fax. When is Nate's acceptance effective?

3. Before Paula starts her first year of college, Ross promises to pay her $50,000 if she graduates. She goes to college, borrowing and spending more than $50,000. At the start of her last semester, she reminds Ross of the promise. Ross sends her a note that says, "I revoke the promise." Is Ross's promise binding?

Chapter 9
Contract Performance, Breach, and Remedies

WHAT THIS CHAPTER IS ABOUT

This chapter begins with a discussion of performance and discharge of contracts. Performance of a contract discharges it. Discharging a contract terminates it. Breach of contract is the failure to perform what a party is under a duty to perform. When this happens, the nonbreaching party can choose one or more remedies.

CHAPTER OUTLINE

I. PERFORMANCE AND DISCHARGE

A. CONDITIONS OF PERFORMANCE
A *condition* is a possible future event, occurrence or nonoccurrence of which triggers performance of an obligation or terminates an obligation. If performance is contingent on a condition and it is not satisfied, a party has to perform.

1. Condition Precedent
`This is a condition that must be fulfilled before a party's performance can be required. Such conditions are common.

2. Condition Subsequent
This is a condition that operates to terminate an obligation to perform. The condition follows a duty to perform. Such conditions are rare.

3. Concurrent Condition
A concurrent condition exists when each party's duty to perform is conditioned on the other's duty to perform. This occurs only when the parties are to perform simultaneously (for example, paying for goods on delivery). No party can recover for breach unless he or she first tenders performance.

B. DISCHARGE BY PERFORMANCE
Most contracts are discharged by performance—the parties' doing what they promised to do.

1. Tender of Performance
Discharge can be accomplished by an unconditional offer to perform by one who is ready, willing, and able to do so. If the other party then refuses to perform, the party making the tender can sue for breach.

2. Degree of Performance Required

a. Complete Performance
Express conditions fully occur in all aspects. Any deviation operates as a discharge.

b. Substantial Performance
Performance that does not vary greatly from the performance promised in the contract. The other party is obligated to perform (but may obtain damages for the deviations).

c. **Performance to the Satisfaction of One of the Parties**
   When the subject matter of the contract is personal, performance must actually satisfy the party. Contracts involving mechanical fitness, utility, or marketability need only be performed to the satisfaction of a reasonable person.

d. **Performance to the Satisfaction of a Third Party**
   When the satisfaction of a third party is required, most courts require the work to be satisfactory to a reasonable person.

3. **Material Breach of Contract**
   A breach of contract is the nonperformance of a contractual duty. A breach is material when performance is not at least substantial; the nonbreaching party is excused from performing. If a breach is minor, the nonbreaching party's duty to perform may be suspended.

4. **Anticipatory Repudiation of a Contract**
   This occurs when, before either party has a duty to perform, one party refuses to perform. It can discharge the nonbreaching party, who can sue to recover damages and can also seek a similar contract elsewhere.

C. DISCHARGE BY AGREEMENT

1. **Discharge by Rescission**
   Rescission is the process by which a contract is canceled and the parties are returned to the positions they occupied prior to forming it.

   a. **Executory Contracts**
      Contracts that are executory on both sides can be rescinded.

      1) **Requirements**
         The parties must make another agreement, which must satisfy the legal requirements for a contract. Their promises not to perform are consideration for the second contract.

      2) **Form**
         Rescission is enforceable if oral (even if the original agreement was in writing), unless it is subject to the UCC and the contract requires written rescission.

   b. **Executed Contracts**
      Contracts that are executed on one side can be rescinded only if the party who has performed receives consideration to call off the deal.

2. **Discharge by Novation**
   This occurs when the parties to a contract and a new party agree to substitute the new party for one of the others. Requirements are (1) a previous obligation, (2) all parties' agreement to a new contract, (3) discharge of the prior party, and (4) a new contract.

3. **Discharge by Substituted Agreement**
   Parties to a contract can execute a new agreement with different terms. The new agreement can expressly or impliedly revoke and discharge the previous contract's obligations.

4. **Discharge by Accord and Satisfaction**
   Parties agree to accept performance that is different from the performance originally promised.

D. DISCHARGE BY OPERATION OF LAW

1. **Alteration of the Contract**
   An innocent party can treat a contract as discharged if the other party materially alters a term (such as quantity or price) without consent.

2. **Statutes of Limitations**
Statutes of limitations limit the period during which a party can sue based on a breach of contract.

3. **Bankruptcy**
A discharge in bankruptcy (see Chapter 12) will bar enforcement of most of a debtor's contracts.

4. **Impossibility or Impracticability of Performance**

   a. **Objective Impossibility of Performance**
   Performance is objectively impossible in the event of (1) a party's death or incapacity, (2) destruction of the specific subject matter, or (3) a change in law that makes performance illegal.

   b. **Commercial Impracticability**
   Performance may be excused if it becomes much more difficult or expensive than contemplated when the contract was formed.

   c. **Frustration of Purpose**
   A contract will be discharged if supervening circumstances make it impossible to attain the purpose the parties had in mind.

   d. **Temporary Impossibility**
   An event that makes it temporarily impossible to perform will suspend performance until the impossibility ceases.

II. DAMAGES FOR BREACH OF CONTRACT

Damages compensate a nonbreaching party for the loss of a bargain and, under special circumstances, for additional losses. Generally, the party is placed in the position he or she would have occupied if the contract had been performed.

A. TYPES OF DAMAGES

1. **Compensatory Damages**
Compensatory damages compensate a party for the loss of a bargain. Incidental damages (expenses caused directly by a breach, such as the cost to obtain performance from another source) may also be recovered.

   a. **Contract for a Sale of Goods**
   The usual measure is the difference between the contract price and the market price. If the buyer breaches and the seller has not yet made the goods, the measure is lost profits.

   b. **Contract for a Sale of Land**
   If specific performance is unavailable, or if the buyer breaches, the measure of damages is usually the difference between the land's contract price and its market price.

   c. **Construction Contracts**

      1) **Owner's Breach Before, During, or After Construction**
      Contractor can recover (1) before construction: only profits (contract price, less cost of materials and labor); (2) during construction: profits, plus cost of partial construction; (3) after construction: the contract price, plus interest.

      2) **Contractor's Breach**
      Owner can recover, before construction is complete, the cost of completion.

2. **Consequential Damages**
These damages give the injured party the entire benefit of the bargain—foreseeable losses caused by special circumstances beyond the contract. The breaching party must know (or have reason to know) that special circumstances will cause the additional loss.

B. MITIGATION OF DAMAGES

The nonbreaching party has a duty to mitigate damages. For example, persons whose employment has been wrongfully terminated have a duty to seek other jobs. The damages they receive are their salaries, less the income they received (or would have received) in similar jobs.

C. LIQUIDATED DAMAGES PROVISIONS

1. Liquidated Damages Provision—Enforceable

Specifies a certain amount to be paid on a contract breach to the nonbreaching party for the loss.

2. Penalty Provision—Unenforceable

Specifies a certain amount to be paid in the event of a breach *to penalize the breaching party.*

3. How to Determine If a Provision Will Be Enforced

(1) When a contract was made, was it clear damages would be difficult to estimate? (2) Was amount set as damages reasonable? If either answer is "no," a provision will not be enforced.

III. EQUITABLE REMEDIES

A. RESCISSION AND RESCISSION

Rescission is an action to undo, or cancel, a contract—to return nonbreaching parties to the positions they occupied prior to the transaction. Rescission is available if fraud, mistake, duress, or failure of consideration is present. The rescinding party must give prompt notice to the breaching party, and the parties must make **restitution** by returning to each other goods, property, or money previously conveyed.

B. SPECIFIC PERFORMANCE

This remedy calls for the performance of the act promised in the contract.

1. When Specific Performance Is Available

Damages must be an inadequate remedy. If goods are unique, a court will decree specific performance. Specific performance is granted to a buyer in a contract for the sale of land (every parcel of land is unique).

2. When Specific Performance Is Not Available

Contracts for a sale of goods (other than unique goods) rarely qualify, because substantially identical goods can be bought or sold elsewhere. Courts normally refuse to grant specific performance of personal service contracts.

C. REFORMATION

This remedy is used when the parties have imperfectly expressed their agreement in writing. It allows the contract to be rewritten to reflect the parties' true intentions.

1. When Reformation Is Available

(1) In cases of fraud or mutual mistake; (2) to prove the correct terms of an oral contract; (3) if a covenant not to compete is for a valid purpose (such as the sale of a business), but the area or time constraints are unreasonable, some courts will reform the restraints to make them reasonable.

2. When Reformation Is Not Available

If the area or time constraints in a covenant not to compete are unreasonable, some courts will throw out the entire covenant.

D. RECOVERY BASED ON QUASI CONTRACT

When there is no enforceable contract, quasi contract prevents unjust enrichment. The law implies a promise to pay the reasonable value for benefits received.

1. When Quasi-Contractual Recovery Is Useful

This remedy is useful when a party has partially performed under a contract that is unenforceable. The party may recover the reasonable value (fair market value).

2. **Requirements of the Doctrine**

A party must show (1) he or she conferred a benefit on the other party, (2) he or she had the reasonable expectation of being paid, (3) he or she did not act as a volunteer in conferring the benefit, and (4) the other party would be unjustly enriched by retaining it without paying.

IV.   ELECTION OF REMEDIES

A nonbreaching party must choose which remedy to pursue. This doctrine has been eliminated in contracts for sales of goods [UCC 2–703, 2–711]—UCC remedies are cumulative (see Chapter 11).

V.   WAIVER OF BREACH

A nonbreaching party may be willing to accept a defective performance of the contract. This relinquishment of a right to full performance is a waiver. A waiver keeps the contract going, but the nonbreaching party can recover damages caused by defective or less-than-full performance.

VI.   CONTRACT PROVISIONS LIMITING REMEDIES

A.   EXCULPATORY CLAUSES

A provision excluding liability for fraudulent or intentional injury or for illegal acts will not be enforced. An exculpatory clause for negligence contained in a contract made between parties who have roughly equal bargaining positions usually will be enforced.

B.   LIMITATION-OF-LIABILITY CLAUSES

A clause excluding liability for negligence may be enforced.

TRUE-FALSE QUESTIONS

(Answers at the Back of the Book)

_T_   1.   Complete performance occurs when a contract's conditions fully occur.

_F_   2.   A material breach of contract does not excuse the nonbreaching party from further performance.

_F_   3.   An executory contract cannot be rescinded.

_T_   4.   Objective impossibility discharges a contract.

_F_   5.   Quasi-contractual recovery is possible only when there is an enforceable contract.

_T_   6.   Damages are designed to compensate a nonbreaching party for the loss of a bargain.

_F_   7.   Liquidated damages are uncertain in amount.

_T_   8.   On a breach of contract, a nonbreaching party has a duty to mitigate damages that he or she suffers.

_T_   9.   Consequential damages are foreseeable damages that arise from a party's breach of a contract.

_F_   10.   Specific performance is the usual remedy when one party has breached a contract for a sale of goods.

FILL-IN QUESTIONS

(Answers at the Back of the Book)

Most contracts are discharged by performance—by doing what was promised. Any contract can be discharged by agreement of the parties. _____ (Rescission/Novation) is the process by which a contract is canceled and the parties are returned to the positions they occupied before forming it.

_____ (Rescission / Novation) substitutes a new party for an original party by agreement of all the parties. _____ (Substitution of a new contract / Accord and satisfaction) revokes and discharges a prior contract. _____ (A substitution / An accord) suspends a contractual duty that has not been discharged. Once the _____ (substitution / accord) is performed, the original contractual obligation is discharged.

MULTIPLE-CHOICE QUESTIONS

(Answers at the Back of the Book)

1. Adam contracts with Beth to deliver Beth's goods to her customers. This contract will, like most contracts, be discharged by

   a. accord and satisfaction.
   b. agreement.
   c. operation of law.
   d. performance.

2. Don contracts to build a store for Pat for $500,000, with payments to be in installments of $50,000 as the work progresses. Don finishes the store except for a cover over a compressor on the roof. A cover can be installed for $500. Pat refuses to pay the last installment. If Don's breach is not material

   a. Don has a claim against Pat, and Pat has a claim against Don.
   b. Don has a claim against Pat for $50,000, but Pat has no claim against Don.
   c. neither party has a claim.
   d. Pat has a claim against Don for the failure to cover the compressor, but Don has no claim against Pat.

3. Tony and Carol contract for the sale of Tony's business. Carol gives Tony a down payment, and Tony gives Carol the keys to one of his stores. Before the contract is fully performed, however, they agree to return the down payment and keys, and cancel the sale. This is

   a. an accord and satisfaction.
   b. an alteration of contract.
   c. a novation.
   d. a rescission.

4. Eve contracts with Frank to act as his personal financial planner. Eve's duties under this contract will be discharged if

   a. Frank declares bankruptcy.
   b. it becomes illegal for Eve to provide the service.
   c. the cost of providing the service doubles.
   d. none of the above.

5. Lee and Mary want Nick to replace Lee as a party to their contract. They can best accomplish this by agreeing to

   a. an accord and satisfaction.
   b. an assignment.
   c. a novation.
   d. a nullification.

_C_   6. Sue contracts to deliver Tom's products to his customers for $1,500, payable in advance. Tom pays the money, but Sue fails to perform. Tom can

   a. obtain restitution of the $1,500 but not rescind the contract.
   b. recover nothing nor rescind the contract.
   c. rescind the contract and obtain restitution of the $1,500.
   d. rescind the contract only.

_C_   7. Eagle Corporation contracts to sell to Frosty Malts, Inc., six steel mixers for $5,000. When Eagle fails to deliver, Frosty buys mixers from Great Company, for $6,500. Frosty's measure of damages is

   a. $6,500.
   b. $5,000.
   c. $1,500 plus incident al damages.
   d. nothing.

_B_   8. Owen contracts with Paul to buy a computer for $1,500. Owen tells Paul that if the goods are not delivered on Monday, he will lose $2,000 in business. Paul ships the computer late. Owen can recover

   a. $3,500.
   b. $2,000.
   c. $1,500.
   d. nothing.

_C_   9. Jay agrees to sell an acre of land to Kim for $5,000. Kim Jay fails to go through with the deal, when the market price of the land is $7,000. If Kim cannot obtain the land through specific performance, Kim may recover

   a. $7,000.
   b. $5,000.
   c. $2,000.
   d. nothing.

_D_   10. Eagle Manufacturing, Inc., contracted with Digital Repair Services to maintain Eagle's computers. A "Liquidated Damages Clause" provides that Digital will pay Eagle $500 for each day that Digital is late in responding to a service request. If Digital is three days late in responding, and Eagle sues to enforce this clause, Eagle will

   a. lose, because liquidated damages clauses violate public policy.
   b. lose, unless the liquidated damages clause is determined to be a penalty.
   c. win, because liquidated damages clauses are always enforceable.
   d. win, unless the liquidated damages clause is determined to be a penalty.

SHORT ESSAY QUESTIONS

1. What effect does a material breach have on the nonbreaching party? What is the effect of a nonmaterial breach?

2. What are damages designed to do in a breach of contract situation?

ISSUE SPOTTERS

(Answers at the Back of the Book)

1.   Eagle Construction contracts with Fred to build a store. The work is to begin on May 1 and be done by November 1, so that Fred can open for the holiday buying season. Eagle does not finish until November 15. Fred opens but, due to the delay, loses some sales. Is Fred's duty to pay for the construction of the store discharged?

2.   Lyle contracts to sell his ranch to Mary, who is to take possession on June 1. Lyle delays the transfer until August 1. Mary incurs expenses in providing for livestock that she bought for the ranch. When they made the contract, Lyle had no reason to know of the livestock. Is Lyle liable for Mary's expenses in providing for the cattle?

3.   Excel Engineering, Inc., signs a contract to design a jet for Flight, Inc. The contract excludes liability for design and construction errors. An error in design causes the jet to crash. Is the clause that excluded liability enforceable?

Chapter 10
Sales, Leases, and E-Contracts

WHAT THIS CHAPTER IS ABOUT

The Uniform Commercial Code (UCC) provides a framework of rules to deal with all the phases arising in an ordinary sales transaction from start to finish—from sale to payment. This chapter outlines the principles of UCC Article 2 and Article 2A.

CHAPTER OUTLINE

I. THE SCOPE OF ARTICLE 2—SALES OF GOODS
Article 2 governs contracts for sales of goods. A *sale* is "the passing of title from the seller to the buyer for a price" [UCC 2–106(1)]. *Title* is the formal right of ownership of property. The price may be payable in money, goods, services, or land. *Goods* are tangible and movable.

II. THE SCOPE OF ARTICLE 2A—LEASES
Article 2A governs contracts for leases of goods. A *lease agreement* is the bargain of the lessor and lessee, in their words and deeds, including course of dealing, usage of trade, and course of performance [UCC 2A–103(k)].

III. THE AMENDMENTS TO ARTICLES 2 AND 2A
Amendments have been proposed to update these articles to accommodate e-commerce.

IV. THE FORMATION OF SALES AND LEASE CONTRACTS
The following sections summarize how UCC provisions *change* the effect of the common law of contracts.

A. OFFER
Verbal exchanges, correspondence, and the actions of the parties may not reveal exactly when a binding contractual obligation arises. An agreement sufficient to constitute a contract can exist even if the moment of its making is undetermined [UCC 2–204(2), 2A–204(2)].

1. Open Terms
A sales contract will not fail for indefiniteness, even if one or more terms are left open, as long as (1) the parties intended to make a contract and (2) there is a reasonably certain basis for the court to grant an appropriate remedy [UCC 2–204(3), 2A–204(3)]. (Without a quantity term, there is no basis for a remedy.)

2. Merchant's Firm Offer
If a merchant gives assurances in a signed writing that an offer will remain open, the offer is irrevocable, without consideration for the stated period of time, or if no definite period is specified, for a reasonable period (not more than three months) [UCC 2–205, 2A–205].

B. ACCEPTANCE

1. Promise to Ship or Prompt Shipment
The UCC permits acceptance of an offer to buy goods for current or prompt shipment by either a promise to ship or prompt shipment of goods to the buyer [UCC 2–206(1)(b)]. Shipment of nonconforming goods is both an acceptance and a breach.

2. **Communication of Acceptance**

   To accept a unilateral offer, the offeree must notify the offeror of performance within a reasonable time if the offeror would not otherwise know [UCC 2–206(2), 2A–206(2)].

3. **Additional Terms**

   If the offeree's response indicates a definite acceptance of the offer, a contract is formed, even if the acceptance includes terms in addition to, or different from, the original offer [UCC 2–207(1)]. If both parties are merchants, the terms may become part of the contract [UCC 2–207(2)].

C. **CONSIDERATION**

An agreement modifying a contract or lease needs no new consideration [UCC 2–209(1), 2A–208(1)]. Modification must be sought in good faith [UCC 1–203]. Good faith in a merchant is honesty in fact and observance of reasonable commercial standards of fair dealing in the trade [UCC 2–103(1)(b)].

V.   THE STATUTE OF FRAUDS

To be enforceable, a sales contract must be in writing if the goods are $500 or more and a lease if the payments are $1,000 or more [UCC 2–201, 2A–201].

A. **SPECIAL RULES FOR CONTRACTS BETWEEN MERCHANTS**

The requirement of a writing is satisfied if one merchant sends a signed written confirmation to the other, unless the merchant who receives the confirmation gives written notice of objection within ten days of receipt.

B. **EXCEPTIONS**

An oral contract for a sale or lease that should otherwise be in writing will be enforceable if [UCC 2–201(3), 2A–201(4)] (1) manufacture of special goods has begun, (2) party against whom enforcement is sought admits in court proceedings a contract was made, or (3) payment is made and accepted or goods are received and accepted (enforceable to that extent).

VI.   PERFORMANCE OF SALES AND LEASE CONTRACTS

The UCC imposes on the performance of all sales or lease contract an obligation of good faith (honesty, and in the case of a merchant the observance of reasonable commercial standards of fair dealing in the trade) [UCC 2–103(b)].

A. **OBLIGATION OF THE SELLER OR LESSOR—PERFECT TENDER OF DELIVERY**

Seller or lessor must have and hold goods that conform exactly to the description in the contract at buyer's or lessee's disposal and give buyer or lessee notice to take delivery [UCC 2–503(1), 2A–508(1)]. If goods or tender fail in any respect, buyer or lessee can accept the goods, reject them, or accept part and reject part [UCC 2–601, 2A–509]. Exceptions—

1. **Agreement of the Parties**

   For example, parties may agree that seller or lessor can repair or replace any defective goods within a reasonable time.

2. **Cure**

   If nonconforming goods are rejected, seller or lessor can notify buyer or lessee of intent to repair or replace the goods and can then do so in the contract time for performance [UCC 2–508, 2A–513].

3. **Substitution of Carriers**

   When an agreed-on manner of delivery becomes impracticable or unavailable through no fault of either party, a commercially reasonable substitute is sufficient [UCC 2–614(1)].

4. **Commercial Impracticability**

   Delay or nondelivery is not a breach if performance is impracticable "by the occurrence of a contingency the nonoccurrence of which was a basic assumption on which the contract was made" [UCC 2–615(a), 2A–405(a)]. Seller must give notice.

5. **Destruction of Identified Goods**

   When goods are destroyed (through no fault of a party) before risk passes, parties are excused from performance [UCC 2–613(a), 2A–221]. If goods are only partially destroyed, a buyer can treat a contract as void or accept damaged goods with a price allowance.

B. **OBLIGATIONS OF THE BUYER OR LESSEE**

   Buyer or lessee must (1) furnish facilities reasonably suited for receipt of the goods [UCC 2–503] and (2) make payment at time and place of delivery, even if it is the same as the place of shipment [UCC 2–310(a), 2A–516(1)].

C. **ANTICIPATORY REPUDIATION**

   A party can (1) treat a repudiation as a final breach by pursuing a remedy or (2) wait, hoping that the repudiating party will decide to honor the contract [UCC 2–610, 2A–402]. If the party decides to wait, the breaching party can retract the repudiation [UCC 2–611, 2A–403].

VII. REMEDIES FOR BREACH OF SALES AND LEASE CONTRACTS

A. **REMEDIES OF THE SELLER OR LESSOR**

1. **The Right to Withhold Delivery**

   Seller or lessor can withhold delivery if buyer or lessee wrongfully rejects or revokes acceptance, fails to pay, or repudiates [UCC 2–703, 2A–523].

2. **The Right to Resell or Dispose of the Goods**

   If seller or lessor still has the goods and buyer or lessee breaches or repudiates the contract, seller or lessor can resell or otherwise dispose of the goods, holding buyer or lessee liable for any loss [UCC 2–703(d), 2–706(1), 2A–523(1)(e), 2A–527(1)].

3. **The Right to Recover the Purchase Price or Lease Payments Due**

   Seller or lessor can bring an action for the price if he or she is unable to resell [UCC 2–709(1), 2A–529(1)]. The buyer then gets the goods, unless the seller or lessor disposes of them before collection of the judgment (with the proceeds credited to the buyer).

4. **The Right to Recover Damages**

   If buyer or lessee repudiates a contract or wrongfully refuses to accept, seller or lessor can recover the difference between the contract price and the market price (at the time and place of tender), plus incidental damages [UCC 2–708, 2A–528]. If the market price is less than the contract price, seller or lessor gets lost profits.

B. **REMEDIES OF THE BUYER OR LESSEE**

1. **The Right of Cover**

   Buyer or lessee can obtain cover (substitute goods) and then sue for damages. The measure of damages is the difference between the cost of cover and the contract price, plus incidental and consequential damages, minus expenses saved by the breach [UCC 2–712, 2–715, 2A–518, 2A–520].

2. **The Right to Obtain Specific Performance**

   Buyer or lessee can obtain specific performance if goods are unique [UCC 2–716(1), 2A–521(1)].

3. **The Right to Recover Damages**

   The measure is the difference between the contract price and, when buyer or lessee learned of the breach, the market price (at the place of delivery), plus incidental and consequential damages, minus expenses saved by the breach [UCC 2–713, 2A–519].

4. **The Right to Reject the Goods**

   If goods or tender fails to conform to the contract, buyer or lessee can reject them. If some of the goods conform, buyer or lessee can keep those and reject the rest [UCC 2–601, 2A–509].

5. **The Right to Recover Damages for Accepted Goods**
   Notice of a breach must be within a reasonable time [UCC 2–607, 2A–516]. The measure of damages is the difference between value of goods as accepted and value if they had been as promised [UCC 2–714(2), 2A–519(4)].

6. **The Right to Revoke Acceptance**
   Acceptance can be revoked if a nonconformity substantially impairs the value of the goods *and* is either not seasonably cured or is difficult to discover [UCC 2–608, 2A–517]. Notice must be given to seller or lessor before goods have undergone substantial change (not caused by their own defects, such as spoilage) [UCC 2–608(2), 2A–517(4)].

VIII. SALES AND LEASE WARRANTIES

A. WARRANTIES OF TITLE

1. **Sellers**
   Sellers warrant (1) they have good title to the goods and transfer of title is rightful [UCC 2–312(1)(a)]; (2) goods are free of a security interest or other lien of which buyer has no knowledge [UCC 2–312(1)(b)]; and (3) goods are free of any third person's patent, trademark, or copyright claims [UCC 2–312(3)].

2. **Lessors**
   Lessors warrant (1) no third party will interfere with the lessee's use of the goods and (2) the goods are free of any third person's patent, trademark, or copyright claims [UCC 2A–211].

3. **Disclaimers**
   Title warranty can be disclaimed or modified only by specific language. In a lease, a disclaimer must be specific, in writing, and conspicuous [UCC 2A–214(4)].

B. EXPRESS WARRANTIES

1. **When Express Warranties Arise**
   Seller or lessor warrants that goods will conform to [UCC 2–313, 2A–210] (1) affirmations or promises of fact (on a label or in a contract, an ad, a brochure, etc.); (2) descriptions (for example, on a label or in a contract, an ad, a brochure, etc.); and (3) samples or models.

2. **Statements of Opinion and Value**
   A statement that relates to the value or worth of goods or a statement of opinion or recommendation about goods is not an express warranty [UCC 2–313(2), 2A–210(2)].

3. **Disclaimers**
   Seller can avoid making express warranties by not promising or affirming anything, describing the goods, or using of a sample or model [UCC 2–313]. A written disclaimer in clear and conspicuous language, called to buyer or lessee's attention, can negate all oral warranties not included in the written contract [UCC 2–316(1), 2A–214(1)].

C. IMPLIED WARRANTIES
An implied warranty is derived by implication or inference from the nature of a transaction or the relative situations or circumstances of the parties.

1. **Implied Warranty of Merchantability**
   This warranty automatically arises in every sale or lease of goods by a merchant who deals in such goods. Goods that are merchantable are "reasonably fit for the ordinary purposes for which such goods are used" [UCC 2–314, 2A–212].

2. **Implied Warranty of Fitness for a Particular Purpose**

Arises when a seller or lessor knows or has reason to know particular purpose for which buyer or lessee will use goods and knows buyer or lessee is relying on seller or lessor to select suitable goods [UCC 2–315, 2A–213]. Goods can be merchantable but not fit for a particular purpose.

3. **Implied Warranty—Dealing, Performance, or Trade Usage**

When the parties know a well-recognized trade custom, it is inferred that they intended it to apply to their contract [UCC 2–314, 2A–212].

4. **Disclaimers**

Implied warranties can be disclaimed by the expression "as is" or a similar phrase [UCC 2–316(3)(a), 2A–214(3)(a)]. Implied warranty of fitness for a particular purpose: disclaimer must be in writing and be conspicuous. Implied warranty of merchantability: disclaimer must mention merchantability; if it is in writing, it must be conspicuous.

IX. E-CONTRACTS

These include contracts entered into in e-commerce, whether business-to-business (B2B) or business-to-consumer (B2C), and contracts involving the computer industry.

A. ONLINE CONTRACT FORMATION

Disputes arising from contracts entered into online concern the terms and the parties' assent to them.

1. **Online Offers**

Terms should be conspicuous and clearly spelled out. On a Web site, this can be done with a link to a separate page that contains the details. The text lists subjects that might be covered, including remedies, forum selection, payment, refund and return policies, disclaimers, and privacy policies.

2. **Online Acceptances**

   a. **Click-On Agreements**

   This is when a buyer, completing a transaction on a computer, indicates his or her assent to be bound by the terms of the offer by clicking on a button that says, for example, "I agree." The terms may appear on a Web site through which a buyer obtains goods or services, or on a computer screen when software is loaded.

   b. **Browse-Wrap Terms**

   These do not require a user to assent to the terms before going ahead with an online transaction. Offerors of these terms generally assert that they are binding without the user's active consent. Critics argue that a user should at least be required to navigate past the terms before they should be considered binding.

B. E-SIGNATURES

How are e-signatures created and verified, and what is their legal effect?

1. **E-Signature Technologies**

The most common methods involve the use of a digitized handwritten signature or a public-key infrastructure base on which a party creates a unique mark with private key code that another can read with a public key. A cybernotary issues the keys.

2. **State Laws Governing E-Signatures**

Most states have laws governing e-signatures, although the laws are not uniform. The Uniform Electronic Transactions Act (UETA), issued in 1999, was an attempt by the National Conference of Commissioners on Uniform State Laws and the American Law Institute to create more uniformity.

3. **Federal Law on E-Signatures and E-Documents**

a. **The E-SIGN Act**

In 2000, Congress enacted the Electronic Signatures in Global and National Commerce (E-SIGN) Act to provide no contract, record, or signature may be denied legal effect solely because it is in an electronic form. Some documents are excluded (such as those under UCC Articles 3, 4, and 9).

b. **Preemption**

If a state enacts the UETA without modifying it, the E-SIGN Act does not preempt it. The E-SIGN Act preempts modified versions of the UETA to the extent that they are inconsistent with the E-SIGN Act.

C. **THE UNIFORM ELECTRONIC TRANSACTIONS ACT**

1. **What the UETA Does**

The UETA removes barriers to e-commerce by giving the same legal effect to e-records and e-signatures as to paper documents and signatures.

2. **The Scope and Applicability of the UETA**

The UETA applies only to e-records and e-signatures in a transaction (an interaction between two or more people relating to business, commercial, or government activities). It does not apply to laws governing wills or testamentary trusts, the UCC (except Articles 2 and 2A), and other laws excluded by states that adopt the UETA, or to agreements that opt out of its provisions.

TRUE-FALSE QUESTIONS

(Answers at the Back of the Book)

____   1.   Article 2 of the UCC governs sales of goods.

____   2.   The UCC governs sales of services and real estate.

____   3.   If a contract for a sale of goods is missing a term, it will not be enforceable.

____   4.   Under the UCC, an offer to buy goods can be accepted only by a prompt shipment of the goods.

____   5.   The duties and obligations of the parties to a contract include those specified in their agreement.

____   6.   Unless the parties agree otherwise, a buyer or lessee must pay for goods in advance.

____   7.   If a buyer wrongfully refuses to accept conforming goods, the seller can recover damages.

____   8.   If a seller wrongfully refuses to deliver conforming goods, the buyer can recover damages.

____   9.   A contract cannot include both an implied warranty and an express warranty.

____   10. A click-on agreement is not normally enforced.

FILL-IN QUESTIONS

(Answers at the Back of the Book)

A seller's obligations include holding _____ (conforming/nonconforming) goods at a buyer's disposal _____ (and/or) giving notice reasonably necessary for the buyer to take delivery. The _____ (seller/buyer) must make payment at the time and place of _____ (delivery/receipt) of the goods _____ (even if/unless) the parties have agreed otherwise.

MULTIPLE-CHOICE QUESTIONS

(Answers at the Back of the Book)

____ 1. AAA Products, Inc. and Best Manufacturing, Inc., enter into a contract for a sale of goods that does not include a price term. In a suit between AAA and Best over this contract and the price, a court will

    a. determine a reasonable price.
    b. impose the lowest market price for the goods.
    c. refuse to enforce the agreement.
    d. return the parties to the positions they held before the contract.

____ 2. Delta Sales Corporation sends its purchase order form to Eagle Company for sixty display stands. Eagle responds with its own form. Additional terms in Eagle's form automatically become part of the contract unless

    a. Eagle objects to the new terms within a reasonable period of time.
    b. Eagle's form expressly required acceptance of its terms.
    c. the additional terms materially alter the original contract.
    d. any of the above.

____ 3. Eagle Products, Inc., assures General Retail Corporation that its offer to sell its products at a certain price will remain open. This is a firm offer only if

    a. General (the offeree) gives consideration for the offer.
    b. General (the offeree) is a merchant.
    c. the offer is made by Eagle (a merchant) in a signed writing.
    d. the offer states the time period during which it will remain open.

____ 4. Adam contracts to buy goods from Beth. Beth wrongfully fails to deliver the goods. Adam can recover damages equal to the difference between the contract price and the market price

    a. at the time the contract was made.
    b. at the time and place of tender.
    c. when Adam learned of the breach.
    d. when Adam filed a suit against Beth.

____ 5. Athletic Goods, Inc. (AGI), agrees to sell sports equipment to Bob's Sports Store. Before the time for performance, AGI tells Bob that it will not deliver. This is

    a. anticipatory repudiation.
    b. assurance and cooperation.
    c. commercial impracticability.
    d. perfect tender.

____ 6. Superior Office stores orders one hundred computers from Total Suppliers. Unless the parties agree otherwise, Total's obligation to Superior is to

    a. deliver the computers to a common carrier.
    b. deliver the computers to Superior's place of business.
    c. hold conforming goods and give notice for Superior's to take delivery.
    d. set aside conforming goods for Superior's inspection before delivery.

____ 7. Alpha Corporation agrees to sell the *updated* version of its word-processing software to Beta Company. Alpha delivers an *outdated* version of the program. Beta's remedies may include

   a. recovering damages only.
   b. rejecting part or all of the goods, or revoking acceptance only.
   c. recovering damages, rejecting the goods, or revoking acceptance.
   d. none of the above.

____ 8. E-Equip, Inc., agrees to lease ten servers to First Bank. When E-Equip tries to deliver, First Bank refuses to accept. There is nothing wrong with the servers. E-Equip sues First Bank, seeking damages. E-Equip is entitled to the difference between

   a. E-Equip's lost profits and First Bank's realized gain.
   b. E-Equip's lost profits and the contract price.
   c. the contract price and the market price.
   d. the market price and E-Equip's lost profits.

____ 9. Great Furniture Company makes and sells furniture. To avoid liability for most implied warranties, their sales agreements should note that their goods are sold

   a. "as is."
   b. by a merchant.
   c. for cash only.
   d. in perfect condition.

____ 10. American Sales Company and B2C Corporation enter into a contract over the Internet. The contract says nothing about the UETA. The UETA applies to

   a. none of the contract.
   b. only the part of the contract that does not involve computer information.
   c. only the part of the contract that involves computer information.
   d. the entire contract.

STARBUCKS COFFEE COMPANY
INTERNATIONAL SALES CONTRACT
APPLICATIONS

(Answers at the Back of the Book)

The following hypothetical situation and multiple-choice questions relate to your text's fold-out exhibit of the international sales contract used by Starbucks Coffee Company. In that contract, Starbucks orders five hundred tons of coffee at $10 per pound from XYZ Co.

____ 1. Starbucks and XYZ would have an enforceable contract even if they did *not* state in writing

   a. the amount of coffee ordered.
   b. the price of the coffee.
   c. both a and b.
   d. none of the above.

____ 2. If Starbucks and XYZ did not include a "DESCRIPTION" of the coffee as "High grown Mexican Altura," then the delivered coffee must met

   a. Starbuck's subjective expectations of their quality.
   b. Starbuck's description of the goods in ads, on labels, and so on.
   c. XYZ's description of the goods in ads, on labels, and so on.
   d. XYZ's subjective belief in their quality.

____   **3.**   Starbucks's incentive to pay on time, according to the terms of this contract, is the clause titled

    a. CLAIMS.
    b. GUARANTEE.
    c. PAYMENT.
    d. PRICE.

____   **4.**   XYZ's incentive to deliver coffee that conforms to the contract is the clause titled

    a. CLAIMS.
    b. GUARANTEE.
    c. PAYMENT.
    d. PRICE.

____   **5.**   Under this contract, until the coffee is delivered to its destination, the party with the risk of loss is

    a. Bonded Public Warehouse.
    b. Green Coffee Association
    c. Starbucks.
    d. XYZ.

SHORT ESSAY QUESTIONS

1.   For purposes of the UCC, who is a merchant?

2.   What is the difference between the implied warranty of merchantability and the implied warranty of fitness for a particular purpose?

ISSUE SPOTTERS

(Answers at the Back of the Book)

1.   E-Design, Inc., orders 150 computer desks. Fine Supplies, Inc., ships 150 printer stands. Is this an acceptance of the offer or a counteroffer? If it is an acceptance, is it a breach of the contract? What if Fine told E-Design it was sending printer stands as "an accommodation"?

2.   Market Distributors, Inc., contracts to sell to National Motor Company (NMC) 10,000 cogwheels at $1 each to be delivered to NMC's factory in Detroit on May 1. Market knows that NMC will use the cogwheels to manufacture specialty motors and that NMC's operation will be at a standstill if it does not receive the goods. When Market fails to deliver, the price of cogwheels in Detroit is $1.20 each. NMC's operation shuts down. NMC sues Market. What is NMC entitled to?

3.   Owen loves Phat Foods, which are cholesterol-rich. When Owen is diagnosed as suffering from heart disease, he sues Phat Foods Company, on the ground that its foods are not fit to eat in violation of the implied warranty of merchantability. Is it likely that the court will agree with Owen?

Chapter 11:
Business Organizations

WHAT THIS CHAPTER IS ABOUT

This chapter sets out features of the major traditional business forms—sole proprietorships, partnerships, and corporations—and other forms for doing business. The chapter includes discussions of private franchises and the rights and duties of corporate directors, officers, and shareholders.

CHAPTER OUTLINE

I. SOLE PROPRIETORSHIPS
The simplest form of business—the owner is the business.

A. ADVANTAGES
The proprietor takes all the profits. Easier to start than other kinds of businesses (few legal forms involved); has more flexibility (proprietor is free to make all decisions); owner pays only personal income tax on profits.

B. DISADVANTAGE
The proprietor has all the risk (unlimited liability for all debts); limited opportunity to raise capital; the business dissolves when the owner dies.

II. PARTNERSHIPS
Arises from an agreement between two or more persons to carry on a business for profit.

A. GENERAL PARTNERSHIPS

1. General Partners Are Co-owners
General partners jointly control the operation and share the profits. No particular form of agreement is necessary to create a general partnership; partners may agree to any terms.

2. A Partnership Is a Legal Entity for Limited Purposes
For example, ownership of property. Partners are personally liable for partnership obligations; partnership is not subject to federal income tax (profit is taxed as individual income to the partners).

B. LIMITED PARTNERSHIPS
Consist of at least one general partner and one or more limited partners. General partners run the business and are subject to personal liability for partnership obligations. Limited partners have limited liability.

III. CORPORATIONS
A corporation consists of shareholders, who own it; directors, who are elected by the shareholders to manage it; and officers, who oversee daily operations.

A. ADVANTAGES
Liability of the owners (shareholders) is usually limited to their investment; corporation can raise capital by selling shares of stock.

B. DISADVANTAGES

1. Corporate Income Is Taxed Twice
(1) As income to the firm and (2) when distributed to shareholders; this may be avoided by electing to be, for tax purposes, an S corporation, which is not taxed at the corporate level.

2. Incorporation Requirements
A corporation must be set up according to specific statutory procedures, have sufficient capitalization, and pay other costs of incorporation; is subject to more governmental supervision and reporting requirements.

3. Credit Limitations
Because of limited liability, creditors may not be willing to extend credit to a new or small corporation (without a personal guarantee).

C. S CORPORATIONS

1. Requirements
Must be a domestic corporation; must not be a member of an affiliated group of corporations; shareholders must be individuals, estates, or certain trusts; must have thirty-five or fewer shareholders; can have only one class of stock; no shareholder can be a nonresident alien.

2. Advantages
Shareholders can use corporate losses to offset other income; only a single tax on corporate income is imposed (at the shareholder level, whether or not the income is distributed).

IV. LIMITED LIABILITY COMPANIES

A limited liability company (LLC) is a hybrid form of business enterprise that offers limited liability of a corporation with tax advantages of a partnership.

A. FORMATION OF AN LLC
Articles of organization must be filed with the state. Certain information is required.

B. ADVANTAGES
Taxed as a partnership; liability of members is limited to the amount of their investment; members can participate in management; corporations, partnerships, and foreign investors can be members; no limit on the number of members (in many states, one is enough).

C. JURISDICTIONAL REQUIREMENTS
An LLC is a citizen of every state of which its members are citizens.

D. THE LLC OPERATING AGREEMENT
Provisions relate to management, division of profits, transfer of membership, what events trigger dissolution, and so on. In the absence of an agreement, state statutes govern. If there is no statute, the principles of partnership law apply.

E. MANAGEMENT OF AN LLC
Unless the articles of organization specify otherwise, an LLC is considered to be member-managed. In a member-managed LLC, all members participate in management. In a manager-managed LLC, the members designate a manager (member or not) to run the firm. These managers owe the fiduciary duties of loyalty and care to the LLC and its members.

V. LIMITED LIABILITY PARTNERSHIPS

Professionals may organize as a limited liability partnership (LLP) to enjoy the tax advantages of a partnership, but avoid personal liability for other partners' wrongdoing (including malpractice). A partner who commits a wrongful act, and his or her supervising partner, is liable, however.

VI.   PRIVATE FRANCHISES

A **franchise** is any arrangement in which the owner of a trademark, a trade name, or a copyright has licensed others to use it in selling goods or services.

A. LAWS GOVERNING FRANCHISING

1. Federal Regulation of Franchising

a. Automobile Dealers' Franchise Act of 1965
Dealership franchisees are protected from manufacturers' bad faith termination of their franchises.

b. Petroleum Marketing Practices Act (PMPA) of 1979
Prescribes the grounds and conditions under which a gasoline station franchiser may terminate or decline to renew a franchise.

c. Antitrust Laws
May apply if there is an anticompetitive agreement (Chapter 20).

d. Federal Trade Commission (FTC) Regulations
Franchisors must disclose material facts necessary to a prospective franchisee's making an informed decision concerning a franchise.

2. State Regulation of Franchising
Similar to federal law. When a franchise exists primarily for the sale of products manufactured by the franchisor, the Uniform Commercial Code applies (see Chapter 10).

B. THE FRANCHISE CONTRACT
A franchise relationship is created by a contract between the franchisor and the franchisee.

1. Payment for the Franchise
A franchisee pays (1) a fee for the franchise license, (2) fees for products bought from or through the franchisor, and (3) a percentage of sales.

2. Business Premises
The agreement may specify whether the premises for the business are leased or purchased and who is to supply equipment and furnishings.

3. Location of the Franchise
The franchisor determines the territory to be served and its exclusivity.

4. Business Organization of the Franchisee
A franchisor may specify requirements for the form and capital structure of the business.

5. Quality Controls
A franchisor may specify standards of operation (such as quality standards) and personnel training methods. Too much control may result in a franchisor's liability for torts of a franchisee's employees.

6. Price Controls
A franchisor may require a franchisee to buy certain supplies from the franchisor at an established price. In some circumstances, a franchisor who sets retail prices for the goods that the franchisee sells may violate antitrust laws.

7. Termination of the Franchise
Determined by the parties. Usually, must be "for cause" (such as breach of the agreement, etc.) and notice must be given. A franchisee must be given reasonable time to wind up the business.

VII. THE NATURE OF THE CORPORATION

A. CORPORATE PERSONNEL
Shareholders elect directors, who are responsible for overall management and hire officers to run daily operations.

B. CORPORATE TAXATION
Corporate profits are taxed twice: as income to the corporation and, when distributed as dividends, as income to the shareholders.

C. CONSTITUTIONAL RIGHTS OF CORPORATIONS
A corporation is recognized by the law as a "person" and, under the Bill of Rights, has the same rights as a natural person (see Chapter 4). Corporations do not have the right against self-incrimination, however, and the privileges and immunities clause does not protect corporations.

D. TORTS AND CRIMINAL ACTS
A corporation is liable for torts committed by its agents within the course and scope of employment. A corporation may be liable for crimes of its employees and agents if punishment for the crimes can be applied to it.

VIII. CLASSIFICATION OF CORPORATIONS
A corporation is a **domestic corporation** in the state in which it incorporated, a **foreign corporation** in other states, and an **alien corporation** in other countries. A foreign corporation normally must obtain a certificate of authority to do business in any state except its home state.

IX. CORPORATE MANAGEMENT—SHAREHOLDERS

A. SHAREHOLDERS' POWERS
Shareholders approve fundamental changes; elect and remove directors.

B. SHAREHOLDERS' MEETINGS
Regular meetings must occur annually; special meetings can be called to handle urgent matters. Rather than attend a meeting, shareholders normally authorize third parties, through a proxy, to vote their shares.

C. SHAREHOLDER VOTING

1. Quorum Requirements
At the meeting, a quorum must be present. A majority vote of the shares present is required to pass resolutions. Fundamental changes require a higher percentage.

2. Cumulative Voting
The number of members of the board to be elected is multiplied by the total number of voting shares. This is the number of votes a shareholder has and can be cast for one or more nominees.

X. CORPORATE MANAGEMENT—DIRECTORS

A. ELECTION OF DIRECTORS
Number of directors are set in a firm's articles or bylaws. First board (appointed by incorporators or named in articles) serves until first shareholders' meeting. Later directors elected by majority vote of shareholders.

B. DIRECTORS' QUALIFICATIONS AND COMPENSATION
A few states have minimum age and residency requirements. Compensation for directors is ordinarily specified in the articles or bylaws.

C. BOARD OF DIRECTORS' MEETINGS

1. **Formal Minutes and Notice**

   A board conducts business by holding formal meetings with recorded minutes. The dates for regular meetings are usually set in the articles and bylaws or by board resolution, and no other notice is required. Special meetings require notice to all directors.

2. **Quorum Requirements and Voting**

   Quorum requirements vary. If the firm specifies none, in most states a quorum is a majority of the number of directors authorized in the articles or bylaws. Voting is done in person, one vote per director.

D. MANAGEMENT RESPONSIBILITIES

1. **Areas of Responsibility**

   Major policy and financial decisions; appointment, supervision, pay, and removal of officers and other managerial employees.

2. **Executive Committee**

   Most states permit a board to elect an executive committee from among the directors to handle management between board meetings. The committee is limited to ordinary business matters.

E. ROLE OF CORPORATE OFFICERS AND DIRECTORS

Officers and executives are hired by the board. Officers act as agents of the corporation. Directors and officers are fiduciaries of the corporation.

1. **Qualifications**

   At the discretion of the firm; included in the articles or bylaws. A person can hold more than one office and also be a director.

2. **Duty of Care**

   Directors and officers must use honest, prudent business judgment and carry out responsibilities in an informed, businesslike manner.

3. **Duty of Loyalty**

   Directors and officers must subordinate their personal interests to the interests of the corporation. They cannot use corporate funds or confidential information for personal advantage.

F. CONFLICTS OF INTEREST

Directors and officers must disclose fully any conflict of interest in a deal involving the firm. A contract may be upheld if it is fair and reasonable when made, there is full disclosure of the officers' or directors' interest, and it is approved by a majority of disinterested directors or shareholders.

G. THE BUSINESS JUDGMENT RULE

Honest mistakes of judgment and poor business decisions do not make directors and officers liable to the firm for poor results, if the decision complies with management's fiduciary duties, has a reasonable basis, and is within managerial authority and the power of the corporation.

XI.   RIGHTS AND DUTIES OF OFFICERS AND MANAGERS

Rights of officers and other top managers are defined by employment contracts. Officers normally can be removed by the board any time (but the firm could be liable for breach of contract). Officers' duties are the same as directors'.

XII.   RIGHTS OF SHAREHOLDERS

A. STOCK CERTIFICATES

Notice of shareholder meetings, dividends, and corporate reports are distributed to owners listed in the corporate books, not on the basis of possession of stock certificates (which most states do not require).

B. PREEMPTIVE RIGHTS

Usually apply only to additional, newly issued stock sold for cash and must be exercised within a specified time (usually thirty days).

C. DIVIDENDS

Dividends can be paid in cash, property, or stock. Once declared, a cash dividend is a corporate debt.

1. Illegal Dividends

A dividend paid when a firm is insolvent is illegal and must be repaid. One paid from an unauthorized account or causing a firm to be insolvent may have to be repaid. In any case, directors may be personally liable.

2. If the Directors Fail to Declare a Dividend

Shareholders can ask a court to compel a declaration of a dividend, but to succeed, the directors' conduct must be an abuse of discretion.

D. INSPECTION RIGHTS

Shareholders (or their attorney, accountant, or agent) can inspect and copy corporate books and records for a proper purpose, with an advance request.

E. TRANSFER OF SHARES

Any restrictions on transferability must be noted on the face of a stock certificate. Restrictions must be reasonable—for example, a right of first refusal remains with the corporation or the shareholders for only a specified time or a reasonable time.

F. SHAREHOLDER'S DERIVATIVE SUIT

If directors fail to sue in the corporate name to redress a wrong suffered by the firm, shareholders can do so (after complaining to the board). Any recovery normally goes into the corporate treasury.

XIII. LIABILITY OF SHAREHOLDERS

In most cases, if a corporation fails, shareholders lose only their investment. Exceptions include payment of illegal dividends (see above) and the following.

A. DISREGARDING THE CORPORATE ENTITY

A court may ignore the corporate structure ("pierce the corporate veil") and impose personal liability for corporate debts on shareholders if—

1. A party is tricked or misled into dealing with the corporation rather than the individual.
2. The corporation is set up never to make a profit or always to be insolvent, or it is too thinly capitalized.
3. Statutory corporate formalities are not followed.
4. Personal and corporate interests are commingled to the extent that the corporation has no separate identity.

B. STOCK-SUBSCRIPTION AGREEMENTS

Once a subscription agreement is accepted, any refusal to pay is a breach, resulting in shareholders' personal liability.

C. WATERED STOCK

In most cases, a shareholder who receives watered stock (stock sold by a corporation for less than par value) must pay the difference to the corporation. In some states, such shareholders may be liable to creditors of the corporation for unpaid corporate debts.

XIV DUTIES OF MAJORITY SHAREHOLDERS

A single shareholder (or a few acting together) who owns enough shares to control the corporation owes a fiduciary duty to the minority shareholders and creditors when they sell their shares.

TRUE-FALSE QUESTIONS

(Answers at the Back of the Book)

F   1.   In a sole proprietorship, the owner and the business are entirely separate.

T   2.   A corporation is not a legal entity separate and distinct from its owners.

F   3.   A franchisee is not subject to the franchisor's control in the area of product quality.

F   4.   A limited liability company does not offer the limited liability of a corporation.

F   5.   A foreign corporation is formed in another country but does business in the United States.

F   6.   S corporations cannot avoid federal taxes at the corporate level.

F   7.   Damages recovered in a shareholder's derivative suit are paid to the shareholder who filed the suit.

T   8.   Generally, shareholders are not personally responsible for the debts of their corporation.

F   9.   Directors, but not officers, owe a duty of loyalty to their corporation.

F   10.   The business judgment rule makes a director liable for losses to the firm in most cases.

FILL-IN QUESTIONS

(Answers at the Back of the Book)

A stock certificate may be lost or destroyed, _____ (and ownership is / but ownership is not) destroyed with it. A new certificate _____ (can / cannot) be issued to replace one that has been lost or destroyed. Notice of meetings, dividends, and operational and financial reports are all distributed according to the individual _____ _____ (in possession of the certificate / recorded as the owner in the corporation's books).

MULTIPLE-CHOICE QUESTIONS

(Answers at the Back of the Book)

D   1.   Ann owns Beta Enterprises, a sole proprietorship. Ann's liability for the obligations of the business is

a.   limited by state statute.
b.   limited to the amount of his original investment.
c.   limited to the total amount of capital Ann invests in the business.
d.   unlimited.

B   2.   Dave and Paul agree to go into business together. They do not formally declare a specific form of organization. Dave and Paul's business is

a.   a proprietorship.
b.   a partnership.
c.   a corporation.
d.   none of the above.

C 3. Aaron invests in a franchise with Big Foods Corporation. With respect to the franchise, Aaron may have legal protection under

    a. federal law only.
    b. state law only.
    c. federal and state law.
    d. none of the above.

B 4. Adam and Beth form A&B, LLC, a limited liability company (LLC). One advantage of an LLC is that it may be taxed as

    a. a corporation.
    b. a partnership.
    c. a sole proprietorship.
    d. none of the above.

A 5. Jill is a shareholder of Kappa Company. As a shareholder, Jill does *not* have a right to

    a. dividends.
    b. inspect corporate books and records.
    c. sue the corporation.
    d. transfer shares.

A 6. Don and Eve are officers of Fine Products Corporation. As officers, their rights are set out in

    a. Don and Eve's employment contracts.
    b. international agreements.
    c. state corporation statutes.
    d. the firm's certificate of authority.

D 7. The management of National Brands, Inc., is at odds with the shareholders over some recent decisions. The shareholders may file a shareholders' derivative suit to

    a. compel dissolution of National.
    b. compel payment of a properly declared dividend.
    c. enforce a right to inspect corporate records.
    d. recover damages from the management for an *ultra vires* act.

C 8. Jiffy Corporation uses cumulative voting in its elections of directors. Kay owns 3,000 Jiffy shares. At an annual meeting at which three directors are to be elected, Mary may cast for any one candidate

    a. 1,000 votes.
    b. 3,000 votes.
    c. 9,000 votes.
    d. 27,000 votes.

A 9. Micro Company makes computer chips. Like most corporations, Micro's officers are hired by the firm's

    a. directors.
    b. incorporators.
    c. officers.
    d. shareholders.

10. Kate is a shareholder of Local Delivery, Inc. A court might "pierce the corporate veil" and hold her personally liable for Local's debts if

    a. Kate's personal interests are commingled with Local's interests to the extent that Local has no separate identity.

    b. Local calls too many shareholders' meetings.

    c. Local is overcapitalized.

    d. none of the above.

SHORT ESSAY QUESTIONS

1. What are the principal characteristics of sole proprietorships, partnerships and corporations?

2. How do franchise agreements generally deal with the following: (1) payment for the franchise, (2) location, (3) price controls, (4) quality control, and (5) termination?

ISSUE SPOTTERS

(Answers at the Back of the Book)

1. Merit Restaurants, Inc., sells franchises. Merit imposes on its franchisees standards of operation and personnel training methods. What is the potential pitfall to Merit if it exercises too much control over its franchisees?

2. Alpha Corporation's board of directors, who include Beth and Carl (officers of the firm), is deadlocked over whether to market a new product. Dan, a minority shareholder, suspects that Beth and Carl are taking advantage of the deadlock to use corporate assets (offices, equipment, supplies, staff time) to initiate a competing enterprise. Can Dan intervene?

3. Beta Corporation has an opportunity to buy stock in Gamma, Inc. The directors decide that, instead of Beta buying the stock, the directors will buy it. Frank, a Beta shareholder, learns of the purchase and wants to sue the directors on Beta's behalf. Can he do it?

Chapter 12:
Creditors' Rights and Bankruptcy

WHAT THIS CHAPTER IS ABOUT

This chapter sets out the rights and remedies available to a creditor, when a debtor defaults, under laws other than federal bankruptcy law. This chapter also covers bankruptcy law. Congressional authority to regulate bankruptcies comes from Article I, Section 8, of the U.S. Constitution. Bankruptcy law (1) protects a debtor by giving him or her a fresh start and (2) ensures equitable treatment to creditors competing for a debtor's assets.

CHAPTER OUTLINE

I. LAWS ASSISTING CREDITORS

A. LIENS
A **lien** is a claim against property to satisfy a debt or to protect a claim for payment of a debt.

1. Mechanic's Lien
A creditor can file this lien on real property when a person contracts for labor, services, or materials to improve the property but does not pay.

a. When Must a Creditor File the Lien?
A creditor must file the lien within a specific period, measured from the last date on which materials or labor were provided (usually within 60 to 120 days).

b. What If the Owner Does Not Pay?
The property can be sold to satisfy the debt. Notice of the foreclosure and sale must be given to the debtor in advance.

2. Artisan's Lien
This is a security device by which a creditor can recover from a debtor for labor and materials furnished in the repair of personal property.

a. The Creditor Must Possess the Property
The lien terminates if possession is voluntarily surrendered, unless the lienholder records notice of the lien in accord with state statutes.

b. What If the Owner Does Not Pay?
The property can be sold to satisfy the debt. Notice of the foreclosure and sale must be given to the debtor in advance.

3. Innkeeper's Lien
This is a security device placed on the baggage of guests for hotel charges that are not paid. The lien terminates when the charges are paid, or the baggage is returned or sold to satisfy the debt.

4. Judicial Liens

a. Attachment
Attachment is a court-ordered seizure and taking into custody of property before the securing of a judgment for a past-due debt. A sheriff or other officer seizes nonexempt property. If the creditor prevails at trial, the property can be sold to satisfy the judgment.

    b. **Writ of Execution**
A **writ of execution** is an order, usually issued by the clerk of court, directing the sheriff to seize and sell any of the debtor's nonexempt property within the court's geographical jurisdiction. Proceeds of the sale pay the debt.

B. GARNISHMENT

Garnishment occurs when a creditor collects a debt by seizing property of the debtor (such as wages or money in a bank account) that a third party (such as an employer or a bank) holds. The creditor obtains a judgment against the debtor and serves it on the third party (known as the garnishee). There are limits on amounts that can be garnished and on the discharge of an employee for a garnishment order.

C. CREDITORS' COMPOSITION AGREEMENTS

A **creditors' composition agreement** is a contract between a debtor and his or her creditors for discharge of the debtor's liquidated debts on payment of a sum less than that owed.

D. MORTGAGE FORECLOSURE

A **mortgagor** (creditor) can foreclose on mortgaged property if the **mortgagee** (debtor) defaults. Usual method is a judicial sale. Proceeds are applied to the debt. If proceeds do not cover the costs and the debt, the mortgagee can recover the difference from the mortgagor with a deficiency judgment.

E. SURETYSHIP AND GUARANTY

    1. **Suretyship**
A promise by a third person to be responsible for a debtor's obligation. Does not have to be in writing. A surety is *primarily* liable—a creditor can demand payment from the surety the moment the debt is due.

    2. **Guaranty**
A promise to be *secondarily* liable for the debt or default of another. A guarantor pays only after the debtor defaults and the creditor has made an attempt to collect from the debtor. A guaranty must be in writing unless the main-purpose exception applies (see Chapter 11).

    3. **Defenses of the Surety and the Guarantor**
To avoid payment, a surety (guarantor) may use the following defenses.

        a. **Material Change to the Contract between Debtor and Creditor**
Without obtaining the consent of the surety (guarantor), a surety is discharged completely or to the extent the surety suffers a loss.

        b. **Principal Obligation Is Paid or Valid Tender Is Made**
The surety (guarantor) is discharged from the obligation.

        c. **Most of the Principal Debtor's Defenses**
Defenses that cannot be used: debtor's incapacity, bankruptcy, and statute of limitations.

        d. **Surety or Guarantor's Own Defenses**

        e. **Surrender or Impairment of Collateral**
Without the surety's (guarantor's) consent, this action on the part of the creditor releases the surety to the extent of any loss suffered.

    4. **Rights of the Surety and the Guarantor**
If the surety (guarantor) pays the debt—

        a. **Right of Subrogation**
The surety (guarantor) has available any remedies that were available to the creditor against the debtor.

b. **Right of Reimbursement**
The surety (guarantor) is entitled to receive from the debtor all outlays made on behalf of the suretyship arrangement.

c. **Right of Contribution**
A surety who pays more than his or her proportionate share on a debtor's default is entitled to recover from co-sureties.

II.   LAWS ASSISTING DEBTORS

A. HOMESTEAD EXEMPTION
Each state allows a debtor to keep the family home (in some states only if the debtor has a family) in its entirety or up to a specified amount.

B. EXEMPT PERSONAL PROPERTY
This includes household furniture up to a specified dollar amount; clothing and other possessions; a vehicle (or vehicles); certain animals; and equipment that the debtor uses in a business or trade.

III.   BANKRUPTCY PROCEEDINGS

A. THE GOALS OF BANKRUPTCY LAW
Federal bankruptcy law has two goals: to protect a debtor by freeing him or her from creditors' claims to make a fresh start and to insure fair treatment to creditors competing for the debtor's assets.

B. BANKRUPTCY PROCEEDINGS
Bankruptcy proceedings are held in federal bankruptcy courts. Current law is based on the Bankruptcy Reform Act of 1978 and a bankruptcy reform act enacted in 2005 (collectively, the Bankruptcy Code, or the Code). Relief can be granted under the Code's Chapter 7, Chapter 11, Chapter 12, or Chapter 13.

IV.   CHAPTER 7—LIQUIDATION
This is the most familiar type of bankruptcy proceeding. A debtor declares his or her debts and gives all assets to a trustee, who sells the nonexempt assets and distributes the proceeds to creditors.

A. WHO CAN FILE FOR A LIQUIDATION
Any "person"—individuals, partnerships, and corporations (spouses can file jointly)—except railroads, insurance companies, banks, savings and loan associations, and credit unions.

B. VOLUNTARY BANKRUPTCY

1. **The Debtor Receives Credit Counseling**
A debtor must receive credit counseling from an approved nonprofit agency within 180 days (six months) before filing a petition.

2. **The Debtor Files a Petition with the Court**
A husband and wife may file jointly.

3. **The Debtor Files Schedules (Lists) with the Court**
Within 45 days, a debtor must file schedules of (1) creditors and the debt to each, (2) the debtor's financial affairs, (3) the debtor's property, (4) current income and expenses, (5) payments from employers within the previous 60 days, (6) a certificate proving the receipt of credit counseling, (7) an itemized calculation of monthly income, and (8) the debtor's most recent federal tax return.

4. **The Debtor's Attorney Files an Affidavit**
The debtor's attorney, if there is one, must attest to a reasonable attempt to verify the accuracy of the debtor's petition and schedules.

5. **The Court or Other Party "of Interest" Asks for More Information**
   Copies of later federal tax returns may be required. A debtor may need to verify his or her identity.

6. **The Court May Dismiss a Petition for Substantial Abuse**

   a. **If the Debtor's Family Income Exceeds the Median Family Income in the Filing State**
      Abuse will be presumed, and a creditor can file a motion to dismiss the petition, if the excess is $6,000 or more, under this "means test." A debtor can rebut the presumption by showing "special circumstances."

   b. **If the Debtor's Family Income Does *Not* Exceed the Median Family Income in the Filing State**
      A court can dismiss a petition on determining that the debtor seeks only an advantage over creditors and his or her financial situation does not warrant a discharge of debts.

7. **Other Grounds on which the Court May Dismiss a Petition**
   If the debtor has been convicted of a crime of violence or drug trafficking, a victim can file a motion to dismiss. Failing to pay post-petition domestic support may also result in a dismissal.

8. **Filing of the Petition Constitutes an Order for Relief**
   The clerk of the court must give the trustee and creditors notice within twenty days.

C. **INVOLUNTARY BANKRUPTCY**
   A debtor's creditors can force the debtor into bankruptcy proceedings.

1. **Who Can Be Forced into Involuntary Proceedings**
   A debtor with twelve or more creditors, three or more of whom (with unsecured claims of at least $12,300) file a petition. A debtor with fewer than twelve creditors, one or more of whom (with a claim of $12,300) files. Not a farmer or a charitable institution.

2. **When an Order for Relief Will Be Entered**
   If the debtor does not challenge the petition, the debtor is generally not paying debts as they come due, or a receiver, assignee, or custodian took possession of the debtor's property within 120 days before the petition was filed.

D. **AUTOMATIC STAY**
   When a petition is filed, an automatic stay suspends all action by creditors against the debtor.

1. **Exceptions**
   These include domestic support obligations (owed to a spouse, former spouse, debtor's child, child's parent or guardian, or the government), related proceedings, securities regulation investigations, property tax liens, prior eviction actions, and withholding to repay retirement account loans.

2. **Limitations**

   a. **Request for Relief**
      A creditor or other party "in interest" can ask for relief from the automatic stay, which then expires in 60 days, unless the court extends it.

   b. **Secured Debts—Adequate Protection Doctrine**
      This doctrine protects secured creditors by requiring payments, or other collateral or relief, to the extent that the stay may cause the value of their collateral to decrease.

   c. **Secured Debts—Other Protection**
      The stay on secured debts may expire within 30 days of a petition if the debtor had a petition dismissed within the prior year. Two dismissed petitions require a finding of good faith in the current filing before the stay takes effect. A stay on secured property terminates 45 days after the creditors' meeting if the debtor does not redeem the property or reaffirm the debt.

E. PROPERTY OF THE ESTATE

1. **What Property Is Included in the Debtor's Estate**
    Interests in property presently held; community property; property transferred in a transaction voidable by the trustee; proceeds and profits; certain after-acquired property; interests in gifts, inheritances, property settlements, and life insurance death proceeds to which the debtor becomes entitled within 180 days after filing.

2. **What Property Is Not Included**
    Property acquired after the filing of the petition except as noted above. Also, withholdings for employee benefit plan contributions are excluded.

F. CREDITORS' MEETING AND CLAIMS

Within "not less than twenty days or more than forty days," the court calls a meeting of creditors, a t which the debtor answers questions. Within ninety days of the meeting, a creditor must file a proof of claim if its amount is disputed. If the debtor's schedules list a claim as liquidated, proof is not needed.

G. EXEMPTIONS

1. **Federal Law**
    Federal law exempts such property as interests in a residence to $18,450, a motor vehicle to $2,950, certain household goods to $9,850, tools of a trade to $1,850, and retirement and education savings accounts, and the rights to receive Social Security, domestic support, and other benefits.

2. **State Law**
    Most states preclude the use of federal exemptions; others allow a debtor to choose between state and federal. State exemptions may include different value limits and exempt different property.

3. **Limits on a State's Homestead Exemption**
    To use this exemption, a debtor must have lived in the state for two years before filing a petition. If the home was acquired within the previous three and a half years, the exemption is limited to $125,000 (except for rolled-over equity). In certain cases of substantial abuse, no amount is exempt.

H. THE TRUSTEE

After the order for relief, an interim trustee is appointed to preside over the debtor's property until the first meeting of creditors, when a permanent trustee is elected. A trustee's duty is to collect and reduce to money the property of the estate and distribute the proceeds.

1. **Initial Duties**
    A trustee must state whether a filing constitutes substantial abuse under the "means test" (see above) within ten days of the creditors' meeting, notify creditors within five days, and file a motion to dismiss or convert a filing to Chapter 11 (or explain why not) within forty days.

2. **Duty with Respect to Domestic Support Obligations**
    A trustee must provide a party to whom this support is owed with certain information.

3. **General Powers**
    A trustee has the same rights as (1) a lien creditor with priority over an unperfected secured party and (2) a bona fide purchaser of real property from the debtor.

4. **Specific Avoidance Powers—Voidable Rights**
    To obtain the return of property, a trustee can use any reason (fraud, duress, etc.) that a debtor can.

5. **Specific Avoidance Powers—Preferences**
    A trustee can recover payments made or property transferred (or the value of the property if a preferred creditor has sold it to an innocent third party) by a debtor (1) within ninety days before the petition and (2) for a preexisting debt.

a. Insiders or Fraud

If a creditor is an insider (partner, corporate officer, relative) or a transfer is fraudulent, a trustee may recover transfers made within one year before filing.

b. Transfers That Are Not Preferences

Payment for services rendered within the previous 10 to 15 days; payment received in the ordinary course of business (such as payment of a phone bill); transfers of property up to $5,000; payment of domestic support debts; and transfers under a credit counselor's negotiated schedule.

6. Liens on Debtor's Property

A trustee can avoid most statutory liens that first took effect on a petition's filing or a debtor's insolvency, and any lien against a bona fide purchaser not enforceable on the date of the filing.

7. Fraudulent Transfers

A trustee can avoid fraudulent transfers made within two years of a petition's filing or if they were made with intent to delay, defraud, or hinder a creditor. Transfers for less than reasonably equivalent consideration may also be avoided if, by making them, a debtor became insolvent or was left in business with little capital.

I. DISTRIBUTION OF PROPERTY

Any amount remaining after the property is distributed to creditors is turned over to the debtor.

1. Secured Creditors

Within 30 days of a petition or before the creditors' meeting (whichever is first), a debtor must state an intent to redeem secured collateral (or not). A trustee must enforce the statement within 45 days. If collateral does not cover a debt, a secured creditor is an unsecured creditor for the rest.

2. Unsecured Creditors

Paid in the order of priority. Each class is paid before the next class is entitled to anything. The order of priority is—

a. Claims for domestic support obligations (subject to certain administrative costs).
b. Administrative expenses (court costs, trustee and attorney fees).
c. In an involuntary bankruptcy, expenses incurred by a debtor in the ordinary course of business from a petition's filing to a trustee's appointment or the issuance of an order for relief.
d. Unpaid wages, salaries, and commissions earned within ninety days of a petition, to $4,925 per claimant. A claim in excess is a claim of a general creditor (no. i below).
e. Unsecured claims for contributions to employee benefit plans, limited to services performed within 180 days before the petition and $4,925 per employee.
f. Claims by farmers and fishers, to $4,925, against storage or processing facilities.
g. Consumer deposits to $2,225 given to a debtor before a petition to buy, lease, or rent property or services that were not received.
h. Taxes and penalties due to the government.
i. Claims for death or injury from an intoxicated debtor's operation of a vehicle or vessel.
j. Claims of general creditors.

J. DISCHARGE

A discharge voids any judgment on a discharged debt and prohibits any action to collect a discharged debt. A co-debtor's liability is not affected.

1. Exceptions—Debts That May Not Be Discharged

Claims for back taxes, amounts borrowed to pay back taxes, goods obtained by fraud, debts that were not listed in a petition, domestic support, student loans, certain cash advances, and others.

2. **Objections—Debtors Who May Not Receive a Discharge**
Those who conceal property with intent to hinder, delay, or defraud creditors; who fail to explain a loss of assets; who have been granted a discharge within eight years prior to filing a petition; or who fail to attend a debt management class (unless no class is available).

3. **Revocation of Discharge**
A discharge may be revoked within one year if the debtor was fraudulent or dishonest during the bankruptcy proceedings.

K. **REAFFIRMATION OF DEBT**
A debtor's agreement to pay a dischargeable debt can be made only after certain disclosures and before a discharge is granted, usually requires court approval, and will be denied if it will cause undue hardship. Can be rescinded within sixty days or before a discharge is granted, whichever is later.

V. CHAPTER 11—REORGANIZATION
The creditors and debtor formulate a plan under which the debtor pays a portion of the debts, is discharged of the rest, and continues in business.

A. **WHO IS ELIGIBLE FOR RELIEF UNDER CHAPTER 11**
Any debtor (except a stockbroker or a commodities broker) who is eligible for Chapter 7 relief is eligible under Chapter 11. With some exceptions, the same principles apply that govern liquidation proceedings (automatic stay, etc.).

B. **WHY A CASE MAY BE DISMISSED**
A case may be dismissed if this is in the creditors' best interest, there is no reasonable likelihood of rehabilitation, a debtor is unable to affect a plan, or there is an unreasonable delay. Creditors may prefer a *workout* (a privately negotiated settlement) to bankruptcy.

C. **DEBTOR IN POSSESSION**
On entry of an order for relief, a debtor continues in business as a debtor in possession (DIP).

1. **If Gross Mismanagement Is Shown**
The court may appoint a trustee (or receiver) to operate the business. This may also be done if it is in the best interests of the estate.

2. **The DIP's Role Is Similar to That of a Trustee in a Liquidation**
The DIP can avoid pre-petition preferential payments and fraudulent transfers and decide whether to cancel pre-petition executory contracts.

3. **Strong-Arm Clause**
A DIP can avoid any obligation or transfer that could be avoided by (1) a creditor who extended credit at the time of bankruptcy and who consequently obtained (a) a lien or (b) a writ of execution that was returned unsatisfied; and (2) a bona fide purchaser of real property, if the transfer was perfected at the time of the bankruptcy.

D. **COLLECTIVE BARGAINING AGREEMENTS**
Can be rejected if the debtor first proposes modifications to the union and the union fails to adopt them without good cause. The debtor must (1) provide the union with information needed to evaluate the proposal and (2) confer in good faith to attempt a mutually satisfactory agreement.

E. **CREDITORS' COMMITTEES**
A committee of unsecured creditors is appointed to consult with the trustee or DIP. Other committees may represent special-interest creditors. Some small businesses can avoid creditors' committees.

F. **THE REORGANIZATION PLAN**

1. **Who Can File a Plan**

   Only a debtor can file within the first 120 days (180 days in some cases) after the date of an order for relief. Any other party can file if a debtor does not meet the deadline or fails to obtain creditor consent within 180 days. A court may extend these time periods.

2. **What the Plan Must Do**

   Be fair and equitable ("in the best interests of the creditors"); designate classes of claims and interests; specify the treatment to be afforded the classes; and provide an adequate means for execution; and provide for the payment of tax claims over a fine-year period.

3. **The Plan Is Submitted to Creditors for Acceptance**

   Each class adversely affected by a plan must accept it (two-thirds of the total claims must approve). If only one class accepts, the court may confirm it under the Code's cram-down provision if the plan does not discriminate unfairly against any creditors.

4. **Discharge**

   The plan is binding on confirmation, but an individual debtor must complete the plan to obtain a discharge. A debtor is discharged from all claims not within the plan (except those that would be denied in a liquidation).

VI. BANKRUPTCY RELIEF UNDER CHAPTER 13 AND CHAPTER 12

A. INDIVIDUALS' REPAYMENT PLAN

1. **Who Is Eligible**

   Individuals (not partnerships or corporations) with regular income and unsecured debts of less than $307,615 or secured debts of less than $922,975 are eligible.

2. **Filing the Petition**

   A Chapter 13 case can be initiated by voluntary filing of a petition or by conversion of a Chapter 7 case. A trustee is appointed.

3. **Automatic Stay**

   On a petition's filing, a stay takes effect, but applies only to consumer debt, not business debt.

4. **The Repayment Plan**

   The plan must provide for (1) turnover to the trustee of the debtor's future income, (2) full payment of all claims entitled to priority, and (3) the same treatment of each claim within a particular class.

   a. **Filing and Confirming the Plan**

      Only a debtor can file a plan, which a court will confirm if (1) the secured creditors accept it, (2) it provides that secured creditors retain their liens until full payment or discharge, or (3) a debtor surrenders property securing claims to the creditors. Also, a creditor with a purchase-money security interest in a car bought within 910 days before a filing must be paid in full.

   b. **Payments under the Plan**

      The time for payment is five years if a debtor's income exceeds the state's median under the "means test" (see above) and three years if it does not. Payments must be timely, or the court can convert the case to a liquidation or dismiss the petition. Before completion of payments, the plan may be modified at the request of the debtor, the trustee, or an unsecured creditor.

   c. **Objection to the Plan**

      Over the objection of the trustee or an unsecured creditor, the court may approve a plan only if (1) the value of the property to be distributed is equal to the amount of the claims, or (2) all the debtor's disposable income (with some exceptions) during the plan will be used to make payments.

5. **Discharge**

After completion of all payments, all debts provided for by the plan are discharged. Many debts (tax claims, domestic support obligations, student loans, and others) are not dischargeable. A hardship discharge may be granted even if a plan is not completed. A discharge obtained by fraud can be revoked within one year.

B. **FAMILY FARMERS AND FISHERMEN**

The procedures and requirements under Chapter 12 are nearly identical to those under Chapter 13. Eligible debtors include family farmers and fishermen.

1. **Family Farmers**

A family farmer is one whose gross income is at least 50 percent farm dependent and whose debts are at least 80 percent farm related (total debt must not exceed $3.237 million), and a partnership or closely held corporation (at least 50 percent owned by a farm family).

2. **Family Fishermen**

A family fisherman is one whose gross income is at least 50 percent dependent on commercial fishing and whose debts are at least 80 percent related to commercial fishing (total debt must not exceed $1.5 million), and a partnership or closely held corporation (at least 50 percent owned by a fishing family).

TRUE-FALSE QUESTIONS

(Answers at the Back of the Book)

_F_ 1. A mechanic's lien involves personal property.

_F_ 2. An employer can dismiss an employee due to garnishment.

_T_ 3. A writ of attachment is a court order to seize a debtor's property *before* the entry of a final judgment in a creditor's lawsuit against the debtor.

_T_ 4. A surety or guarantor is discharged from his or her obligation when the principal debtor pays the debt.

_F_ 5. A surety cannot use defenses available to the debtor to avoid liability on an obligation to a creditor.

_T_ 6. A debtor must be insolvent to file a voluntary petition under Chapter 7.

_T_ 7. With some exceptions, the same principles cover liquidations and reorganizations.

_T_ 8. Under Chapter 13, the automatic stay applies only to consumer debt, not business debt.

_F_ 9. When a business debtor files for Chapter 11 protection, the debtor is not allowed to continue in business.

_F_ 10. No small business can avoid creditors' committees under Chapter 11.

FILL-IN QUESTIONS

(Answers at the Back of the Book)

A _____ (contract of suretyship/guaranty contract) is a promise to a creditor made by a third person to be responsible for a debtor's obligation. A _____ (guarantor/surety) is primarily liable: the creditor can hold the _____ (guarantor/surety) responsible for payment of the debt when the debt is due, without first exhausting all remedies against the debtor. A _____ (contract of suretyship/guaranty contract) also includes a promise to answer for a principal's obligation, but a _____ (guarantor/surety) is secondarily liable—that is, the principal must first default, and ordinarily, a creditor must have attempted to collect from the principal, because ordinarily a debtor would not otherwise be declared in default.

MULTIPLE-CHOICE QUESTIONS

(Answers at the Back of the Book)

 1. Ann borrows money from Best Credit, Inc. Ann defaults. To use attachment as a remedy Best must first

   a. be unable to collect the amount of a judgment against Ann.
   b. file a suit against Ann.
   c. lose a suit against Ann.
   d. succeed in a suit against Ann.

 2. Ed's $2,500 debt to Owen is past due. To collect money from Ed's wages to pay the debt, Owen can use

   a. an order of receivership.
   b. a writ of attachment.
   c. a writ of execution.
   d. garnishment.

 3. Eve owes Fred $200,000. A court awards Fred a judgment in this amount. To satisfy the judgment, Eve's home is sold at public auction for $150,000. The state homestead exemption is $50,000. Fred gets

   a. $0.
   b. $50,000.
   c. $100,000.
   d. $150,000.

 4. Eagle Company wants to borrow money from First State Bank. The bank insists that Holly, Eagle's president, agree to be personally liable for payment if Eagle defaults. Holly agrees. She is

   a. a guarantor and a surety.
   b. a guarantor only.
   c. a surety only.
   d. neither a guarantor nor a surety.

 5. Ira and Jill agree to act as guarantors on a loan made by Ken. Ken defaults on the payments and Jill refuses to pay. If Ira pays the debt, he can recover from

   a. Ken and Jill under the right of reimbursement.
   b. Ken and Jill under the right of proportionate liability.
   c. Ken under the right of subrogation and Jill under the right of contribution.
   d. neither Ken nor Jill.

6. Bob files a bankruptcy petition under Chapter 7 to have his debts discharged. Assuming Bob passes the appropriate test, the debts most likely to be discharged include claims for

   a. back taxes accruing within three years before the petition was filed.
   b. certain fines and penalties payable to the government.
   c. domestic support.
   d. student loans, if the payment would impose undue hardship on Bob.

7. Carol is the sole proprietor of Diners Cafe, which owes debts in an amount more than Carol believes she and the cafe can repay. The creditors agree that liquidating the business would not be in their best interests. To stay in business, Lora could file for bankruptcy under

   a. Chapter 7 only.
   b. Chapter 11 only.
   c. Chapter 13 only.
   d. Chapter 11 or Chapter 13.

8. Pat files a Chapter 7 petition for a discharge in bankruptcy. Pat may be denied a discharge if Pat

   a. fails to explain a loss of assets.
   b. fails to list a debt.
   c. owes back taxes.
   d. owes domestic support payments.

9. Dora and Ed make down payments on goods to be received from Fine Furniture Store. Before the goods are delivered, Fine files for bankruptcy. Besides consumers like Dora and Ed, Fine owes wages to its employees and taxes to the government. The order in which these debts will be paid is

   a. consumer deposits, unpaid wages, and taxes.
   b. taxes, consumer deposits, and unpaid wages.
   c. unpaid wages, consumer deposits, and taxes.
   d. unpaid wages, taxes, and consumer deposits.

10. Regional Stores, Inc., files for bankruptcy. A corporation can file a petition for bankruptcy under

    a. Chapter 7 only.
    b. Chapter 11 only.
    c. Chapter 13 only.
    d. Chapter 7 or Chapter 11.

SHORT ESSAY QUESTIONS

1. What is a lien? What are the four ways in which a lien can arise? What is a lienholder's priority compared to other creditors?

2. What are the differences between contracts of suretyship and guaranty contracts?

ISSUE SPOTTERS

(Answers at the Back of the Book)

1. Joe contracts with Larry of Midwest Roofing to fix Joe's roof. Joe pays half of the contract price in advance. Larry and Midwest complete the job, but Joe refuses to pay the rest of the price. What can Larry and Midwest do?

2. Pat wants to borrow $10,000 from Quality Loan Company to buy a new car, but Quality refuses to lend the money unless Ron cosigns the note. Ron cosigns and makes three of the payments when Pat fails to do so. Can Ron get this money from Pat?

3. Ada is a vice president for Beta, Inc. On May 1, Ada loans Beta $10,000. On June 1, the firm repays the loan. On July 1, Beta files for bankruptcy. Cole is appointed trustee. Can Cole recover the $10,000 paid to Ada on June 1?

CUMULATIVE HYPOTHETICAL PROBLEM FOR UNIT THREE—INCLUDING CHAPTERS 7–12

(Answers at the Back of the Book)

Adam, Beth, and Carl pool their resources to make and sell customized software. They do business under the name "Computer Data" (CD).

____   1.   To protect the rights that CD has in the software it produces, CD's best protection is offered by

    a. bankruptcy law.
    b. intellectual property law.
    c. contract law.
    d. sales law.

____   2.   CD sends e-mail to Doe & Roe, an accounting firm, offering to contract for its services for a certain price. The offer is sent on June 1 and is seen by Doe on June 2. The offer states that it will be open until July 1. This offer

    a. cannot be revoked because it is a firm offer.
    b. cannot be revoked because it is an option contract.
    c. could have been revoked only before Doe saw it.
    d. may be revoked any time before it is accepted.

____   3.   Digital Products Company (DPC) writes to CD to order customized software, which it plans to sell to its customer, Eagle Corporation. CD writes to accept but adds a clause providing for interest on any overdue invoices (a common practice in the industry). If there is no further communication between the parties

    a. CD has made a counteroffer.
    b. there is a contract but without CD's added term.
    c. there is a contract that includes CD's added term.
    d. there is no contract because DPC did not expressly accept the added term.

____   4.   After the news about Eagle's losses is publicized, CD loses business and files a voluntary petition in bankruptcy under Chapter 11. A reorganization plan is filed with the court. The court will confirm the plan if it is accepted by

    a. CD.
    b. CD's secured creditors.
    c. CD's shareholders.
    d. CD's unsecured creditors.

____   5.   CD's Chapter 11 plan is confirmed, and a final decree is entered. CD will be

    a. discharged from all debts except as otherwise provided by the law.
    b. liquidated.
    c. operated in business by the bankruptcy trustee.
    d. required to change its business purpose.

Chapter 13:
Employment Relationships

WHAT THIS CHAPTER IS ABOUT

This chapter covers agency relationships, including how they are formed and the duties involved. An agency relationship involves two parties: the principal and the agent. Employment relationships are agency relationships. This chapter also discusses some of the significant employment laws.

CHAPTER OUTLINE

I. AGENCY RELATIONSHIPS
In an agency relationship, the parties agree that the agent will act on behalf and instead of the principal in negotiating and transacting business with third persons.

A. EMPLOYER-EMPLOYEE RELATIONSHIPS
Normally, all employees who deal with third parties are deemed to be agents. Statutes covering workers' compensation and so on apply only to employer-employee relationships.

B. EMPLOYER–INDEPENDENT CONTRACTOR RELATIONSHIPS
Those who hire independent contractors have no control over the details of their physical performance. Independent contractors can be agents.

C. CRITERIA FOR DETERMINING EMPLOYEE STATUS
The greater an employer's control over the work, the more likely it is that the worker is an employee. Another key factor is whether the employer withholds taxes from payments to the worker and pays unemployment and Social Security taxes covering the worker.

II. AGENCY FORMATION
Consideration is not required. A principal must have capacity to contract. An agency can be created for any legal purpose.

A. AGENCY BY AGREEMENT
Normally, an agency must be based on an agreement that the agent will act for the principal. Such an agreement can be an express written contract, can be implied by conduct, or can be oral.

B. AGENCY BY RATIFICATION
A person who is not an agent (or who is an agent acting outside the scope of his or her authority) may make a contract on behalf of another (a principal). If the principal approves or affirms that contract by word or by action, an agency relationship is created by ratification.

C. AGENCY BY ESTOPPEL
When a principal causes a third person to believe that another person is his or her agent, and the third person deals with the supposed agent, the principal is estopped to deny the agency relationship.

D. AGENCY BY OPERATION OF LAW
An agency relationship in the absence of a formal agreement may occur in family relationships or in an emergency, if the agent's failure to act outside the scope of his or her authority would cause the principal substantial loss.

III. DUTIES OF AGENTS AND PRINCIPALS
The principal-agent relationship is fiduciary.

A. AGENT'S DUTIES TO THE PRINCIPAL

1. Performance
An agent must perform with reasonable diligence and skill.

2. Notification
An agent must notify the principal of all matters concerning the agency.

3. Loyalty
An agent must act solely for the benefit of the principal.

4. Obedience
An agent must follow all lawful instructions of the principal.

5. Accounting
An agent must keep and make available to the principal an account of everything received and paid out on behalf of the principal.

B. PRINCIPAL'S DUTIES TO THE AGENT

1. Compensation
A principal must pay the agent for services rendered.

2. Reimbursement and Indemnification
A principal must (1) reimburse the agent for money paid at the principal's request or for necessary expenses and (2) indemnify an agent for liability incurred because of authorized acts.

3. Cooperation
A principal must cooperate with his or her agent.

4. Safe Working Conditions
A principal must provide safe working conditions.

IV. AGENT'S AUTHORITY

A. ACTUAL AUTHORITY
Express authority may be oral or in writing. Implied authority may be conferred by custom, can be inferred from the position an agent occupies, or is implied as reasonably necessary to carry out express authority.

B. APPARENT AUTHORITY
An agent has apparent authority when a principal, by word or action, causes a third party reasonably to believe that an agent has authority, though the agent has no authority. The principal may be estopped from denying it if the third party changes position in reliance.

V. LIABILITY IN AGENCY RELATIONSHIPS

A. LIABILITY FOR CONTRACTS
Who is liable to third parties for contracts formed by an agent?

1. If an Agent Acts within the Scope of His or Her Authority

    a. Disclosed Principal
    If a principal's identity is known to a third party when an agent makes a contract, the principal is liable. The agent is not liable.

    b. Partially Disclosed Principal
    If a principal's identity is not known to a third party when an agent makes a contract but the third party knows the agent is acting for a principal, the principal is liable. In most states, the agent is also liable.

c. **Undisclosed Principal**
If a principal's identity is not known to a third party when an agent makes a contract, the principal *and* the agent are liable (with some exceptions).

2. **If the Agent Has No Authority**
The principal is not liable in contract to a third party. The agent is liable, unless the third party knew the agent did not have authority.

B. **LIABILITY FOR TORTS AND CRIMES**
An agent is liable to third parties for his or her torts and crimes. Is the principal also liable?

1. **Liability for Agent's Torts**

a. **The Doctrine of *Respondeat Superior***
An employer is liable for harm caused (negligently or intentionally) to a third party by an employee acting within the scope of employment, without regard to the fault of the employer.

b. **Scope of Employment**
Factors for determining whether an act is within the scope of employment are—

1) the time, place, and purpose of the act.
2) whether the act was authorized by the employer.
3) whether the act is one commonly performed by employees on behalf of their employers.
4) whether the employer's interest was advanced by the act.
5) whether the private interests of the employee were involved.
6) whether the employer furnished the means by which an injury was inflicted.
7) whether the employer had reason to know that the employee would do the act in question.
8) whether the act involved the commission of a serious crime.

c. **Misrepresentation**
A principal is responsible for an agent's misrepresentation made within the scope of the agent's authority.

2. **Liability for Independent Contractor's Torts**
An employer is not liable for physical harm caused to a third person by an independent contractor's tort (except for hazardous activities—blasting operations, transportation of volatile chemicals, and use of poisonous gases—in which strict liability is imposed).

3. **Liability for Agent's Crimes**
A principal is not liable for an agent's crime, unless the principal participated. In some states, a principal may be liable for an agent's violating, in the course and scope of employment, such regulations as those governing sanitation, prices, weights, and the sale of liquor.

VI.   WAGE-HOUR LAWS
Davis-Bacon Act of 1931 requires "prevailing wages" for employees of some government contractors. Walsh-Healey Act of 1936 requires minimum wage and overtime for employees of some government contractors. Fair Labor Standards Act of 1938 (FLSA) covers all employees and regulates—

A. **CHILD LABOR**
Children under fourteen can deliver newspapers, work for their parents, and work in entertainment and agriculture. Children fourteen and older cannot work in hazardous occupations.

B. **MAXIMUM HOURS**
Employees who work more than forty hours per week must be paid no less than one and a half times their regular pay for all hours over forty. Executives, administrative employees, professional employees, computer employees, and outside salespersons are exempt if they meet certain requirements.

C. **MINIMUM WAGE**
A specified amount (periodically revised) must be paid to employees in covered industries. Wages include the reasonable cost to furnish employees with board, lodging, and other facilities.

VII. WORKER HEALTH AND SAFETY

A. THE OCCUPATIONAL SAFETY AND HEALTH ACT OF 1970
Attempts to ensure safe and healthful work conditions for most employees.

1. Enforcement Agencies

a. Occupational Safety and Health Administration (OSHA)
Inspects workplaces and issues safety standards, including standards covering employee exposure to harmful substances.

b. National Institute for Occupational Safety and Health
Researches safety and health problems and recommends standards for OSHA to adopt.

c. Occupational Safety and Health Review Commission
Hears appeals from actions taken by OSHA administrators.

2. Procedures and Violations
Employees file complaints of OSHA violations (employers cannot retaliate); employers must keep injury and illness records; employers must file accident reports directly to OSHA. Penalties are limited.

B. WORKERS' COMPENSATION
State laws establish procedure for compensating workers injured on the job.

1. No State Covers All Employees
Often excluded are domestic workers, agricultural workers, temporary employees, and employees of common carriers.

2. Requirements for Recovery
There must be an employment relationship, and the injury must be accidental and occur on the job or in the course of employment.

3. Filing a Claim
An employee must notify the employer of an injury (usually within thirty days), and file a claim with a state agency within a certain period (sixty days to two years) from the time the injury is first noticed.

4. Acceptance of Workers' Compensation Benefits Bars Suits
An employee's acceptance of benefits bars the employee from suing for injuries caused by the employer's negligence.

VIII. INCOME SECURITY

A. SOCIAL SECURITY
The Social Security Act of 1935 provides for payments to persons who are retired, widowed, disabled, etc. Employers and employees must contribute under the Federal Insurance Contributions Act (FICA).

B. MEDICARE
A health insurance program administered by the Social Security Administration for people sixty-five years of age and older and for some under sixty-five who are disabled.

C. PRIVATE PENSION PLANS
The Employee Retirement Income Security Act (ERISA) of 1974 empowers the Labor Management Services Administration of the Department of Labor to oversee those who operate private pension funds.

1. Vesting
Generally, employee contributions to pension plans vest immediately; employee rights to employer contributions vest after five years.

2. Investing
Pension-fund managers must be cautious in investing and refrain from investing more than 10 percent of the fund in securities of the employer.

D. **UNEMPLOYMENT INSURANCE**
The Federal Unemployment Tax Act of 1935 created a state system that provides unemployment compensation to eligible individuals.

E. **COBRA**
The Consolidated Omnibus Budget Reconciliation Act (COBRA) of 1985 prohibits the elimination of most workers' medical, optical, or dental insurance on the termination of their employment. Coverage must continue for up to 18 months (29 months in some cases). A worker pays the premium plus 2 percent.

IX.   FAMILY AND MEDICAL LEAVE ACT (FMLA) OF 1993
Employers with fifty or more employees must provide them with up to twelve weeks of family or medical leave during any twelve-month period, continue health-care coverage during the leave, and guarantee employment in the same, or a comparable, position when the employee returns to work.

X.   EMPLOYEE PRIVACY RIGHTS
A right to privacy has been inferred from constitutional guarantees provided by the First, Third, Fourth, Fifth, and Ninth Amendments to the Constitution.

A. **ELECTRONIC MONITORING IN THE WORKPLACE**
The Electronic Communications Privacy Act (ECPA) of 1986 bars interception of any wire or electronic communication or the disclosure or use of information obtained by interception. Excepted are employers' monitoring of *business* phone conversations and cases in which employees consent. With e-mail, it has not seemed to matter whether employees were aware of being monitored, however.

B. **OTHER TYPES OF MONITORING**

1. **Lie-Detector Tests**
Under the Employee Polygraph Protection Act of 1988, most employers cannot, among other things, require, request, or suggest that employees or applicants take lie-detector tests, except when investigating theft, including theft of trade secrets.

2. **Drug Testing**

a. **Protection for the Privacy Rights of Private Employees**
Some state constitutions may prohibit private employers from testing for drugs. State statutes may restrict drug testing by private employers. Other sources of protection include collective bargaining agreements and tort actions for invasion of privacy (see Chapter 4).

b. **Protection for Government Employees**
Constitutional limitations (the Fourth Amendment) apply. Drug tests have been upheld when there was a reasonable basis for suspecting employees of using drugs, or when drug use could threaten public safety.

3. **AIDS Testing**
Some state laws restrict AIDS testing. The federal Americans with Disabilities Act of 1990 and other statutes protect employees or applicants who have tested positive from discrimination.

4. **Genetic Testing**
This may violate the Americans with Disabilities Act of 1990 or other privacy provisions.

TRUE-FALSE QUESTIONS
(Answers at the Back of the Book)

1. Unless the parties agree otherwise, a principal must pay for an agent's services.

2. An agent must keep separate accounts for the principal's funds.

3. A disclosed principal is liable to a third party for a contract by an agent within the scope of authority.

F 4. A principal is not liable for an agent's torts committed within the scope of his or her employment.

T 5. An undisclosed principal is liable to a third party for a contract by an agent within the scope of authority.

T 6. Federal wage-hour laws cover all employers engaged in interstate commerce.

F 7. Under federal law, employers can monitor employees' personal communications.

F 8. Workers' compensation laws cover all employees in all states.

T 9. Except in investigating theft, employers cannot tell employees or job applicants take lie-detector tests.

F 10. Children fourteen and older can work in hazardous occupations.

FILL-IN QUESTIONS

(Answers at the Back of the Book)

An agent's use of reasonable diligence and skill is part of the agent's duty of _____ (obedience / performance). Informing a principal of all material matters that come to the agent's attention concerning the subject matter of the agency is an aspect of the agent's duty of _____ (accounting / notification). Acting solely for the benefit of the principal and not in the interest of the agent or a third party is part of the agent's duty of _____ (loyalty / performance). Following all lawful and clearly stated instructions of the principal is an aspect of the agent's duty of _____ (loyalty / obedience). If an agent is required to keep and make available to the principal a record of all property and money received and paid out on behalf of the principal, this is part of the agent's duty of _____ (accounting / notification).

MULTIPLE-CHOICE QUESTIONS

(Answers at the Back of the Book)

A 1. Carol is a salesperson who works for Delta Products, Inc. In determining whether Carol is Delta's employee or an independent contractor, the most important factor is

   a. the degree of control that Delta exercises over Carol.
   b. the distinction between Delta's business and Carol's occupation.
   c. the length of the working relationship between Delta and Carol.
   d. the method of payment.

A 2. Greg, a salesperson at Home Electronics Company, tells Irma, a customer, "Buy your computer here, and I'll set it up for less than what Home would charge." Irma buys the computer, Greg sets it up, and Irma pays Greg, who keeps the money. Greg has breached the duty of

   a. loyalty.
   b. notification.
   c. obedience.
   d. performance.

C 3. Elle acts within the scope of her authority to enter into a contract with Fidelity Builders, Inc., on behalf of Elle's undisclosed principal, General Engineering, Inc. General is

   a. liable on the contract only if General ratifies the contract.
   b. liable on the contract only if General's identity is later disclosed.
   c. liable on the contract under the stated circumstances.
   d. not liable on the contract.

A   4.   Quality Products Company requires its customers to pay by check. Ray, a Quality agent, tells customers that they can pay him with cash. Quality learns of Ray's collections, but takes no action to stop them. Ray steals some of the cash. Quality may be liable for the loss under the doctrine of

    a.   apparent authority.
    b.   express authority.
    c.   imagined authority.
    d.   implied authority.

C   5.   Standard Delivery Company employs Tina as a driver. While driving within the scope of employment, Tina causes an accident in which Vic is injured. Vic can recover from

    a.   neither Standard nor Tina
    b.   Standard only.
    c.   Standard or Tina.
    d.   Tina only.

A   6.   Fast Jack is a fast-food restaurant. To verify Fast Jack's compliance with statutes governing employees' wages and hours, personnel records should be checked against the provisions of

    a.   the Fair Labor Standards Act.
    b.   the Family and Medical Leave Act.
    c.   the National Labor Relations Act.
    d.   the Taft-Hartley Act.

B   7.   Eve, an employee of First Bank, is injured. For Eve to receive *workers' compensation*, the injury must be

    a.   accidental and arise out of a preexisting disease or condition.
    b.   accidental and occur on the job or in the course of employment.
    c.   intentional and arise out of a preexisting disease or condition.
    d.   intentional and occur on the job or in the course of employment.

C   8.   Ron is an employee of Super Sales Company. Ron and Super contribute to the federal social security system under

    a.   the Employee Payments Act.
    b.   the Employment Retirement Income Security Act.
    c.   the Federal Insurance Contributions Act.
    d.   the Federal Unemployment Tax Act.

B   9.   Eagle, Inc., sets up a pension fund for its employees. Eagle's operation of the fund is regulated by

    a.   the Employer Payments Act.
    b.   the Employment Retirement Income Security Act.
    c.   the Federal Insurance Contributions Act.
    d.   the Federal Unemployment Tax Act.

B   10.   ABC Corporation provides health insurance for its 150 employees, including Dian. When Dian takes twelve weeks' leave to care for her child, she

    a.   can collect "leave pay" equal to twelve weeks' of health insurance coverage.
    b.   can continue her heath insurance at ABC's expense.
    c.   can continue her heath insurance at her expense.
    d.   loses her heath insurance immediately on taking leave.

SHORT ESSAY QUESTIONS

1.   What are the essential differences among the relationships of principal and agent, employer and employee, and employer and independent contractor? What factors indicate whether an individual is an employee or an independent contractor?

2. What protection do employees have from the financial impact of retirement, disability, death, hospitalization, and unemployment?

ISSUE SPOTTERS

(Answers at the Back of the Book)

1. Don contracts with Eve to buy a certain horse for Eve, who asks Don not to reveal her identity. Don makes a deal with Farm Stables, the owner of the horse, and makes a down payment. Eve fails to pay the rest of the price. Farm Stables sues Don for breach of contract. Can Don hold Eve liable for whatever damages he has to pay?

2. Alpha Corporation wants to build a new mall on a specific tract of land. Alpha enters into a contract with Beth to buy the land. When Beth learns the difference between the price that Alpha is willing to pay and the price at which the owner is willing to sell, she wants to buy the land and sell it to Alpha herself. Can she do this?

3. Workers' compensation laws establish a procedure for compensating workers who are injured on the job. Instead of suing, the worker files a claim with the appropriate state agency. Does the injury have to have been caused by the employer's negligence?

Chapter 14:
Equal Employment Opportunities

WHAT THIS CHAPTER IS ABOUT

The law restricts employers and unions from discriminating against workers on the basis of race, color, religion, national origin, gender, age, or handicap. A class of persons defined by one or more of these criteria is known as a **protected class**. This chapter outlines these laws.

CHAPTER OUTLINE

I. TITLE VII OF THE CIVIL RIGHTS ACT OF 1964

Prohibits employment discrimination against employees, applicants, and union members on the basis of race, color, national origin, religion, and gender.

A. WHO IS SUBJECT TO TITLE VII?

Employers with fifteen or more employees, labor unions with fifteen or more members, labor unions that operate hiring halls, employment agencies, and federal, state, and local agencies.

B. PROCEDURES UNDER TITLE VII

(1) A victim files a claim with the Equal Employment Opportunity Commission (EEOC); (2) the EEOC investigates and seeks a voluntary settlement; (3) if no settlement is reached, the EEOC may sue the employer; (4) if the EEOC chooses not to sue, the victim may file a lawsuit.

C. INTENTIONAL AND UNINTENTIONAL DISCRIMINATION

Title VII prohibits both intentional and unintentional discrimination.

1. Intentional Discrimination

Intentional discrimination by one employer against another is disparate-treatment discrimination.

a. *Prima Facie* Case—Plaintiff's Side of the Case

A plaintiff must show (1) he or she is a member of a protected class, (2) he or she applied and was qualified for the job, (3) he or she was rejected by the employer, (4) the employer continued to seek applicants or filled the job with a person not in a protected class.

b. Defense—Employer's Side of the Case

An employer must articulate a legal reason for not hiring the plaintiff. To prevail, a plaintiff must show that this reason is a pretext and discriminatory intent motivated the decision.

2. Unintentional Discrimination

Unintentional discrimination is known as disparate-impact discrimination.

a. Types of Unintentional Discrimination

Disparate-impact discrimination results if, because of a requirement or hiring practice—

1) an employer's work force does not reflect the percentage of members of protected classes that characterizes qualified individuals in the local labor market, or

2) members of a protected class are excluded from an employer's work force at substantially higher rate than nonmembers (under EEOC's "four-fifths rule," selection rate for protected class must be at least 80 percent of rate for group with the highest rate).

b. *Prima Facie* Case—Plaintiff's Side of the Case

Plaintiff must show a connection between a requirement or practice and a disparity; no evidence of discriminatory intent is needed.

D. **DISCRIMINATION BASED ON RACE, COLOR, AND NATIONAL ORIGIN**

Employers cannot effectively discriminate against employees on the basis of race, color, national origin, or religion (absent a substantial, demonstrable relationship between the trait and the job, etc.).

E. **DISCRIMINATION BASED ON RELIGION**

Title VII prohibits employers and unions from discriminating against persons because of their religions.

F. **DISCRIMINATION BASED ON GENDER**

Employers cannot discriminate against employees on the basis of gender (unless the gender of the applicant can be proved essential to the job, etc.). The Pregnancy Discrimination Act of 1978 amended Title VII: employees affected by pregnancy or related conditions must be treated the same as persons not so affected but similar in ability to work.

G. **SEXUAL HARASSMENT**

1. **Forms of Harassment**

(1) *Quid pro quo* harassment: when promotions, etc., are doled out on the basis of sexual favors; (2) hostile-environment harassment: when an employee is subjected to offensive sexual comments, etc. Plaintiffs can sue for same-gender harassment.

2. **Harassment by Supervisors, Co-Workers, or Nonemployees**

a. **When Is an Employer Liable?**

If anyone (employee or nonemployee) harasses an employee, and the employer knew, or should have known, and failed to take immediate corrective action, the employer may be liable. To be liable for a supervisor's harassment, the supervisor must have taken a tangible employment action against the employee.

b. **Employer's Defense**

(1) Employer took "reasonable care to prevent and correct promptly any sexually harassing behavior," and (2) employee suing for harassment failed to follow employer's policies and procedures.

H. **ONLINE HARASSMENT**

Employers may avoid liability if they take prompt remedial action. Privacy rights must be considered if the action includes electronic monitoring of employees.

I. **REMEDIES UNDER TITLE VII**

Remedies under Title VII include job reinstatement, back pay, retroactive promotions, and damages.

1. **Damages**

Compensatory damages are available only in cases of intentional discrimination. Punitive damages are available only if an employer acted with malice or reckless indifference

2. **Limitations**

Total damages are limited to specific amounts against specific employers (from $50,000 against those with one hundred or fewer employees to $300,000 against those with more than five hundred employees).

II. EQUAL PAY ACT OF 1963

Prohibits gender-based discrimination in wages for equal work (work requiring equal skill, effort, responsibility under similar conditions) in the same workplace. Different wages are acceptable because of any factor but gender (seniority, merit, etc.).

III. DISCRIMINATION BASED ON AGE

A. THE AGE DISCRIMINATION IN EMPLOYMENT ACT (ADEA) OF 1967

Prohibits employment discrimination on the basis of age (including mandatory retirement), by employers with twenty or more employees, against individuals forty years of age or older. Administered by the EEOC, but private causes of action are also possible.

B. PRINCIPLES ARE SIMILAR TO TITLE VII

Requires the establishment of a *prima facie* case: plaintiff must show that he or she was (1) forty or older, (2) qualified for a position, and (3) rejected in circumstances that infer discrimination. The employer must articulate a legal reason; the plaintiff may show it is a pretext.

C. STATE EMPLOYEES

Under the Eleventh Amendment to the Constitution, a state is immune from suits brought by private individuals in federal court unless the state consents to the suit. A state agency sued by a state employee for age discrimination may have the suit dismissed on this ground.

IV. DISCRIMINATION BASED ON DISABILITY

Under the Americans with Disabilities Act (ADA) of 1990, an employer cannot refuse to hire a person who is qualified but disabled.

A. PROCEDURES AND REMEDIES UNDER THE ADA

1. Procedures

A plaintiff must show he or she (1) has a disability, (2) is otherwise qualified for a job and (3) was excluded solely because of the disability. A suit may be filed only after a claim is pursued through the EEOC (which may file a suit even if the employee agrees to arbitration).

2. Remedies

These include reinstatement, back pay, some compensatory and punitive damages (for intentional discrimination), and certain other relief. Repeat violators may be fined up to $100,000.

B. WHAT IS A DISABILITY?

"(1) [A] physical or mental impairment that substantially limits one or more of the major life activities . . . ; (2) a record of such impairment; or (3) being regarded as having such an impairment," based on how a person functions with medication or corrective devices. Includes AIDS, morbid obesity, etc.; not kleptomania.

C. REASONABLE ACCOMMODATION

For a person with a disability, an employer may have to make a reasonable accommodation (more flexible working hours, new job assignment, different training materials or procedures)—but not an accommodation that will cause *undue hardship* ("significant difficulty or expense").

1. Job Applications

The application process must be accessible to those with disabilities.

2. Preemployment Physical Exams

Employers cannot require a disabled person to take a preemployment physical (unless all applicants do). Disqualification must be from problems that render a person unable to perform the job.

3. Dangerous Workers

An employer need not hire disabled workers who would pose a "direct threat to the health or safety" of co-workers or to themselves.

4. Substance Abusers

The ADA protects addicts who have completed or are in supervised rehabilitation, and alcoholics to the extent of equal treatment.

5. Health-Insurance Plans

Workers with disabilities must be given equal access to insurance plans provided to other workers. If a plan includes a disability-based distinction, an employer must show (1) limiting coverage keeps the plan financially sound, (2) coverage would otherwise be too expensive for many workers, or (3) the distinction is justified by the risk and costs.

V. DEFENSES TO EMPLOYMENT DISCRIMINATION

The first defense is to assert that the plaintiff did not prove discrimination. If discrimination is proved, an employer may attempt to justify it as—

A. BUSINESS NECESSITY

An employer may show that there is a legitimate connection between a job requirement that discriminates and job performance.

B. BONA FIDE OCCUPATIONAL QUALIFICATION (BFOQ)

Another defense applies when discrimination against a protected class is essential to a job—that is, when a particular trait is a BFOQ. Generally restricted to cases in which gender is essential. Race can never be a BFOQ.

C. SENIORITY SYSTEMS

An employer with a history of discrimination may have no members of protected classes or disabled workers in upper-level positions. If no present intent to discriminate is shown, and promotions, etc., are distributed according to a fair seniority system, the employer has a good defense.

D. AFTER-ACQUIRED EVIDENCE

Evidence of an employee's prior misconduct acquired after a lawsuit is filed may limit damages but is not otherwise a defense.

VI. AFFIRMATIVE ACTION

An affirmative action program attempts to make up for past discrimination by giving members of protected classes preferential treatment in hiring or promotion. Such a program cannot use quotas or preferences for unqualified persons, and once a program has succeeded, it must be changed or dropped.

VII. STATE STATUTES

Most states have statutes that prohibit the kinds of discrimination prohibited under federal legislation. State statutes also often protect individuals, such as homosexuals, who are not protected under Title VII.

TRUE-FALSE QUESTIONS

(Answers at the Back of the Book)

_T_ 1. Once an affirmative action program has succeeded, it must be changed or dropped.

_F_ 2. In a sexual harassment case, an employer cannot be held liable if an employee did the harassing.

_F_ 3. In a sexual harassment case, an employer cannot be held liable if a nonemployee did the harassing.

_T_ 4. Women affected by pregnancy must be treated for all job-related purposes the same as persons not so affected but similar in ability to work.

_T_ 5. Employment discrimination against persons with a physical or mental impairment that substantially limits their everyday activities is prohibited.

_T_ 6. Discrimination complaints under federal law must be filed with the Equal Opportunity Employment Commission.

F 7. If the Equal Employment Opportunity Commission decides not to investigate a claim, the victim has no other option.

F 8. All employers are subject to Title VII of the Civil Rights Act of 1964.

T 9. Disparate-treatment discrimination occurs when an employer intentionally discriminates against an employee.

T 10. Title VII prohibits employers and unions from discriminating against persons because of their religions.

FILL-IN QUESTIONS

(Answers at the Back of the Book)

The Equal Employment Opportunity Commission (EEOC) monitors compliance with the federal antidiscrimination laws. The EEOC _____ (can/cannot) sue organizations that violate these laws. A victim files a claim with the EEOC, which investigates and _____ _____ (must sue/may sue if a settlement between the parties is not reached). If the EEOC does not sue, the victim may sue. On proof of discrimination, a victim may be awarded _____ _____ (reinstatement and back pay/reinstatement, back pay, and retroactive promotions).

MULTIPLE-CHOICE QUESTIONS

(Answers at the Back of the Book)

A 1. Ann is an employee of Beta Communications Corporation. Ann attempts to resolve a gender-based discrimination claim with Beta, whose representative denies the claim. Ann's next best step is to

a. ask the Equal Opportunity Employment Commission whether a claim is justified.
b. file a lawsuit.
c. forget about the matter.
d. secretly sabotage company operations for revenge.

A 2. Bob and Carol work for Delta Company. Bob is Carol's supervisor. During work, Bob touches Carol in ways that she perceives as sexually offensive. Carol resists the advances. Bob cuts her pay. Delta is

a. liable, because Bob's conduct constituted sexual harassment.
b. liable, because Carol resisted Bob's advances.
c. not liable, because Bob's conduct was not job-related.
d. not liable, because Carol resisted Bob's advances.

A 3. Under the Age Discrimination in Employment Act of 1967, Alpha Corporation is prohibited from

a. committing unintentional age discrimination.
b. forcing an employee to retire.
c. terminating an employee between the ages of sixty-five and seventy for cause.
d. terminating an employee as part of a rational business decision.

C 4. National Company requires job applicants to pass certain physical tests. Only a few female applicants can pass the tests, but it they pass, they are hired. To successfully defend against a suit on this basis under Title VII, National must show that

a. any discrimination is not intentional.
b. being a male is a BFOQ.
c. passing the tests is a business necessity.
d. some men cannot pass the tests.

5. Kay, who is hearing impaired, applies for a position with Local Company. Kay is qualified but is refused the job and sues Local. To succeed under the Americans with Disabilities Act, Kay must show that

   a. Kay was willing to make a "reasonable accommodation" for Local.
   b. Kay would not have to accept "significant additional costs" to work for Local.
   c. Local refused to make a "reasonable accommodation" for Kay.
   d. Local would not have to accept "significant additional costs" to hire Kay.

 6. Omega Sales, Inc., promotes employees on the basis of color. Employees with darker skin color are passed over in favor of those with lighter skin color, regardless of their race. This is prohibited by

   a. the Americans with Disabilities Act of 1990.
   b. the Equal Pay Act of 1963.
   c. Title VII of the Civil Rights Act of 1964.
   d. none of the above.

 7. Curt, personnel director for Digital Products, Inc., prefers to hire Asian Americans, because "they're smarter and work harder" than other minorities. This is prohibited by

   a. the Age Discrimination in Employment Act of 1967.
   b. the Americans with Disabilities Act of 1990.
   c. Title VII of the Civil Rights Act of 1964 .
   d. none of the above.

 8. Greg and Holly work for Interstate Services, Inc. (ISI), as electrical engineers. Greg is paid more than Holly because, according to ISI, he is a man with a family to support. This is prohibited by

   a. the Age Discrimination in Employment Act of 1967.
   b. the Americans with Disabilities Act of 1990.
   c. the Equal Pay Act of 1963.
   d. none of the above.

 9. Donna applies to Eagle Corporation for an administrative assistant's job, which requires certain typing skills. Donna cannot type but tells Eagle that she is willing to learn. Eagle does not hire Donna, who later sues. To successfully defend against the suit under Title VII, Eagle must show that

   a. being a member of the majority is a BFOQ.
   b. Donna was not willing to learn to type.
   c. Eagle has a valid business necessity defense.
   d. Eagle's work force reflects the same percentage of members of a protected class that characterizes qualified individuals in the local labor market.

10. Standard Corporation terminates Tom, who sues on the basis of age discrimination. To succeed under the Age Discrimination in Employment Act, Tom must show that at the time of the discharge, he was

   a. forty or older.
   b. forty or younger.
   c. replaced with someone forty or older.
   d. replaced with someone forty or younger.

SHORT ESSAY QUESTIONS

1. Compare and contrast disparate-treatment discrimination and disparate-impact discrimination, and Title VII's response to each in the context of employment.

2. What does the Americans with Disabilities Act require employers to do?

ISSUE SPOTTERS

(Answers at the Back of the Book)

1.   Phil applies for a job at Quality Corporation for which he is well qualified, but for which he is rejected. Quality continues to seek applicants and eventually fills the position with a person who is not a member of a minority. Could Phil succeed in a suit against Quality for discrimination?

2.   Ruth is a supervisor for Subs & Suds, a restaurant. Tim is a Subs employee. The owner announces that some employees will be discharged. Ruth tells Tim that if he has sex with her, he can keep his job. Is this sexual harassment?

3.   Paula, a disabled person, applies for a job at Quantity Corporation for which she is well qualified, but for which she is rejected. Quantity continues to seek applicants and eventually fills the position with a person who is not disabled. Could Paula succeed in a suit against Quantity for discrimination?

Chapter 15:
Labor-Management Relations

WHAT THIS CHAPTER IS ABOUT

This chapter outlines labor law and legal recognition of the right to form unions, the process of unionizing a company, the process of collective bargaining, and labor practices considered fair and unfair under federal law.

CHAPTER OUTLINE

I. FEDERAL LABOR LAW

All employers whose businesses involve or affect interstate commerce are subject to these laws. Agricultural workers and domestic servants are excluded.

A. NORRIS-LaGUARDIA ACT OF 1932

This law restricts federal courts' power to issue injunctions against unions engaged in peaceful strikes, picketing, and boycotts.

B. NATIONAL LABOR RELATIONS ACT OF 1935 (NLRA)

The NLRA established the right of employees to bargain collectively and to strike; prescribed unfair employer practices; created the NLRB to oversee union elections, prevent employers from engaging in unfair practices, investigate employers in response to employee charges of unfair labor practices, issue cease-and-desist orders.

C. LABOR-MANAGEMENT RELATIONS ACT OF 1947 (TAFT-HARTLEY ACT)

This act prohibits unions from refusing to bargain with employers, engaging in certain types of picketing, featherbedding, and other unfair union practices. Expressly preserves union shops, but allows states to pass right-to-work laws, which make it illegal to require union membership for employment.

D. LABOR-MANAGEMENT REPORTING AND DISCLOSURE ACT OF 1959

This law requires regular elections of union officers, under secret ballot; prohibits ex-convicts and Communists from holding union office; makes union officials accountable for union property; allows members to participate in union meetings, nominate officers, vote in proceedings.

II. THE DECISION TO FORM OR TO SELECT A UNION

A. PRELIMINARY ORGANIZING

1. Workers Sign Authorization Cards
A majority of the relevant workers must sign authorization cards, which state that they want a certain union to represent the workforce.

2. The Employer Is Asked to Recognize the Union
If the employer refuses, unionizers must present authorization cards from at least 30 percent of the workers to the NLRB regional office with a petition for an election.

B. APPROPRIATE BARGAINING UNIT
The NLRB determines this, which requires a mutuality of interest among the workers to be represented. Mutuality of interest requires—

1. **Job Similarity**

   Similar levels of skill, wages, benefits, working conditions.

2. **Work-Site Proximity**

   It may be a problem if the workers are at many different sites.

3. **No Management Employees**

   Members of management cannot be part of a union.

C. **MOVING TOWARD CERTIFICATION**

   If no other union has been certified within the past twelve months to represent the workers, the NLRB schedules an election.

III. UNION ELECTION

The NLRB supervises the election.

A. **UNION ELECTION CAMPAIGN**

1. **Employer Limits**

   Employers may limit the campaign activities of union supporters (such as where on company property and when campaigning may occur).

2. **Restrictions on Employer Limits**

   An employer may prohibit *all* solicitation during work time or in certain places but may not prohibit *only* union solicitation. Workers also have a right to a reasonable opportunity to campaign (nonworking areas on the employer's property during nonworking time).

B. **MANAGEMENT ELECTION CAMPAIGN**

1. **Employer Advantages**

   Employers may campaign on company property on company time without giving union supporters an opportunity for rebuttal.

2. **Restrictions on Employer Advantages**

   a . **No Threats**

      An employer may not make threats of reprisals if employees vote to unionize. Employers may not question individual workers about their positions on unionization.

   b. **No Last-minute Speeches**

      An employer cannot make an election speech on company time to assembled workers within twenty-four hours of an election, unless employees attend voluntarily on their own time.

   c. **No Surveillance**

      An employer may not undertake certain types of surveillance of workers or even create the impression of observing workers.

3. **NLRB Options**

   If the employer commits an unfair labor practice, the NLRB may invalidate an election (order a new election; direct the employer to recognize the union).

C. **DECERTIFICATION ELECTION**

   May be sought by employees, by a petition to the NLRB, with a showing of 30 percent employee support and no certification within the past year.

D. **ELECTION RESULTS**

   If a fair election is held and the union wins, the NLRB will certify the union as the exclusive bargaining representative of the workers polled.

IV.   COLLECTIVE BARGAINING

The central legal right of a union is to serve as the sole representative of the group of workers in bargaining with the employer over the workers' rights.

A.   SUBJECTS OF BARGAINING

1.   Appropriate Subjects

a.   Terms and Conditions of Employment
Wages, hours of work, safety rules, insurance coverage, pension and other benefits plans, procedures for discipline, and procedures for grievances against the company.

b.   Decision to Relocate a Plant
An employer must bargain over relocation if it does not involve a basic change in the nature of the operation (with exceptions).

2.   Illegal Subjects
These include featherbedding (hiring unnecessary excess workers) and a closed shop (requiring union membership as a condition of employment).

3.   Possible Subjects
Management may choose to bargain over decisions otherwise within its discretion (such as severance pay or rights of transfer to other plants in the event of plant shut-down) to obtain concessions on other subjects.

B.   NO UNILATERAL CHANGES DURING BARGAINING

Management may not make unilateral changes in important working conditions, such as wages or hours of employment, unless bargaining reaches an impasse or in cases of business necessity.

C.   GOOD FAITH BARGAINING

1.   Bad Faith Bargaining Is an Unfair Labor Practice
Includes refusing to meet with union representatives; excessive delaying tactics; insisting on unreasonable contract terms; engaging in a campaign to undermine the union; constantly shifting positions on disputed terms; sending bargainers who lack authority to commit to a contract.

2.   Options If a Party Refuses to Bargain in Good Faith
The NLRB can order a party to bargain in good faith. The other party may be excused from bargaining.

V.   STRIKES

When bargaining reaches an impasse, the union may call a strike to pressure the employer to make concessions.

A.   THE RIGHT TO STRIKE

The right to strike is guaranteed by the NLRA, within limits, and strike activities, such as picketing, are protected by the First Amendment. Nonworkers have a right to participate in picketing. Workers can also refuse to cross a picket line of fellow workers who are engaged in a lawful strike.

B.   ILLEGAL STRIKES

Illegal strikes include violent strikes, massed picketing, sitdown strikes, and—

1.   Secondary Boycotts
Picketing cannot be directed against a secondary employer, but common situs picketing (at site occupied by both primary and secondary employers) is permitted.

2. **Hot-Cargo Agreements**
   Employers cannot agree with unions not to handle, use, or deal in non-union-produced goods of other employers.

3. **Wildcat Strikes**
   A minority of employees cannot call their own strike.

4. **Strikes That Threaten National Health or Safety**
   These strikes are not illegal, but to encourage their settlement, the president of the United States can obtain an injunction to last for eighty days, during which the government can work to produce a settlement.

5. **Strikes That Contravene No-strike Clauses in Previous Collective Bargaining Agreements**

C. **REPLACEMENT WORKERS**
   An employer may hire substitute workers to replace strikers.

D. **RIGHTS OF STRIKERS AFTER A STRIKE**
   Strikers have no right to return to their jobs (but former strikers must be given preference to any vacancies and also retain their seniority rights) unless the strike is due to employer unfair labor practice.

VI. LOCKOUTS

An employer can shut down to prevent employees from working, but may not use a lockout to break a union and pressure employees into decertification.

VII. UNFAIR LABOR PRACTICES

A. **EMPLOYER'S UNFAIR PRACTICES**

1. **Refusal to Recognize Union and Negotiate**
   For one year after certification, it is presumed that the union enjoys majority support; after this period, the presumption is can be rebutted. With evidence to support a good faith belief that union has no majority support, an employer can refuse to recognize the union.

2. **Interference in Union Activities**
   An employer may not interfere with, restrain, or coerce employees in the exercise of their rights to form a union and bargain collectively.

3. **Domination of Unions**
   The NLRA forbids company unions and other forms of employer domination of workers' unions.

4. **Discrimination against Union Employees**
   Employers cannot discriminate against union workers (in layoffs, hiring, or closing a union plant).

B. **UNION'S UNFAIR PRACTICES**

1. **Secondary Boycotts**

2. **Discrimination against Nonunion Workers**
   A union cannot threaten employees with violence, use economic coercion, picket, or otherwise discriminate (or influence employers to discriminate) against workers who refuse to join a union.

3. **Featherbedding**

4. **Picketing to Coerce Unionization without Majority Support**

5. **Refusal to Bargain in Good Faith with Employer**

6. **Excessive Fees or Dues**
    A nonunion employee subject to a union shop clause who must pay dues cannot be required to contribute to causes or to lobby politicians.

VIII.   RIGHTS OF NONUNION EMPLOYEES

A. CONCERTED ACTIVITY
This activity must be for employees' mutual aid regarding wages, hours, or terms and conditions of employment. A single employee's action may be protected if it is taken for the benefit of other employees and the employee discussed it with other approving workers.

B. SAFETY
An employee can walk off the job if he or she has a good faith belief that working conditions are abnormally dangerous.

C. EMPLOYEE COMMITTEES
The central problem with employee committees is that they may become the functional equivalent of a union that is dominated by management. Thus, these committees cannot perform union functions.

TRUE-FALSE QUESTIONS
(Answers at the Back of the Book)

F   1. Employers can agree with unions not to handle, use, or deal in non-union-produced goods.

F   2. Management serves as the representative of workers in bargaining with a union.

T   3. Federal labor law protects employees' rights to strike, to picket, and to boycott.

F   4. Employees have no right to engage in collective bargaining through elected representatives.

T   5. Similarity of workers' jobs is a factor in determining which workers are to be represented by a union.

T   6. Supervisors and managers cannot be members of a union.

T   7. An employer cannot consider union participation as a criterion for deciding which workers to hire.

F   8. An employer can use a lockout to break a union and pressure employees into decertifying it.

T   9. An employer may make unilateral changes in important working conditions if bargaining negotiations reach an impasse.

T   10. If an employer commits an unfair labor practice during a union election campaign, the election may be invalidated.

FILL-IN QUESTIONS
(Answers at the Back of the Book)

Peaceful strikes, picketing, and boycotts are protected under the _____ _____ (National Labor Relations/Norris-LaGuardia) Act, which also restricts federal courts in enjoining unions engaged in peaceful strikes. Employees' rights to organize, to engage in collective bargaining through elected representatives, and to engage in concerted activities for those and other purposes were established in the _____ (National Labor Relations/Norris-LaGuardia) Act. Requiring union membership as a condition of employment is prohibited by the Labor-Management _____ (Relations/Reporting and Disclosure) Act. This act also _____ (allows/prohibits) requiring workers to join the union after a certain time on the job. This act also _____ (allows/prohibits) laws making it illegal to require union membership for continued employment.

MULTIPLE-CHOICE QUESTIONS

(Answers at the Back of the Book)

1. Standard Manufacturer, Inc., refuses to pay its workers for time spent on union activities. This violates

   a. the Labor-Management Relations Act.
   b. the National Labor Relations Act.
   c. the Norris-LaGuardia Act.
   d. no federal labor law.

2. The employees of Top Products, Inc. (TPI), designate United Machinists Union (UMU) as their bargaining representative. TPI refuses to bargain with UMU and fires several workers for "choosing the wrong side." This violates

   a. the Labor-Management Relations Act.
   b. the National Labor Relations Act.
   c. the Norris-LaGuardia Act.
   d. no federal labor law.

3. During a union election campaign, Alpha Company asks its employees to openly declare their views on the union, so that "everyone knows where everyone stands." This is an unfair labor practice

   a. only if it is a condition of continued employment.
   b. only if the employees do not want to do it.
   c. under any circumstances.
   d. under no circumstances.

4. Assembly Workers of America (AWA) represents employees of Beta Company. During collective bargaining, AWA wants to negotiate changes to Beta's health insurance plan and safety rules. Beta can refuse to bargain over changes to

   a. the plan only.
   b. the rules only.
   c. the plan and the rules.
   d. neither the plan nor the rules.

5. Federated Union Workers (FUW) represents employees of Gamma Company. During collective bargaining, FUW wants to negotiate to the closure of a Gamma plant and the procedure for employee grievances. Gamma can refuse to negotiate over

   a. the closure only.
   b. the procedure only.
   c. the closure and the procedure.
   d. neither the closure nor the procedure.

6. Metalcraft Employees Union (MEU) represents workers of National Production Company. Bargaining reaches an impasse, and MEU calls a strike. Strikers circle the plant to prevent nonunion workers from entering. This is an unfair labor practice

   a. only if the nonunion workers are replacements.
   b. only if the nonunion workers are supervisors.
   c. under any circumstances.
   d. under no circumstances.

P 7.   Consolidated Employees Union (CEU) represents workers of Delta Company. Bargaining reaches an impasse, and CEU calls a strike. During the strike, it would be an unfair labor practice

 a. only to send nonworkers to picket Delta's plant.
 b. only to set up a twenty-four hour picket line around Delta's plant.
 c. to send nonworkers to picket and to set up a twenty-four hour picket line around Delta's plant.
 d. neither to send nonworkers to picket nor to set up a twenty-four hour picket line.

P 8.   During a union election campaign at Omega Corporation, Omega may

 a. not campaign against the union.
 b. not give a speech against the union within twenty-hours of the election.
 c. not limit the campaign activities of union supporters.
 d. campaign against the union, speak against the union within twenty-hours of the election, and limit the campaign activities of union supporters.

P 9.   During a union election campaign at Eagle Corporation, Eagle may *not*

 a. designate where and when campaigning may occur.
 b. prohibit all solicitation during work time.
 c. promise to hire more workers if the union loses the election.
 d. threaten employees with the loss of their jobs if the union wins the election.

P 10. National Workers Union (NWU) represents the employees of Office Company, Inc. NWU calls an economic strike, and Office hires replacement workers. After the strike, the replacement workers

 a. must be retained and the former strikers must be rehired.
 b. must be terminated and the former strikers must be rehired.
 c. must be terminated whether or not the former strikers are rehired.
 d. may be retained or terminated whether or not the former strikers are rehired.

SHORT ESSAY QUESTIONS

1. What are the four basic federal labor laws and what do they provide?

2. Which types of strikes are illegal?

ISSUE SPOTTERS

(Answers at the Back of the Book)

1.   Ann applies for work with Beta Company, which tells her that it requires union membership as a condition of employment. Ann applies for work with Omega, Inc., which does not require union membership as a condition of employment but requires employees to join a union after six months on the job. Are these conditions legal?

2.   Beth, an employee of Computer Digital, Inc. (CDI), is a vocal union advocate. CDI fires Beth, on the ground that she did not work the exact hours reported on her time card—although CDI has never discharged an employee for this reason. Can CDI be required to prove that it did not have a discriminatory motive in discharging Beth?

3.   Tasty Bakery has five nonunion employees. The employees discuss working conditions with Tasty, which refuses to make any changes. The employees agree that one of them should walk out in protest. When the employee walks out, Tasty fires him. Has Tasty committed an unfair labor practice?

CUMULATIVE HYPOTHETICAL PROBLEM
FOR UNIT FOUR—INCLUDING CHAPTERS 13–15

(Answers at the Back of the Book)

Donna, Earl, Frank, Gail, Hal, Ira, Jane, Karen, Larry, and Mike work for International Sales Corporation (ISC).

____ 1. Donna, who works in ISC's warehouse, is injured on the job. Donna may NOT collect workers' compensation benefits if she

 a. files a civil suit against a third party based on the injury.
 b. intentionally caused her own injury.
 c. was injured as a result of a co-worker's act.
 d. worked for ISC for less than sixty days.

____ 2. Earl retires from ISC at the age of sixty-five. Frank retires at sixty-seven. Because of a disability, Gail, after fifteen years, is unable to continue working for ISC. Hal is discharged from ISC as part of a reduction in force. All of the following benefits are part of Social Security EXCEPT

 a. Earl's government retirement payments.
 b. Frank's Medicare payments.
 c. Gail's government disability payments.
 d. Hal's unemployment benefits.

____ 3. Ira works for ISC as a sales representative at a salary of $3,000 per month, plus a 10 percent commission. As ISC's agent, Ira

 a. cannot be dismissed during the six-month period without cause.
 b. cannot enforce the agency unless it is in writing and signed by Delta.
 c. is an agent coupled with an interest.
 d. must act solely in Delta's interest in matters concerning Delta's business.

____ 4. Four employees file suits against ISC, alleging discrimination. Title VII of the Civil Rights Act of 1964 covers all of the following EXCEPT Jane's suit alleging discrimination on the basis of

 a. age.
 b. gender.
 c. race.
 d. religion.

____ 5. Karen, an ISC manager, wants to institute a policy of mandatory retirement for all employees at age sixty-four. Larry, an ISC manager, wants to discharge Mike, who is age sixty-seven, for cause. Under federal anti-discrimination law

 a. only Karen's wish can be granted.
 b. only Larry's wish can be granted.
 c. both Karen's and Larry's wishes can be granted.
 d. neither Karen's nor Larry's wishes can be granted.

Chapter 16:
Powers and Functions of Administrative Agencies

WHAT THIS CHAPTER IS ABOUT

Federal, state, and local administrative agencies regulate virtually every aspect of a business's operation. Agencies' rules, orders, and decisions make up the body of administrative law. How agencies function is the subject of this chapter.

CHAPTER OUTLINE

I. AGENCY CREATION AND POWERS

Congress delegates some of its authority to make and implement laws, particularly in highly technical areas, to administrative agencies.

A. ENABLING LEGISLATION

To create an agency, Congress passes enabling legislation, which specifies the powers of the agency.

B. TYPES OF AGENCIES

1. Executive Agencies

Includes cabinet departments and their subagencies. Subject to the authority of the president, who can appoint and remove their officers.

2. Independent Regulatory Agencies

Includes agencies outside the major executive departments. Their officers serve for fixed terms and cannot be removed without just cause.

C. AGENCY POWERS AND THE CONSTITUTION

Agency powers include functions associated with the legislature (rulemaking), executive branch (enforcement), and courts (adjudication). Under Article I of the Constitution and the delegation doctrine, Congress has the power to establish agencies to create rules for implementing laws.

II. ADMINISTRATIVE PROCESS

Rulemaking, investigation, and adjudication make up the administrative process. The Administrative Procedure Act (APA) of 1946 imposes procedural requirements that agencies must follow.

A. RULEMAKING

Rulemaking is the formulation of new regulations. Legislative rules are as binding as the laws that Congress makes. Interpretive rules are not binding but indicate how an agency will apply a statute.

1. Notice of the Proposed Rulemaking

An agency begins by publishing, in the *Federal Register,* a notice that states where and when proceedings will be held, terms or subject matter of the proposed rule, the agency's legal authority for making the rule.

2. Comment Period

Interested parties can express their views. An agency must respond to significant comments by modifying the final rule or explaining, in a statement accompanying the final rule, why it did not.

3. **The Final Rule**
The agency publishes the final rule in the *Federal Register*. The final rule has binding legal effect unless overturned by a court.

B. **INVESTIGATION**
Agencies must have knowledge of facts and circumstances pertinent to proposed rules. Agencies must also obtain information and investigate conduct to ascertain whether its rules are being violated.

1. **Inspections and Tests**
Through on-site inspections and testing, agencies gather information to prove a regulatory violation or to correct or prevent a bad condition.

2. **Subpoenas**
With subpoenas, agencies compel witnesses to testify and compel individuals or organizations to hand over specified books, papers, records, or documents. Limits on agency demands include—

   a. An investigation must have a legitimate purpose.
   b. The information that is sought must be relevant.
   c. Demands must be specific.
   d. The party from whom the information is sought must not be unduly burdened by the request.

3. **Search Warrants**
A search warrant directs an officer to search a specific place for a specific item and present it to the agency.

   a. **Fourth Amendment**
   The Fourth Amendment protects against unreasonable searches and seizures by requiring that in most instances a physical search must be conducted under the authority of a search warrant.

   b. **Warrantless Searches**
   Warrants are not required to conduct searches in businesses in highly regulated industries, in certain hazardous operations, and in emergencies.

C. **ADJUDICATION**
Adjudication involves the resolution of disputes by an agency.

1. **Formal Complaints**
If there is no settlement, the agency may issue a formal complaint. The party charged in the complaint may respond with an answer. The case may go before an administrative law judge (ALJ).

2. **The Role of an Administrative Law Judge (ALJ)**
Presides over the hearing. Has the power to administer oaths, take testimony, rule on questions of evidence, and make determinations of fact. An ALJ works for the agency, but must be unbiased. Certain safeguards in the APA prevent bias and promote fairness.

3. **Hearing Procedures**
Procedures vary widely from agency to agency. Agencies exercise substantial discretion over the type of procedures used. A formal hearing resembles a trial, but more items and testimony are admissible in an administrative hearing.

4. **Agency Orders**
After a hearing, the ALJ issues an initial order. Either side may appeal to the commission that governs the agency and ultimately to a federal appeals court. If there is no appeal or review, the initial order becomes final.

III.   LIMITATIONS ON AGENCY POWERS
Because of the concentration of so much authority in administrative agencies, the three branches of the government exercise control over agency powers.

A. JUDICIAL CONTROLS

The APA provides for judicial review of most agency decisions.

1. Requirements for Judicial Review

a. The action must be reviewable (under the APA, agency actions are presumed reviewable).
b. The party must have standing (a direct stake in the outcome).
c. The party must have exhausted all administrative remedies.
d. An actual controversy must be at issue.

2. Scope of Review

In most cases, a court defers to the facts as found in an agency proceeding. A court will review whether an agency has —

a. Exceeded its authority under its enabling legislation.
b. Properly interpreted laws applicable to the action under review.
c. Violated any constitutional provisions.
d. Acted in accord with procedural requirements.
e. Taken actions that were arbitrary, capricious, or an abuse of discretion.
f. Reached conclusions that are not supported by substantial evidence.

B. EXECUTIVE CONTROLS

The president may veto enabling legislation or subsequent modifications to agency authority that Congress seeks to enact. The president appoints and removes many federal officers, including those in charge of agencies.

C. LEGISLATIVE CONTROLS

Congress can give power to an agency, take power away, reduce or increase agency finances, abolish an agency, investigate the implementation of the laws, investigate agencies, and affect policy through individual legislators' attempts to help their constituents deal with agencies.

IV. PUBLIC ACCOUNTABILITY

A. FREEDOM OF INFORMATION ACT (FOIA) OF 1966

The federal government must disclose certain records to any person on request. A failure to comply may be challenged in federal district court.

B. GOVERNMENT IN THE SUNSHINE ACT OF 1976

Requires (1) that "every portion of every meeting of an agency" that is headed by a "collegial body" is open to "public observation" and (2) procedures to ensure that the public is provided with adequate advance notice of meetings and agendas (with exceptions).

C. REGULATORY FLEXIBILITY ACT OF 1980

Whenever a new regulation will have a "significant impact upon a substantial number of small entities," the agency must conduct a regulatory flexibility analysis. The analysis must measure the cost imposed by the rule on small businesses and must consider less burdensome alternatives.

D. SMALL BUSINESS REGULATORY ENFORCEMENT FAIRNESS ACT

Under this act, passed in 1996—

1. Congress Reviews New Federal Regulations

Congress reviews new regulations for at least sixty days before they take effect. Opponents have time to present arguments to Congress.

2. Agencies Must Issue "Plain English" Guides

Agencies must prepare guides that explain how small businesses can comply with their regulations.

3. **Regional Boards Rate Federal Agencies**
    The National Enforcement Ombudsman receives comments from small businesses about agencies. Based on the comments, Regional Small Business Fairness Boards rate the agencies.

4. **Small Businesses May Recover Expenses and Fees**
    Small businesses may recover expenses and legal fees from the government if an agency makes excessive demands for fines or penalties.

V.   STATE ADMINISTRATIVE AGENCIES

A state agency often parallels a federal agency, providing similar services on a localized basis. The supremacy clause requires that the federal agency's operation prevail over an inconsistent state agency's action.

TRUE-FALSE QUESTIONS

(Answers at the Back of the Book)

____   1.   Enabling legislation specifies the powers of an agency.

____   2.   Most federal agencies are part of the executive branch of government.

____   3.   To create an agency, Congress enacts enabling legislation.

____   4.   Agency rules are not as legally binding as the laws that Congress enacts.

____   5.   After an agency adjudication, the administrative law judge's order must be appealed to become final.

____   6.   Congress has no power to influence agency policy.

____   7.   The Administrative Procedure Act provides for judicial review of most agency actions.

____   8.   When a new regulation will have a significant impact on a substantial number of small entities, an analysis must be conducted to measure the cost imposed on small businesses.

____   9.   State administrative agency operations prevail over federal agency actions.

____   10.   An agency cannot conduct a search without a warrant.

FILL-IN QUESTIONS

(Answers at the Back of the Book)

The rulemaking process begins with the publication in the _____ (*Congressional Record/Federal Register*) of a notice of the proposed rulemaking. The agency may conduct a public hearing at which it presents evidence to justify the proposed rule, and _____ (anyone/no one) may present opposing evidence. The agency _____ (must/need not) respond to significant comments. After the hearing, the agency publishes the final draft of the rule in the _____ (*Congressional Record/Federal Register*).

MULTIPLE-CHOICE QUESTIONS

(Answers at the Back of the Book)

____ 1. Ann, a congressperson, believes a new federal agency is needed to perform a certain function. Congress has the power to establish an agency to

a. adjudicate disputes arising from rules only.
b. make rules only.
c. adjudicate disputes arising from rules and make rules.
d. none of the above.

____ 2. Like other federal agencies, the Securities and Exchange Commission may obtain information concerning activities and organizations that it oversees by compelling disclosure through

a. a search only.
b. a subpoena only.
c. a search or a subpoena.
d. neither a search nor a subpoena.

____ 3. In making rules, the procedures of the Equal Employment Opportunity Commission and other federal agencies normally includes

a. notice and opportunity for comments by interested parties only.
b. publication of the final draft of the rule only.
c. notice and opportunity for comments by interested parties, and publication of the final draft of the rule.
d. none of the above.

____ 4. The Occupational Safety and Health Administration (OSHA) issues a subpoena for Alpha Corporation to hand over its files. Alpha's possible defenses against the subpoena include

a. OSHA cannot issue a subpoena.
b. OSHA is a federal agency, but Alpha only does business locally.
c. OSHA's request is not specific enough.
d. OSHA's request violates Alpha's right to privacy.

____ 5. The National Oceanic and Atmospheric Administration (NOAA) is a federal agency. To limit the authority of NOAA, the president can

a. abolish NOAA.
b. take away NOAA's power.
c. refuse to appropriate funds to NOAA.
d. veto legislative modifications to NOAA's authority.

____ 6. The Federal Energy Regulatory Commission (FERC) wants to close a series of its meetings to the public. To open the meetings, a citizen could sue the FERC under

a. the Freedom of Information Act.
b. the Government-in-the-Sunshine Act.
c. the Regulatory Flexibility Act.
d. the Small Business Regulatory Enforcement Fairness Act.

____ 7. The U.S. Fish and Wildlife Service orders Ed to stop using a certain type of fishing net from his boat. To appeal this order to a court, Ed must

   a. appeal simultaneously to the agency and the court.
   b. bypass all administrative remedies and appeal directly to the court.
   c. exhaust all administrative remedies.
   d. ignore the agency and continue using the net.

____ 8. The Federal Trade Commission (FTC) issues an order relating to the advertising of Great Sales, Inc. Great Sales appeals the order to a court. The court may review whether the FTC's action is

   a. arbitrary, capricious, or an abuse of discretion.
   b. discourteous, disrespectful, or dissatisfying to one or more parties.
   c. flippant, wanton, or in disregard of social norms.
   d. impious, non-utilitarian, or in violation of ethical precepts.

____ 9. The Environmental Protection Agency (EPA) publishes notice of a proposed rule. When comments are received about the rule, the EPA must respond to

   a. all of the comments.
   b. any significant comments that bear directly on the proposed rule.
   c. only comments by businesses engaged in interstate commerce.
   d. only comments by businesses that will be affected by the rule.

____ 10. Mary is an administrative law judge (ALJ) for the National Labor Relations Board. In hearing a case, Mary has the authority to make

   a. decisions binding on the federal courts.
   b. determinations of fact.
   c. new laws.
   d. new rules.

SHORT ESSAY QUESTIONS

1. What are the conditions to judicial review of an agency enforcement action?

2. How does Congress hold agency authority in check?

ISSUE SPOTTERS

(Answers at the Back of the Book)

1. The Securities and Exchange Commission (SEC) makes rules regarding what disclosures must be made in a stock prospectus, prosecutes and adjudicates alleged violations, and prescribes punishment. This gives the SEC considerable power. What checks are there against this power?

2. The U.S. Department of Transportation (DOT) sometimes hears an appeal from a party whose contract with the DOT is canceled. An administrative law judge (ALJ), who works for the DOT, hears this appeal. What safeguards promote the ALJ's fairness?

3. The U.S. Department of Justice holds formal hearings concerning the deportation and exclusion of immigrants. How do such formal hearings resemble a trial? How are they different?

Chapter 17:
Consumer Protection

WHAT THIS CHAPTER IS ABOUT

Federal and state laws protect consumers from unfair trade practices, unsafe products, discriminatory or unreasonable credit requirements, and other problems related to consumer transactions. This chapter focuses on *federal* consumer law.

CHAPTER OUTLINE

I. ADVERTISING

The Federal Trade Commission Act of 1914 created the Federal Trade Commission (FTC) to prevent unfair and deceptive trade practices.

A. DECEPTIVE ADVERTISING

This is advertising that would mislead a consumer—such as scientifically untrue claims and misleading half-truths. Puffing (vague generalities, obvious exaggeration) does not qualify.

B. BAIT-AND-SWITCH ADVERTISING

This occurs when a seller refuses to show an advertised item, fails to have adequate quantities on hand, fails to promise to deliver within a reasonable time, or discourages employees from selling the item. The FTC has issued rules to prevent this practice.

C. ONLINE DECEPTIVE ADVERTISING

The same laws that apply to other forms of advertising apply to online ads, under FTC guidelines.

D. FTC ACTIONS AGAINST DECEPTIVE ADVERTISING

If the FTC believes that an ad is unfair or deceptive, it sends a complaint to the advertiser, who may settle. If not, the FTC can, after a hearing, issue a cease-and-desist order or require counteradvertising.

E. TELEMARKETING AND ELECTRONIC ADVERTISING

1. Telephone Consumer Protection Act (TCPA) of 1991

The TCPA prohibits (1) phone solicitation using an automatic dialing system or a prerecorded voice and (2) transmission of ads via fax without the recipient's permission. For each violation, consumers can recover actual losses or $500, whichever is greater. If a defendant willfully or knowingly violated the act, a court can award treble damages.

2. Telemarketing and Consumer Fraud and Abuse Prevention Act of 1994

This act authorized FTC to set rules for telemarketing and bring actions against fraudulent telemarketers. The FTC's Telemarketing Sales Rule of 1995 makes it illegal to misrepresent information and requires disclosure. In 2003, the FTC set up a "National Do Not Call Registry," which prohibits telemarketers from calling consumers whose names are listed.

F. STATE LAWS

Most states also have laws regulating phone solicitation.

II. LABELING AND PACKAGING

A. FAIR PACKAGING AND LABELING ACT OF 1966

Requires that product labels identify the product; net quantity of contents; quantity of servings, if the number of servings is stated; manufacturer; packager or distributor. More can be required (such as fat content).

B. OTHER FEDERAL LAWS

Fur Products Labeling Act of 1951, Wool Products Labeling Act of 1939, Flammable Fabrics Act of 1953, Smokeless Tobacco Health Education Act of 1986.

III. SALES

Federal agencies that regulate sales include the FTC and the Federal Reserve Board of Governors (Regulation Z governs credit provisions in sales contracts). All states have some form of consumer protection laws.

A. DOOR-TO-DOOR SALES

States' "cooling-off" laws permit a buyer to rescind a door-to-door purchase within a certain time. The FTC has a three-day period. The FTC requires a seller to notify a buyer of the right to cancel (if the sale is in Spanish, notice must be in Spanish).

B. TELEPHONE AND MAIL-ORDER SALES

Consumers are partly protected by federal laws prohibiting mail fraud and by state law that parallels federal law.

1. FTC "Mail or Telephone Order Merchandise Rule" of 1993

For goods bought via phone lines or through the mail, merchants must ship orders within the time promised in their ads, notify consumers when orders cannot be shipped on time, and issue a refund within a specified time if a consumer cancels an order.

2. Postal Reorganization Act of 1970

Unsolicited merchandise sent by the mail may be retained, used, discarded, or disposed of, without obligation to the sender.

C. ONLINE SALES

The federal and state laws that apply to other media generally protect consumers online.

IV. CONSUMER HEALTH AND SAFETY

A. FOOD AND DRUGS

The Federal Food, Drug, and Cosmetic Act (FFDCA) of 1938 sets food standards, levels of additives, classifications of food and food ads; regulates medical devices. Drugs must be shown to be effective and safe. Enforced by the Food and Drug Administration (FDA).

B. CONSUMER PRODUCT SAFETY

The Consumer Product Safety Act of 1972 includes a scheme for the regulation of consumer products and safety by the Consumer Product Safety Commission (CPSC). The CPSC—

1. Conducts research on product safety.
2. Sets standards for consumer products and bans the manufacture and sale of a product that is potentially hazardous to consumers.
3. Removes from the market any products imminently hazardous and requires manufacturers to report on any products already sold or intended for sale if the products have proved to be hazardous.
4. Administers other product safety legislation.

V. CREDIT PROTECTION

A. TRUTH-IN-LENDING ACT (TILA) OF 1968

The TILA, administered by the Federal Reserve Board, requires the disclosure of credit terms.

1. Who Is Subject to the TILA?

The TILA covers creditors who, in the ordinary course of business, lend money or sell goods on credit to consumers, or arrange for credit for consumers.

2. **What Does the TILA Require?**

   Under Regulation Z, in any transaction involving a sales contract in which payment is to be made in more than four installments, a lender must disclose all the credit terms clearly and conspicuously.

3. **Equal Credit Opportunity Act of 1974**

   This act prohibits (1) denial of credit on the basis of race, religion, national origin, color, sex, marital status, age and (2) credit discrimination based on whether an individual receives certain forms of income.

4. **Credit-Card Rules**

   Liability of a cardholder is $50 per card for unauthorized charges made before the issuer is notified the card is lost. An issuer cannot bill for unauthorized charges if a card was improperly issued. If a cardholder wishes to withhold payment for a faulty product, there are specific procedures to follow.

5. **Consumer Leasing Act of 1988**

   Those who lease consumer goods in the ordinary course of their business, if the goods are priced at $25,000 or less and the lease term exceeds four months, must disclose all material terms in writing.

B. FAIR CREDIT REPORTING ACT (FCRA) OF 1970

1. **What the FCRA Provides**

   Consumer credit reporting agencies may issue credit reports only for certain purposes (extension of credit, etc.); a consumer who is denied credit, or is charged more than others would be, on the basis of a report must be notified of the fact and of the agency that issued the report.

2. **Consumers Can Have Inaccurate Information Deleted**

   If a consumer discovers that the report contains inaccurate information, the agency must delete it within a reasonable period of time.

C. FAIR AND ACCURATE CREDIT TRANSACTIONS ACT (FACT ACT) OF 2003

The FACT Act established a national "fraud alert" system so that consumers who suspect ID theft can place an alert on their credit files. Also—

1. **Credit-Reporting Agencies' Responsibilities**

   Consumer credit-reporting agencies must provide consumers with free copies of their reports and stop reporting allegedly fraudulent information once a consumer shows that ID theft occurred.

2. **Other Businesses' Responsibilities**

   Businesses must include shortened ("truncated") account numbers on credit card receipts and provide consumers with copies of records to help prove an account or transaction was fraudulent.

D. FAIR DEBT COLLECTION PRACTICES ACT (FDCPA) OF 1977

Applies only to debt-collection agencies that, usually for a percentage of the amount owed, attempt to collect debts on behalf of someone else.

1. **What the FDCPA Prohibits**

   a. Contacting the debtor at the debtor's place of employment if the employer objects.
   b. Contacting the debtor during inconvenient times or at any time if an attorney represents the debtor.
   c. Contacting third parties other than the debtor's parents, spouse, or financial advisor about payment unless a court agrees.
   d. Using harassment, or false and misleading information.
   e. Contacting the debtor any time after the debtor refuses to pay the debt, except to advise the debtor of further action to be taken.

2. **What the FDCPA Requires**

Collection agencies must give a debtor notice that he or she has thirty days to dispute the debt and request written verification of it.

3. **Remedies**

A debt collector may be liable for actual damages, plus additional damages not to exceed $1,000 and attorneys' fees.

VI.   STATE CONSUMER PROTECTION LAWS

State laws (typically directed at deceptive trade practices) may provide more protection for consumers than do federal laws.

TRUE-FALSE QUESTIONS

(Answers at the Back of the Book)

1. Advertising will be deemed deceptive if a consumer would be misled by the advertising claim.

2. In general, labels must be accurate.

3. A consumer cannot rescind a contract freely entered into.

4. The TILA applies to creditors who, in the ordinary course of business, sell goods on credit to consumers.

5. Misinformation in a consumer's credit file cannot be deleted.

6. Consumers may have more protection under state laws than federal laws.

7. The Fair Debt Collection Practices Act applies to anyone who attempts to collect a debt.

8. There are no federal agencies that regulate sales.

9. One who leases consumer goods in the ordinary course of business does not have to disclose any material terms in writing.

10. An advertiser cannot fax ads to consumers without their permission.

FILL-IN QUESTIONS

(Answers at the Back of the Book)

The Truth-in-Lending Act contains provisions regarding credit cards. One provision limits the liability of the cardholder to _____ ($50/$500) per card for unauthorized charges made _____ (after/before) the credit card issuer is notified that the card has been lost. Another provision _____ (allows/prohibits) a credit card company _____ (from billing/to bill) a consumer for any unauthorized charges _____ (unless/if) the credit card was improperly issued by the company.

MULTIPLE-CHOICE QUESTIONS

(Answers at the Back of the Book)

1. Tasty Treat Company advertises that its cereal, "Fiber Rich," reduces cholesterol. After an investigation and a hearing, the FTC finds no evidence to support the claim. To correct the public's impression of Fiber Rich, the most appropriate action would be

a. a cease-and-desist order.
b. a civil fine.
c. a criminal fine.
d. counteradvertising.

B   2.   ABC Corporation sells consumer products. Generally, the labels must use words as they are

a.   normally used in the scientific community.
b.   ordinarily understood by consumers.
c.   reasonably approved by ABC's officers.
d.   typically explained by the marketing department.

B   3.   Maria does not speak English. Nick comes to her home and, after a long presentation in Spanish, sells her a vacuum cleaner. He hands her a paper that contains only in English a notice of the right to cancel a sale within three days. This transaction is

a.   not proper, because ignorance of your rights is a defense.
b.   not proper, because the deal was in Spanish but the notice was in English.
c.   proper, because ignorance of your rights is no defense.
d.   proper, because Nick gave Maria notice of her rights.

C   4.   Ed takes out a student loan from First National Bank. After graduation, Ed goes to work, but he does not make payments on the loan. The bank agrees with Good Collection Agency (GCA) that if GCA collects the debt, it can keep a percentage of the amount. To collect the debt, GCA can contact

a.   Ed at his place of employment, even if his employer objects.
b.   Ed at unusual or inconvenient times or any time if he retains an attorney.
c.   Ed only to advise him of further action that GCA will take.
d.   third parties, including Ed's parents, unless ordered otherwise by a court.

B   5.   The ordinary business of Ace Credit Company is to lend money to consumers. Ace must disclose all credit terms clearly and conspicuously in

a.   all credit transactions.
b.   any credit transaction in which payments are to be made in more than four installments.
c.   any credit transaction in which payments are to be made in more than one installment.
d.   no credit transaction.

    6.   Eve borrows money to buy a car and to pay for repairs to the roof of her house. She also buys furniture in a transaction financed by the seller whom she will repay in installments. If all of the parties are subject to the Truth-in-Lending Act, Regulation Z applies to

a.   the car loan only.
b.   the home improvement loan only.
c.   the retail installment sale only.
d.   the car loan, the home improvement loan, and the retail installment sale.

C   7.   Qwik Food, Inc., sells snack foods. Qwik must include on the packages

a.   no nutrition information.
b.   the identity of the product only.
c.   the identity of the product, the net quantity of the contents, and the number of servings.
d.   the net quantity of the contents and the number of servings only.

    8.   General Tobacco Corporation (GTC) sells tobacco products. On the packages of its *smokeless* tobacco products, GTC must include warnings about health hazards associated with

a.   cigarettes.
b.   smokeless products.
c.   tobacco products generally.
d.   none of the above.

A   9.   Best Toy Company begins marketing a new toy that is highly flammable. The Consumer Product Safety Commission may

    a.   ban the toy's future manufacture and sale, and order that the toy be removed from the market.
    b.   ban the toy's future manufacture and sale only.
    c.   do nothing until there is an injury or damage on which to base an action.
    d.   order that the toy be removed from the market only.

D   10. Ann receives an unsolicited credit card in the mail and tosses it on her desk. Without Ann's permission, her roommate uses the card to buy new clothes for $1,000. Ann is liable for

    a. $1,000.
    b. $500.
    c. $50.
    d. $0.

SHORT ESSAY QUESTIONS

1.   What are some of the more common deceptive advertising techniques and the ways in which the FTC may deal with such conduct?

2.   What are the primary provisions of the Truth-In-Lending Act?

ISSUE SPOTTERS

(Answers at the Back of the Book)

1.   Alpha Electronics, Inc., advertises Beta computers at a low price. Alpha keeps only a few in stock and tells its sales staff to switch consumers attracted by the price to more expensive brands. Alpha tells its staff that if all else fails, refuse to show the Betas, and if a consumer insists on buying one, do not promise delivery. Has Alpha violated a law?

2.   Carol buys a notebook computer from Alpha Electronics. She pays for it with her credit card. When it proves defective, she asks Alpha to repair or replace it, but Alpha refuses. What can Carol do?

3.   ABC Pharmaceuticals, Inc., believes it has developed a new drug that will be effective in the treatment of AIDS patients. The drug has had only limited testing, but ABC wants to make the drug widely available as soon as possible. To market the drug, what must ABC show the Food and Drug Administration?

Chapter 18:
Protecting the Environment

WHAT THIS CHAPTER IS ABOUT

This chapter covers environmental law, which is the law that relates to environmental protection—common law actions and federal statutes and regulations.

CHAPTER OUTLINE

I.   COMMON LAW ACTIONS

A. NUISANCE
Persons cannot use their property in a way that unreasonably interferes with others' rights to use or enjoy their own property. An injured party may be awarded damages or an injunction.

B. NEGLIGENCE AND STRICT LIABILITY
A business that fails to use reasonable care may be liable to a party whose injury was foreseeable. Businesses that engage in ultrahazardous activities are strictly liable for whatever injuries the activities cause.

II. FEDERAL, STATE, AND LOCAL REGULATION

A. FEDERAL REGULATION

1. Environmental Regulatory Agencies
The Environmental Protection Agency (EPA) coordinates federal environmental responsibilities and administers most federal environmental policies and statutes. State and local agencies implement environmental statutes and regulations. Citizens can sue to enforce the regulations.

2. Environmental Impact Statements
The National Environmental Policy Act (NEPA) of 1969 requires all federal agencies to consider environmental factors in making significant decisions.

a. When Must an Environmental Impact Statement (EIS) Be Prepared?
When a major federal action significantly affects the quality of the environment. An action is *major* if it involves substantial commitment of resources. An action is *federal* if a federal agency has the power to control it.

b. What Must an EIS Analyze?
(1) The impact on the environment that the action will have, (2) any adverse effects to the environment and alternative actions that might be taken, (3) irreversible effects the action might generate.

c. Can an Agency Decide Not to Issue an EIS?
Yes, but it must issue a statement explaining why an EIS is unnecessary.

B. STATE AND LOCAL REGULATION
States regulate the environment through zoning or more direct regulation. City, county, and other local governments control some aspects through zoning laws, waste removal and disposal regulations, aesthetic ordinances, and so on.

III. AIR POLLUTION

The Clean Air Act of 1963 (and amendments) is the basis for regulation.

A. MOBILE SOURCES OF POLLUTION

Regulations governing air pollution from automobiles and other mobile sources specify standards and time schedules. For example, under the 1990 amendments to the Clean Air Act—

1. **New Automobiles' Exhaust**
    Manufacturers have to cut emission of nitrogen oxide by 10 percent by 2007.

2. **EPA Action**
    If a vehicle does not meet the standards, the EPA can order a recall and repair or replacement of pollution-control devices.

3. **Sport Utility Vehicles and Light Trucks**
    These vehicles are now subject to the same standards as cars.

4. **Gasoline**
    Service stations must sell gasoline with higher oxygen content.

5. **New Standards**
    The EPA attempts to update these and other standards when new scientific evidence is available.

B. STATIONARY SOURCES OF POLLUTION

The EPA sets air quality standards for stationary sources (such as industrial plants), and the states formulate plans to achieve them. For example, under the 1990 amendments to the Clean Air Act—

1. **Major New Sources**
    Must use the maximum achievable control technology (MACT) to reduce emissions from the combustion of fossil fuels (coal and oil).

2. **110 of the Oldest Coal-burning Power Plants in the United States**
    Must cut emissions by 40 percent by the year 2001 to reduce acid rain.

3. **Utilities**
    Granted "credits" to emit certain amounts of sulfur dioxide, and those that emit less can sell their credits to other polluters.

4. **Other Factories and Businesses**
    Production of chlorofluorocarbons, carbon tetrachloride, and methyl chloroform (linked to depleting the ozone layer) must stop.

5. **Hazardous Air Pollutants**
    Industrial emissions of 189 specific hazardous air pollutants must be reduced (through MACT). Certain landfills must install air-pollution collection and control systems.

C. PENALTIES

Civil penalties of up to $25,000 per day, or an amount equal to a violator's economic benefits from noncompliance, plus up to $5,000 per day for other violations. Criminal fines up to $1 million and imprisonment up to two years are possible. Private citizens can sue.

IV. WATER POLLUTION

A. NAVIGABLE WATERS

The Clean Water Act of 1972 amended the Federal Water Pollution Control Act (FWPCA) of 1948 to provide—

1. **Goals**
   (1) Make waters safe for swimming, (2) protect fish and wildlife, (3) eliminate the discharge of pollutants into the water.

2. **Limits on Discharges Based on Best Available Control Technology**
   Time schedules (extended by amendment in 1977 and by the Water Quality Act of 1987) limit discharges of pollutants.

3. **Permits**
   Municipal and industrial polluters must obtain permits before discharging wastes into navigable waters. Filling or dredging wetlands requires a permit from the Army Corps of Engineers.

4. **Penalties and Remedies**
   Civil penalties from $10,000 per day (up to $25,000 per violation) to $25,000 per day. Criminal penalties from fines of $2,500 per day to $1 million total and one to fifteen years' imprisonment. Injunctions, damages, and clean-up costs can be imposed.

B. **DRINKING WATER**
The Safe Drinking Water Act of 1974 requires the EPA to set maximum levels for pollutants in public water systems. Operators must come as close as possible to the standards using the best available technology.

C. **OCEAN DUMPING**
The Marine Protection, Research, and Sanctuaries Act of 1972—

1. **Radiological Waste and Other Materials**
   Dumping of radiological, chemical, and biological warfare agents, and high-level radioactive waste is banned. Transporting and dumping other materials (with exceptions) requires a permit.

2. **Penalties**
   Civil penalties of not more than $50,000 or revocation or suspension of a permit. Criminal penalties of up to a $50,000 fine, imprisonment for not more than a year, or both. Injunctions can be imposed.

D. **OIL SPILLS**
The Oil Pollution Act of 1990 provides that any oil facility, oil shipper, vessel owner, or vessel operator that discharges oil may be liable for clean-up costs, damages, and fines of up to $25,000 per day.

V.   TOXIC CHEMICALS

A. **PESTICIDES AND HERBICIDES**
Under the Federal Insecticide, Fungicide, and Rodenticide Act (FIFRA) of 1947—

1. **Registration, Certification, and Use**
   Pesticides and herbicides must be (1) registered before they can be sold, (2) certified and used only for approved applications, and (3) used in limited quantities when applied to food crops.

2. **Labels**
   Labels must include directions for use of a pesticide or herbicide, warnings to protect human health and the environment, a statement of treatment in the case of poisoning, and a list of the ingredients.

3. **Penalties**
   For registrants and producers: fine of up to $50,000, imprisonment up to one year. For commercial dealers: $25,000, one year. For farmers and other private users: $1,000, thirty days.

B. **TOXIC SUBSTANCES**
Under the Toxic Substances Control Act of 1976, for substances that potentially pose an imminent hazard or an unreasonable risk of injury to health or the environment, the EPA may require special labeling, set production quotas, or limit or prohibit the use of a substance.

VI.   HAZARDOUS WASTE DISPOSAL

A.   RESOURCE CONSERVATION AND RECOVERY ACT (RCRA) OF 1976

The EPA determines which forms of solid waste are hazardous, and sets requirements for disposal, storage, and treatment. Penalties include up to $25,000 (civil) per violation, $50,000 (criminal) per day, imprisonment up to two years (may be doubled for repeaters), and up to $250,000 and fifteen years for knowingly violating the RCRA and endangering another's life.

B.   SUPERFUND

The Comprehensive Environmental Response, Compensation, and Liability Act (CERCLA) of 1980 regulates the clean-up of leaking hazardous waste disposal sites. If a release or a threatened release occurs, the EPA can clean up a site and recover the cost from—

1.   Potentially Responsible Parties
(1) The person who generated the wastes disposed of at the site, (2) the person who transported the wastes to the site, (3) the person who owned or operated the site at the time of the disposal, or (4) the current owner or operator.

2.   Joint and Several Liability
One party can be charged with the entire cost (which that party may recover in a contribution action against others).

TRUE-FALSE QUESTIONS

(Answers at the Back of the Book)

____ 1.   No common law doctrines apply against polluters today.

____ 2.   Local governments can control some aspects of the environment through zoning laws.

____ 3.   Under federal environmental laws, there is a single standard for all polluters and all pollutants.

____ 4.   The Toxic Substances Control Act of 1976 regulates clean-ups of leaking hazardous waste disposal sites.

____ 5.   The Environmental Protection Agency (EPA) can clean up a release of hazardous waste at a hazardous waste disposal site and recover the entire cost from the site's owner or operator.

____ 6.   States may restrict discharge of chemicals into the water or air.

____ 7.   A party who violates the Clean Air Act may realize economic benefits from the noncompliance.

____ 8.   The Environmental Protection Agency sets limits on discharges of pollutants into water.

____ 9.   A party who only transports hazardous waste to a disposal site cannot be held liable for any costs to clean up the site.

____ 10.   States may regulate the disposal of toxic wastes.

FILL-IN QUESTIONS

(Answers at the Back of the Book)

The National Environmental Policy Act requires _____ (federal/state and local) agencies to prepare environmental impact statements (EIS) when major _____ (federal/state and local) actions significantly affect the quality of the environment. An EIS analyzes (1) the _____ (environmental impact that an action will have/environment's impact on a project), (2) any adverse effects to the _____ (environment/project) and alternative courses of action, and (3) irreversible effects that _____ (an action might cause to the environment/the environment might cause to the project). If an agency decides that an EIS is unnecessary, it must issue a statement announcing that decision _____ (and reasons/but it need not provide reasons) supporting the conclusion.

MULTIPLE-CHOICE QUESTIONS

(Answers at the Back of the Book)

____ 1. The U.S. Department of the Interior's approval of coal mining operations in several eastern states requires an environmental impact statement

a. because it affects the quality of the environment, is "federal," and is "major."
b. only because it affects the quality of the environment.
c. only because it is "federal."
d. only because it is "major."

____ 2. Red Glow Power Plant burns fossil fuels. Under the Clean Air Act and EPA regulations, as a major new source of possible pollution, to reduce emissions the plant must use

a. the best available technology (BAT).
b. the lowest common denominator (LCD).
c. the maximum achievable control technology (MACT).
d. the minimum allowable technology (MAT).

____ 3. Auto Motors, Inc. (AMI) makes sport utility vehicles (SUVs). Under the Clean Air Act, AMI is required to makes its SUVs comply with standards that, with respect to automobile exhaust emissions, are

a. different but neither more nor less strict.
b. less strict.
c. more strict.
d. the same.

____ 4. Eagle Industries, Inc., fails to obtain a permit before discharging waste into navigable waters. Under the Clean Water Act, Eagle can be required

a. only to clean up the pollution.
b. only to pay for the cost of cleaning up the pollution.
c. to clean up the pollution or pay for the cost of doing so.
d. to do nothing.

____ 5. Petro, Inc., ships unlabeled containers of hazardous waste to off-site facilities for disposal. If the containers later leak, Petro could be found to have violated

a. neither the Comprehensive Environmental Response, Compensation, and Liability Act (CERCLA) nor the Resource Conservation and Recovery Act (RCRA).
b. the CERCLA and the RCRA.
c. the CERCLA only.
d. the RCRA only.

____   6. Beta Company operates a hazardous waste storage facility. If Beta buries unlabeled containers without determining their contents and the containers leak, Beta could be found to have violated

     a. neither the Comprehensive Environmental Response, Compensation, and Liability Act (CERCLA) nor the Resource Conservation and Recovery Act (RCRA).
     b. the CERCLA and the RCRA.
     c. the CERCLA only.
     d. the RCRA only.

____   7. The U.S. Department of the Interior approves minor landscaping around a federal courthouse in St. Louis. This does *not* require an environmental impact statement

     a. only because it does not affect the quality of the environment.
     b. only because it is not "major."
     c. only because it is not "federal."
     d. because it does not affect the quality of the environment, is not "major," and is not "federal."

____   8. Standard Corporation's factory emits toxic air pollutants. Under the Clean Air Act and EPA regulations, Standard is required to

     a. eliminate all air polluting emissions.
     b. install emission control equipment on its products.
     c. reduce emissions by installing the maximum achievable control technology.
     d. remove all pollutants from its factories.

____   9. Alpha Development Company owns wetlands that it wants to fill in and develop as a site for homes. Under the Clean Water Act, before filling and dredging, Alpha must obtain a permit from

     a. no one.
     b. the Army Corps of Engineers.
     c. the EPA.
     d. the U.S. Department of the Navy.

____   10. Gamma Company owns a hazardous waste disposal site that it sells to Omega Properties, Inc. Later, the EPA discovers a leak at the site and cleans it up. The EPA can recover the cost from

     a. Gamma only.
     b. Gamma or Omega.
     c. neither Gamma nor Omega.
     d. Omega only.

SHORT ESSAY QUESTIONS

1. What does the National Environmental Policy Act require?

2. What federal laws regulate toxic chemicals?

ISSUE SPOTTERS

(Answers at the Back of the Book)

1. ChemCorp generates hazardous wastes from its operations. Central Trucking Company transports those wastes to Intrastate Disposal, Inc., which owns a hazardous waste disposal site. Intrastate sells the property on which the disposal site is located to ABC Properties, Inc. If the EPA cleans up the site, from whom can it recover the cost?

2.   ABC Company's plant emits smoke and fumes. ABC's operation includes a short railway system, and trucks enter and exit the grounds continuously. Constant vibrations from the trains and trucks rattle a nearby residential neighborhood. The residents sue ABC. Are there any reasons that the court might *refuse* to enjoin ABC's operation?

3.   What federal agencies have authority to regulate environmental matters?

Chapter 19:
Land-Use Control and Real Property

WHAT THIS CHAPTER IS ABOUT

This chapter covers ownership rights in real property, including the nature of those rights and their transfer. The chapter also outlines the right of the government to take private land for public use, zoning laws, and other restrictions on ownership.

CHAPTER OUTLINE

I. THE NATURE OF REAL PROPERTY
Real property consists of land and the buildings, plants, and trees on it. It is immovable.

A. LAND
Land includes the soil on the surface of the earth, natural products or artificial structures attached to it, the water on or under it, and the air space above.

B. AIR AND SUBSURFACE RIGHTS
Limitations on air rights or subsurface rights normally must be indicated on the document transferring title at the time of purchase.

1. Air Rights
Flights over private land do not normally violate the owners' rights.

2. Subsurface Rights
Ownership of the surface can be separated from ownership of the subsurface. In excavating, if a subsurface owner causes the land to subside, he or she may be liable to the owner of the surface.

C. PLANT LIFE AND VEGETATION
A sale of land with growing crops on it includes the crops, unless otherwise agreed. When crops are sold separately, they are personal property governed by the Uniform Commercial Code.

D. FIXTURES
Personal property so closely associated with certain real property that it is viewed as part of it (such as plumbing in a building). Fixtures are included in a sale of land unless a contract provides otherwise.

II. OWNERSHIP OF REAL PROPERTY

A. OWNERSHIP IN FEE SIMPLE
An owner in fee simple absolute has the most rights possible—he or she can give the property away, sell it, transfer it by will, use it for almost any purpose, and possess it to the exclusion of all the world—potentially forever.

B. LIFE ESTATE
Lasts for the life of a specified individual ("to A for his life"). A life tenant can use the land (but not commit waste), or mortgage or lease the life estate (but for no longer than the life estate).

C. NONPOSSESSORY INTERESTS
Easement: the right of a person to make limited use of another person's land without taking anything from the property. **Profit**: the right to go onto another's land and take away a part or product of the land. **License**: the revocable right of a person to come onto another person's land.

III. TRANSFER OF OWNERSHIP

A. DEEDS
Possession and title to land can be passed by deed without consideration.

1. Requirements
(1) Names of the seller and buyer, (2) words evidencing an intent to convey, (3) legally sufficient description of the land, (4) seller's (and sometimes spouse's) signature, and (5) delivery.

2. Warranty Deed
Provides the most protection against defects of title—covenants that seller has title to, and power to convey, the property; that the property is not subject to any outstanding interests that diminish its value; and that the buyer will not be disturbed in his or her possession.

3. Quitclaim Deed
Warrants less than any other deed. Conveys to the buyer only whatever interest the seller had.

4. Recording Statutes
Recording statutes require transfers to be recorded in public records (generally in the county in which the property is located) to give notice to the public that a certain person is the owner. Many states require the seller's signature and two witnesses' signatures.

B. WILL OR INHERITANCE
Transfer of real property may also occur by will or inheritance.

C. ADVERSE POSSESSION
A person who possesses another's property acquires title good against the original owner if the possession is (1) actual and exclusive; (2) open, visible, and notorious; (3) continuous and peaceable for a required period of time; and (4) hostile, as against the whole world.

IV. LEASEHOLD ESTATES
Created when an owner or landlord conveys a right to possess and use property to a tenant. The tenant's interest is a leasehold estate.

A. TENANCY FOR YEARS
A tenancy for years is created by an express contract by which property is leased for a specific period (a month, a year, a period of years). At the end of the period, the lease ends (without notice). If the tenant dies during the lease, the lease interest passes to the tenant's heirs.

B. PERIODIC TENANCY
A periodic tenancy is created by a lease that specifies only that rent is to be paid at certain intervals. Automatically renews unless terminated. Terminates, at common law, on one period's notice.

C. TENANCY AT WILL
This is a tenancy for as long as the landlord and tenant agree. Exists when a tenant for years retains possession after termination with the landlord's consent before payment of the next rent (when it becomes a periodic tenancy). Terminates on the death of either party or tenant's commission of waste.

D. TENANCY AT SUFFERANCE
A tenancy at sufferance is possession of land without right (without the owner's permission). The true owner can immediately evict the tenant.

V. LANDLORD-TENANT RELATIONSHIPS

A. FORM OF THE LEASE
To ensure the validity of a lease, it should be in writing and—

   1. Express an intent to establish the relationship.
   2. Provide for transfer of the property's possession to the tenant at the beginning of the term.
   3. Provide for the landlord to retake possession at the end of the term.
   4. Describe the property (include the address).
   5. Indicate the length of term and the amount and due dates of rent.

B. ILLEGALITY

A landlord cannot discriminate against tenants on the basis of race, color, religion, national origin, or sex. A tenant cannot promise to do something against these (or other) laws.

C. RIGHTS AND DUTIES

1. Possession

a. Landlord's Duty to Deliver Possession
A landlord must give a tenant possession of the property at the beginning of the term.

b. Tenant's Right to Retain Possession
The tenant retains possession exclusively until the lease expires.

c. Covenant of Quiet Enjoyment
The landlord promises that during the lease term no one having superior title to the property will disturb the tenant's use and enjoyment of it. If so, the tenant can sue for damages for breach.

d. Eviction
If the landlord deprives the tenant of possession of the property or interferes with his or her use or enjoyment of it, an eviction occurs. *Constructive eviction* occurs when this results from a landlord's failure to perform adequately his or her duties under the lease.

2. Use and Maintenance of the Premises

a. Tenant's Use
Generally, a tenant may make any legal use of the property, as long as it is reasonably related to the purpose for which the property is ordinarily used and does not harm the landlord's interest. A tenant is not responsible for ordinary wear and tear.

b. Landlord's Maintenance
A landlord must comply with local building codes.

3. Implied Warranty of Habitability
In most states, a landlord must furnish residential premises that are habitable. This applies to substantial defects that the landlord knows or should know about and has had a reasonable time to repair.

4. Rent
A tenant must pay rent even if he or she moves out or refuses to move in (if the move is unjustifiable). If the landlord violates the implied warranty of habitability, a tenant may withhold rent, pay for repair and deduct the cost, cancel the lease, or sue for damages.

D. TRANSFERRING RIGHTS TO LEASED PROPERTY

1. Transferring the Landlord's Interest
A landlord can sell, give away, or otherwise transfer his or her real property. If complete title is transferred, the tenant becomes the tenant of the new owner, who must also abide by the lease.

2. Transferring the Tenant's Interest
Before a tenant can assign or sublet his or her interest, the landlord's consent may be required (it cannot be unreasonably withheld). If the assignee or sublessee later defaults, the tenant must pay the rent.

VI. LAND-USE CONTROL

A. POLICE POWER
A state can regulate uses of land within its jurisdiction.

1. General Plans
Land-use laws typically follow a local government general plan, which may be supplemented by special, area, or community plans.

2. Zoning Laws
Divide an area into districts to which land-use regulations apply.

a. Types of Restrictions
Use restrictions—kind of use (commercial, residential). Structural restrictions —engineering features and architectural design.

b. Variances
An owner can obtain a variance if (1) it is impossible to realize a reasonable return on the land as zoned, (2) the ordinance adversely affects only the owner (not all owners), (3) granting a variance will not substantially alter the essential character of the zoned area.

3. Other Regulations
Subdivision regulations—local requirements for dedication of land for schools, etc. Growth-management ordinances—limit building permits.

4. Limits on the State's Power
Regulation cannot be (1) confiscatory (or the owner must be paid just compensation); (2) arbitrary or unreasonable (taking without due process under the Fourteenth Amendment); or (3) discriminatory, under the Fourteenth Amendment.

B. EMINENT DOMAIN
The government can take private property for public use. To obtain title, a condemnation proceeding is brought. The Fifth Amendment requires that just compensation be paid for a taking; thus, in a separate proceeding a court determines the land's fair value (usually market value) to pay the owner.

TRUE-FALSE QUESTIONS

(Answers at the Back of the Book)

_T_ 1. A fee simple absolute is potentially infinite in duration and can be disposed of by deed or by will.

_F_ 2. The owner of a life estate has the same rights as a fee simple owner.

_F_ 3. An easement allows a person to use land and take something from it, but a profit allows a person only to use land.

_T_ 4. Deeds offer different degrees of protection against defects of title.

_F_ 5. The government can take private property for *public* use without just compensation.

_F_ 6. The government can take private property for *private* uses only.

_T_ 7. A covenant of quiet enjoyment guarantees that a tenant will not be disturbed in his or her possession of leased property by the landlord or any third person.

_T_ 8. If the covenant of quiet enjoyment is breached, the tenant can sue the landlord for damages.

_T_   **9.**   Generally, a tenant must pay rent even if he or she moves out, if the move is unjustifiable.

_F_   **10.**   To obtain a variance, a landowner must show that his or her alternative use of the land would substantially alter its essential character.

FILL-IN QUESTIONS

(Answers at the Back of the Book)

The deed that provides the most protection against defects of title is the _____ (warranty/ quitclaim) deed. Among other things, it covenants that the transfer is made without any unknown adverse claims of third parties. The deed that warrants less than any other deed is the _____ (warranty/ quitclaim) deed. This deed conveys to the grantee only whatever interest the grantor had.

MULTIPLE-CHOICE QUESTIONS

(Answers at the Back of the Book)

_C_   **1.**   Lou owns two hundred acres next to Mark's mill. Lou sells to Mark the privilege of removing timber from his land to refine into lumber. The privilege of removing the timber is

   a.   a license.
   b.   an easement.
   c.   a profit.
   d.   a taking.

_A_   **2.**   Gamma Company buys forty acres of land to build a corporate complex. After construction begins, the county zones the surrounding, undeveloped area for a nature preserve, in which it includes 75 percent of Gamma's land. The county owes Gamma

   a.   just compensation.
   b.   land of equivalent value.
   c.   private use of the preserve.
   d.   nothing.

_C_   **3.**   Ann owns a cabin on Long Lake. Bob takes possession of the cabin without Ann's permission and puts up a sign that reads "No Trespassing by Order of Bob, the Owner." The statutory period for adverse possession is ten years. Bob is in the cabin for eleven years. Ann sues to remove Bob. She will

   a.   win, because Ann sued Bob after the statutory period for adverse possession.
   b.   win, because Bob did not have permission to take possession of the cabin.
   c.   lose, because Bob acquired the cabin by adverse possession.
   d.   lose, because the no-trespassing sign misrepresented ownership of the cabin.

_B_   **4.**   Dan owns a half-acre of land fronting on Eagle Lake. Fred owns the property behind Dan's land. No road runs to Dan's land, but Fred's driveway runs between a road and Dan's property, so Dan uses Fred's driveway. The right-of-way that Dan has across Fred's property is

   a.   a license.
   b.   an easement.
   c.   a profit.
   d.   a taking.

5. Alpha Corporation wants to convert a warehouse near Bay City into a shopping mall and to construct an apartment tower on adjacent land. Local policy concerning growth, and building requirements and restrictions can be found in Bay City's

   a. area and general development plans only.
   b. zoning ordinances only.
   c. area and development plans, and zoning ordinances.
   d. covenant of quiet enjoyment.

 6. Beta Construction, Inc., wants to develop a suburban tract, subdividing the land to build single-family homes. Formation of the subdivision and such public facilities as streets and schools are responsibilities of

   a. Beta only.
   b. the local agency that oversees the zoning process only.
   c. Beta and the local agency that oversees the zoning process.
   d. the individuals who buy the homes only.

7. Susan signs a lease for an apartment, agreeing to make rental payments before the fifth of each month. The lease does not specify a termination date. This tenancy is

   a. a periodic tenancy.
   b. a tenancy at sufferance.
   c. a tenancy at will.
   d. a tenancy for years.

8. Sam owns an acre of land on Red River. The federal government dams the river. A lake forms behind the dam, covering Sam's land. The federal government owes Sam

   a. just compensation.
   b. land of equivalent value.
   c. private use of the lake.
   d. nothing.

 9. Evan owns an apartment building in fee simple. Evan can

   a. give the building away, but not sell it or transfer it by will.
   b. sell the building or transfer it by a will, but not give it away.
   c. give the building away, sell it, or transfer it by will.
   d. not give, sell, or transfer the building by will.

10. Gina conveys her warehouse to Sam under a warranty deed. Later, Rosa appears, holding a better title to the warehouse than Sam's. Rosa proceeds to evict Sam. Sam can recover from Gina

   a. the purchase price of the property only.
   b. damages from being evicted only.
   c. the purchase price of the property and damages from being evicted.
   d. neither the purchase price of the property nor damages from being evicted.

SHORT ESSAY QUESTIONS

1. Describe the power of eminent domain and the process by which private property is condemned for a public purpose.

2. What does the implied warranty of habitability require, and when does it apply?

ISSUE SPOTTERS

(Answers at the Back of the Book)

1. Gary owns a commercial building in fee simple. Gary transfers temporary possession of the building to Holding Corporation (HC). Can HC transfer possession for even less time to Investment Company?

2. Metro City designates certain areas within its limits for industrial, commercial, residential, and mixed uses. Nick owns a small plot of land in a mixed-use area. Can Metro limit only Nick's land to residential use?

3. Eve owns an acre of land in an area that allows houses on half-acres. She proposes to divide her property and build a house on each half-acre. To do so, Eve must obtain residential building permits from the local zoning authorities. On what grounds, unrelated to Eve, can the authorities refuse to grant the permits?

Chapter 20:
Promoting Competition

WHAT THIS CHAPTER IS ABOUT

This chapter outlines aspects of the major antitrust statutes, including the Sherman Act and the Clayton Act. Keep in mind that the basis of the antitrust laws is a desire to foster competition (to result in lower prices and so on) by limiting restraints on trade (agreements that have the effect of reducing competition).

CHAPTER OUTLINE

I. THE SHERMAN ANTITRUST ACT
Enacted in 1890, the Sherman Act is one of the government's most powerful weapons to maintain a competitive economy.

A. MAJOR PROVISIONS OF THE SHERMAN ACT
Section 1 requires two or more persons; cases often concern agreements (written or oral) that have a wrongful purpose and lead to a restraint of trade. Section 2 cases deal with monopolies that already exist.

B. JURISDICTIONAL REQUIREMENTS
The Sherman Act applies to restraints that substantially affect interstate commerce. The act also covers activities by nationals that have an effect on U.S. foreign commerce.

II. SECTION 1 OF THE SHERMAN ACT

A. *PER SE* VIOLATIONS VERSUS THE RULE OF REASON
Some trade restraints are deemed *per se* violations. Others are subject to analysis under the rule of reason.

1. *Per Se* Violations
Agreements that are blatantly anticompetitive are illegal *per se*.

2. Rule of Reason
A court considers the purpose of an agreement, the power of the parties, the effect of the action on trade, and in some cases, whether there are less restrictive alternatives to achieve the same goals. If the competitive benefits outweigh the anticompetitive effects, the agreement is held lawful.

B. HORIZONTAL RESTRAINTS
Agreements that restrain competition between rivals in the same market.

1. Price Fixing
Any agreement among competitors to fix prices is a *per se* violation.

2. Group Boycotts
An agreement by two or more sellers to refuse to deal with a particular person or firm is a *per se* violation, if it is intended to eliminate competition or prevent entry into a given market.

3. Horizontal Market Division
An agreement between competitors to divide up territories or customers is a *per se* violation.

4. **Trade Associations**
Businesses within the same industry or profession organized to pursue common interests. The rule of reason is applied.

C. VERTICAL RESTRAINTS
A vertical restraint is a restraint of trade that results from an agreement between firms at different levels in the manufacturing and distribution process.

1. **Territorial or Customer Restrictions**
This is an agreement between a manufacturer and a distributor or retailer to restrict sales to certain areas or customers. Judged under a rule of reason.

2. **Resale Price Maintenance Agreements**
This is an agreement between a manufacturer and a distributor or retailer in which the manufacturer specifies the retail prices of its products. Subject to the rule of reason.

3. **Refusals to Deal**
A firm is free to deal, or not, unilaterally, with whomever it wishes.

III. SECTION 2 OF THE SHERMAN ACT
This section of the Sherman Act applies to individuals and to several people; cases concern the structure of a monopoly in the marketplace and the misuse of monopoly power. Covers two distinct types of behavior: monopolization and attempts to monopolize.

A. MONOPOLIZATION
This requires two elements: (1) the possession of monopoly power in the relevant market and (2) the willful acquisition or maintenance of that power.

1. **Monopoly Power**
Monopoly power is sufficient market power to control prices and exclude competition.

   a. **Market-Share Test**
   A firm has monopoly power if its share of the relevant market is 70 percent or more.

   b. **The Relevant Market Has Two Elements—**

      1) **Relevant Product Market**
      All products with identical attributes and those that are sufficient substitutes for each other are included.

      2) **Relevant Geographical Market**
      If competitors sell in only a limited area, the geographical market is limited to that area.

2. **The Intent Requirement**
If a firm has market power as a result of a purposeful act to acquire or maintain that power through anticompetitive means, it is a violation of Section 2. Intent may be inferred from evidence that the firm had monopoly power and engaged in anticompetitive behavior.

B. ATTEMPTS TO MONOPOLIZE
Any action challenged as an attempt to monopolize must (1) be intended to exclude competitors and garner monopoly power and (2) have a dangerous probability of success.

IV. THE CLAYTON ACT
Enacted in 1914, the Clayton Act is aimed at practices not covered by the Sherman Act. Conduct is illegal only if it substantially tends to lessen competition or create monopoly power.

A. SECTION 2—PRICE DISCRIMINATION
Price discrimination occurs when a seller charges different prices to competitive buyers for identical goods.

1. Elements
(1) The seller must be engaged in interstate commerce, (2) the effect of the price discrimination must be to substantially lessen competition or create a competitive injury, and (3) a seller's pricing policies must include a reasonable prospect of the seller's recouping its losses.

2. Exception
When a lower price is charged temporarily and in good faith to meet another seller's equally low price to the buyer's competitor.

B. SECTION 3—EXCLUSIONARY PRACTICES

1. Exclusive-Dealing Contracts
This is a contract in which a seller forbids the buyer to buy products from the seller's competitors. Prohibited if the effect is "to substantially lessen competition or tend to create a monopoly."

2. Tying Arrangements
These exist when a seller conditions the sale of a product on the buyer's agreement to buy another product produced or distributed by the same seller. Legality depends on the agreement's purpose and its likely effect on competition in the relevant markets.

C. SECTION 7—MERGERS
A person or firm cannot hold stock or assets in another firm if the effect may be to substantially lessen competition. A crucial consideration in most cases is **market concentration** (percentage of market shares of firms in the relevant market).

1. Horizontal Mergers
These are mergers between firms that compete with each other in the same market. If a merger creates an entity with more than a small percentage market share, it is presumed illegal. Factors include—

- **a.** The degree of concentration in the relevant market.
- **b.** The ease of entry into the relevant market.
- **c.** Economic efficiency.
- **d.** The financial condition of the merging firms.
- **e.** The nature and prices of the products.

2. Vertical Mergers
This occurs when a company at one stage of production acquires a company at a higher or lower stage of production. Legality depends on market concentration, barriers to entry into that market, and the parties' intent.

D. SECTION 8—INTERLOCKING DIRECTORATES
No person may be a director in two or more corporations at the same time if either firm has capital, surplus, or undivided profits of more than $22,276,000 or if a firm's competitive sales are $22,761,000 or more (as of 2006).

V. ENFORCEMENT OF ANTITRUST LAWS

A. U.S. DEPARTMENT OF JUSTICE (DOJ)
The DOJ prosecutes violations of the Sherman Act as criminal or civil violations. Violations of the Clayton Act are not crimes; the DOJ can enforce it only through civil proceedings. Remedies include divestiture and dissolution.

B. FEDERAL TRADE COMMISSION (FTC)
The FTC enforces the Clayton Act; has the sole authority to enforce the Federal Trade Commission Act of 1914 (Section 5 condemns all forms of anticompetitive behavior that are not covered by other federal antitrust laws); issues administrative orders; can seek court sanctions.

C. PRIVATE PARTIES

  1. Treble Damages and Attorneys' Fees
  Private parties can sue for treble damages and attorneys' fees under the Clayton Act if they are injured by a violation of any federal antitrust law (except the FTC Act).

  2. Injunctions
  Private parties may seek an injunction to prevent an antitrust violation if it will injure business activities protected by the antitrust laws.

VI. EXEMPTIONS FROM ANTITRUST LAWS

A. LABOR ACTIVITIES
A labor union can lose its exemption if it combines with a nonlabor group.

B. AGRICULTURAL ASSOCIATIONS AND FISHERIES
Except exclusionary practices or restraints of trade against competitors.

C. INSURANCE COMPANIES
Exempt in most cases when state regulation exists.

D. FOREIGN TRADE
U.S. exporters may cooperate to compete with similar foreign associations (if it does not restrain trade in the United States or injure other U.S. exporters).

E. PROFESSIONAL BASEBALL
Players may sue team owners for anticompetitive practices. Other professional sports are not exempt.

F. OIL MARKETING
States set quotas on oil to be marketed in interstate commerce.

G. COOPERATIVE RESEARCH AND PRODUCTION
Cooperative research among small business firms is exempt.

H. JOINT EFFORTS TO OBTAIN LEGISLATIVE OR EXECUTIVE ACTION
Joint efforts by businesspersons to obtain executive or legislative action are exempt (*Noerr-Pennington* doctrine). Exception: an action is not protected if "no reasonable [person] could reasonably expect success on the merits" and it is an attempt to make anticompetitive use of government processes.

I. OTHER EXEMPTIONS

  1. Activities approved by the president in furtherance of defense.
  2. State actions, when the state policy is clearly articulated and the policy is actively supervised by the state.
  3. Activities of regulated industries when federal commissions, boards, or agencies have primary regulatory authority.

TRUE-FALSE QUESTIONS
(Answers at the Back of the Book)

____ **1.** A horizontal restraint results from an agreement between firms at different levels in the manufacturing and distribution process.

_____ 2. An agreement that restrains competition between rivals in the same market is a vertical restraint.

_____ 3. Monopoly power is market power sufficient to control prices and exclude competition.

_____ 4. An exclusive dealing contract is a contract under which competitors agree to divide up customers.

_____ 5. Price discrimination occurs when a seller forbids a buyer to buy products from the seller's competitors.

_____ 6. A horizontal merger results when a company at one stage of production acquires another company at a higher or lower stage in the chain of production and distribution.

_____ 7. A merger between firms that compete with each other in the same market is a vertical merger.

_____ 8. A relevant product market consists of all products with identical attributes and those that are sufficient substitutes for each other.

_____ 9. An agreement that is inherently anticompetitive is illegal *per se*.

_____ 10. An agreement between competitors to fix prices is a *per se* violation.

FILL-IN QUESTIONS

(Answers at the Back of the Book)

_____ (Monopoly power/Restraint of trade) is any agreement that has the effect of reducing competition in the marketplace. _____ (Monopoly power/ Restraint of trade) is an extreme amount of market power. A firm that can raise its prices somewhat without too much concern for its competitors' response has some degree of market power. Whether such power is sufficient to call it _____ (monopoly power/ a restraint of trade) is one of the most difficult tasks in antitrust law.

MULTIPLE-CHOICE QUESTIONS

(Answers at the Back of the Book)

_____ 1. National Coal Association (NCA) is a group of independent coal mining companies. Demand for coal falls. The price drops. Coal Refiners Association, a group of coal refining companies, agrees to buy NCA's coal and sell it according to a schedule that will increase the price. This agreement is

a. a *per se* violation of the Sherman Act.
b. exempt from the antitrust laws.
c. subject to continuing review by the appropriate federal agency.
d. subject to the rule of reason.

_____ 2. International Sales, Inc. (ISI), is charged with a violation of antitrust law. ISI's conduct is a *per se* violation

a. if the anticompetitive harm outweighs the competitive benefits.
b. if the competitive benefits outweigh the anticompetitive harm.
c. if the conduct is blatantly anticompetitive.
d. only if it qualifies as an exemption.

____ 3. Tech, Inc., sells its brand-name computer equipment directly to its franchised retailers. Depending on how existing franchisees do, Tech may limit the number of franchisees in a given area to reduce intrabrand competition. Tech's restrictions on the number of dealers is

   a. a *per se* violation of the Sherman Act.
   b. exempt from the antitrust laws.
   c. subject to continuing review by the appropriate federal agency.
   d. subject to the rule of reason.

____ 4. Gamma Corporation is charged with a violation of antitrust law that requires evaluation under the rule of reason. The court will consider

   a. only the effect of the conduct on trade.
   b. only the power of the parties to accomplish what they intend.
   c. only the purpose of the conduct.
   d. the effect of the conduct, the power of the parties, and the purpose of the conduct.

____ 5. Omega, Inc., controls 80 percent of the market for telecommunications equipment in the southeastern United States. To show that Omega is monopolizing that market in violation of the Sherman Act requires proof of

   a. only the possession of monopoly power in the relevant market.
   b. only the willful acquisition or maintenance of monopoly power.
   c. the possession of monopoly power in the relevant market *and* its willful acquisition or maintenance.
   d. none of the above.

____ 6. Handy Tools, Inc., charges Jack's Hardware five cents per item and Irma's Home Store ten cents per item for the same product. The two stores are competitors. If this substantially lessens competition, it constitutes

   a. a market division.
   b. an exclusionary practice.
   c. a tying arrangement.
   d. price discrimination.

____ 7. Standard Company is charged with violating antitrust law, subject to evaluation under the rule of reason. Standard's conduct is unlawful

   a. if the anticompetitive harm outweighs the competitive benefits.
   b. if the competitive benefits outweigh the anticompetitive harm.
   c. if the conduct is blatantly anticompetitive.
   d. only if it does not qualify for an exemption.

____ 8. Central Data Corporation and Digital, Inc., are competitors. They form a joint venture to research, develop, and produce new software for a particular line of computers. This joint venture is

   a. a *per se* violation of the Sherman Act.
   b. exempt from the antitrust laws.
   c. subject to continuing review by the appropriate federal agency.
   d. subject to the rule of reason.

____   **9.**   The Sherman and Clayton Acts can be enforced through civil proceedings by

a.   the U.S. Department of Justice (DOJ) only.
b.   the Federal Trade Commission (FTC) only.
c.   private parties only.
d.   the DOJ, the FTC, and private parties.

____   **10.**   Alpha, Inc., and Beta Corporation are competitors. They merge, and after the merger, Alpha is the surviving firm. To assess whether this is in violation of the Clayton Act requires a look at the market

a.   concentration.
b.   discrimination.
c.   division.
d.   power.

SHORT ESSAY QUESTIONS

1.   How does Section 1 of the Sherman Act deal with horizontal restraints?

2.   How does the Clayton Act deal with exclusionary practices?

ISSUE SPOTTERS

(Answers at the Back of the Book)

1.   Able Company, a bicycle manufacturer, refuses to deal with Baker Bikes, a retailer. In what circumstances might Able's refusal to deal with Baker violate antitrust law?

2.   Under what circumstances would Pop's Market, a small store in a small, isolated town, be considered a monopolist? If Pop's is a monopolist, is it in violation of Section 2 of the Sherman Act?

3.   Maple Corporation conditions the sale of its syrup on the buyer's agreement to buy Maple's pancake mix. What factors would a court consider to decide whether this arrangement violates the Clayton Act?

Chapter 21:
Investor Protection and Corporate Governance

WHAT THIS CHAPTER IS ABOUT

The general purpose of securities laws is to provide sufficient, accurate information to investors to enable them to make informed buying and selling decisions about securities. This chapter provides an outline of federal securities laws. This chapter also discusses issues of corporate governance.

CHAPTER OUTLINE

I. THE SECURITIES AND EXCHANGE COMMISSION (SEC)
The SEC administers the federal securities laws and regulates the sale and purchase of securities.

A. THE SEC'S BASIC FUNCTIONS

1. Require disclosure of facts concerning offerings of certain securities.

2. Regulate national securities trading.

3. Investigate securities fraud.

4. Regulate securities brokers, dealers, and investment advisers.

5. Supervise mutual funds.

6. Recommend sanctions in cases involving violations of securities laws. (The U.S. Department of Justice prosecutes violations.)

B. THE SEC'S EXPANDING REGULATORY POWERS
The SEC's powers include the power to seek sanctions against those who violate foreign securities laws; to suspend trading if prices rise and fall in short periods of time; to exempt persons, securities, and transactions from securities law requirements; and to require more corporate disclosure.

II. SECURITIES ACT OF 1933
This act requires that all essential information concerning the issuance (sales) of new securities be disclosed to investors.

A. WHAT IS A SECURITY?

1. **Courts' Interpretation of the Securities Act**
   Securities includes investment contracts, which exist in any transaction in which a person (1) invests (2) in a common enterprise (3) reasonably expecting profits (4) derived *primarily* or *substantially* from others' managerial or entrepreneurial efforts.

2. **A Security Is an Investment**
   Examples: stocks, bonds, investment contracts in condominiums, franchises, limited partnerships, and oil or gas or other mineral rights.

B. REGISTRATION STATEMENT

Before offering securities for sale, issuing corporations must (1) file a registration statement with the Securities and Exchange Commission (SEC) and (2) provide investors with a prospectus that describes the security being sold, the issuing corporation, and the investment or risk. These documents must be written in "plain English."

1. Contents of a Registration Statement

   a. Description of the significant provisions of the security and how the registrant intends to use the proceeds of the sale.
   b. Description of the registrant's properties and business.
   c. Description of the management of the registrant; its security holdings; its remuneration and other benefits, including pensions and stock options; and any interests of directors or officers in any material transactions with the corporation.
   d. Financial statement certified by an independent public accountant.
   e. Description of pending lawsuits.

2. Twenty-Day Waiting Period after Registration

Securities cannot be sold for twenty days (oral offers can be made).

3. Advertising

During the waiting period, very limited written advertising is allowed. After the period, no written advertising is allowed, except a tombstone ad, which simply tells how to obtain a prospectus.

C. EXEMPT SECURITIES

Securities that can be sold (and resold) without being registered include—

1. Small Offerings under Regulation A

An issuer's offer of up to $5 million in securities in any twelve-month period (including up to $1.5 million in nonissuer resales). The issuer must file with the SEC a notice of the issue and an offering circular (also provided to investors before the sale). A company can "test the waters" (determine potential interest) before preparing the circular.

2. Other Exempt Securities

   a. All bank securities sold prior to July 27, 1933.
   b. Commercial paper if maturity does not exceed nine months.
   c. Securities of charitable organizations.
   d. Securities resulting from a reorganization issued in exchange for the issuer's existing securities and certificates issued by trustees, receivers, or debtors in possession in bankruptcy (see Chapter 12).
   e. Securities issued exclusively in exchange for the issuer's existing securities, provided no commission is paid (such as stock splits).
   f. Securities issued to finance the acquisition of railroad equipment.
   g. Any insurance, endowment, or annuity contract issued by a state-regulated insurance company.
   h. Government-issued securities.
   i. Securities issued by banks, savings and loan associations, farmers' cooperatives, and similar institutions.

D. EXEMPT TRANSACTIONS

Securities that can be sold without being registered include those sold in transactions that consist of—

1. Limited Offers (Regulation D)

Offers that involve a small amount of money or are not made publicly.

   a. Small Offerings

   Noninvestment company offerings up to $1 million in a twelve-month period [Rule 504].

b. **Blank-Check Company Offerings**

Offerings up to $500,000 in any one year by companies with no specific business plans are exempt if (1) no general solicitation or advertising is used, (2) the SEC is notified of the sales, and (3) precaution is taken against nonexempt, unregistered resales [Rule 504a].

c. **Small Offerings**

Private, noninvestment company offerings up to $5 million in a twelve-month period if (1) no general solicitation or advertising is used; (2) the SEC is notified of the sales; (3) precaution is taken against nonexempt, unregistered resales; and (4) there are no more than thirty-five unaccredited investors. If the sale involves any unaccredited investors, all investors must be given material information about the company, its business, the securities [Rule 505].

d. **Private Offerings**

Essentially the same requirements as Rule 505, except (1) there is no limit on the amount of the offering and (2) the issuer must believe that each unaccredited investor has sufficient knowledge or experience to evaluate the investment [Rule 506].

2. **Small Offerings to Accredited Investors Only**

An offer up to $5 million is exempt if (1) no general solicitation or advertising is used; (2) the SEC is notified of the sales; (3) precaution is taken against nonexempt, unregistered resales; and (4) there are no unaccredited investors [Section 4(6)].

3. **Intrastate Issues**

Offerings in the state in which the issuer is organized and doing business are exempt [Rule 147] if, for nine months after the sale, no resale is made to a nonresident.

4. **Resales—"Safe Harbors"**

Most securities can be resold without registration. Resales of blank-check company offerings [Rule 504a], small offerings [Rule 505], private offerings [Rule 506], and offers to accredited investors only [Section 4(6)] are exempt from registration if—

a. **The Securities Have Been Owned for Three Years or More**

If seller is not an affiliate (in control with the issuer) [Rule 144].

b. **The Securities Have Been Owned for at Least Two Years**

There must be adequate public information about the issuer, the securities must be sold in limited amounts in unsolicited brokers' transactions, and the SEC must be notified of the resale [Rule 144].

c. **The Securities Are Sold Only to an Institutional Investor**

The securities, on issue, must not have been of the same class as securities listed on a national securities exchange or a U.S. automated interdealer quotation system, and the seller on resale must take steps to tell the buyer they are exempt [Rule 144A].

E. **VIOLATIONS AND PENALTIES**

The SEC can bring civil actions. The U.S. Department of Justice enforces the criminal provisions. Private parties can also sue. Penalties include fines to $10,000, imprisonment for five years, or both.

III. SECURITIES EXCHANGE ACT OF 1934

This act regulates the markets in which securities are traded by requiring disclosure by Section 12 companies (corporations with securities on the exchanges and firms with assets in excess of $5 million and five hundred or more shareholders).

A. **INSIDER TRADING—SECTION 10(b) AND SEC RULE 10b-5**

Section 10(b) proscribes the use of "any manipulative or deceptive device or contrivance in contravention of such rules and regulations as the [SEC] may prescribe." Rule 10b-5 prohibits the commission of fraud in connection with the purchase or sale of any security (registered or unregistered).

1. **What Triggers Liability**
   Any material omission or misrepresentation of material facts in connection with the purchase or sale of any security.

2. **What Does Not Trigger Liability**
   Under the Private Securities Litigation Reform Act of 1995, financial forecasts and other forward-looking statements do not trigger liability if they include "meaningful cautionary statements identifying factors that could cause actual results to differ materially."

3. **Who Can Be Liable**
   Those who take advantage of inside information when they know it is unavailable to the person with whom they are dealing.

   a. **Insiders**
      Officers, directors, majority shareholders, and persons having access to or receiving information of a nonpublic nature on which trading is based (accountants, attorneys).

   b. **Outsiders**

      1) **Tipper/Tippee Theory**
         A party who acquires inside information as a result of an insider's breach of fiduciary duty to the firm whose shares are traded can be liable, if he or she knows or should know of the breach.

      2) **Misappropriation Theory**
         A party who wrongfully obtains inside information and trades on it to his or her gain can be liable, if a duty to the lawful possessor of information was violated and harm to another results.

B. **INSIDER REPORTING AND TRADING—SECTION 16(b)**
   Officers, directors, and shareholders owning 10 percent of the securities registered under Section 12 are required to file reports with the SEC concerning their ownership and trading of the securities.

   1. **Corporation Is Entitled to All Profits**
      A firm can recapture *all* profits realized by an insider on *any* purchase and sale or sale and purchase of its stock in any six-month period.

   2. **Applicability of Section 16(b)**
      Applies to stock, warrants, options, and securities convertible into stock.

C. **PROXY STATEMENTS—SECTION 14(A)**
   This section regulates the solicitation of proxies from shareholders of Section 12 companies. Whoever solicits a proxy must disclose, in the proxy statement, all of the pertinent facts.

D. **VIOLATIONS OF THE 1934 ACT**

   1. **Criminal Penalties**
      Maximum jail term is five years; fines up to $5 million for individuals and $2.5 million for partnerships and corporations.

   2. **Civil Sanctions**

      a. **Insider Trading Sanctions Act of 1984**
         The SEC can bring a suit in federal court against anyone violating or aiding in a violation of the 1934 act or SEC rules. Penalties include triple the profits gained or the loss avoided by the guilty party.

    b. Insider Trading and Securities Fraud Enforcement Act of 1988
    This act enlarged the class of persons subject to civil liability for insider-trading violations, increased criminal penalties, and gave the SEC authority to (1) reward persons providing information and (2) make rules to prevent insider trading.

IV. CORPORATE GOVERNANCE

Corporate governance is the system by which corporations are governed and controlled, according to the Organization of Economic Cooperation and Development. Effective governance requires more than compliance with the law.

A. THE NEED FOR GOOD CORPORATE GOVERNANCE

Because corporate ownership is separated from corporate control, conflicts of interest can arise.

B. ATTEMPTS AT ALIGNING THE INTERESTS OF SHAREHOLDERS AND OFFICERS

Providing stock options to align the financial interests of shareholders and officers has proved to be an imperfect control device. Officers have manipulated circumstances to artificially inflate stock prices to keep the value of options high, or the options have been "repriced" to avoid losses when stock prices dropped. "Outside" directors are often the friends of corporate officers.

C. CORPORATE GOVERNANCE AND CORPORATE LAW

Corporate oversight involves (1) the audited reporting of corporate financial progress so that managers can be evaluated and (2) legal protection for shareholders.

    1. The Practical Significance of Good Corporate Governance
    Firms with greater shareholder rights have higher profits, higher sales growth, higher firm value, and other economic advantages.

    2. Governance and Corporation Law
    Under the law, a corporation must have a board of directors elected by the shareholders. Thus, the key element of corporate structure is the board, which makes important decisions about the firm.

    3. The Board of Directors
    Directors, who must operate for the shareholders' benefit, are responsible for monitoring officers and can be sued for failing to do their jobs effectively.

    4. Importance of the Audit Committee
    An audit committee oversees the corporate accounting and financial reporting processes, including the internal controls designed to ensure that the reports are accurate.

    5. The Compensation Committee
    This committee determines the amount of compensation to be paid to the officers and is responsible for assessing those officers' performance.

D. THE SARBANES-OXLEY ACT OF 2002

This act imposes strict disclosure requirements and harsh penalties for violations of securities laws.

    1. Responsible Parties
    Chief corporate executives (CEOs and CFOs) are responsible for the accuracy and completeness of financial statements and reports filed with the SEC [Sections 302 and 906]. Penalties for knowingly certifying a report or statement that does not meet statutory requirements include up to $1 million in fines and ten years imprisonment ($5 million and twenty years for "willful" certification). Altering or destroying documents is also subject to fines and imprisonment.

    2. Public Company Accounting Oversight Board
    The SEC oversees this entity, which regulates and oversees public accounting firms.

3. **Limitations on Private Actions**

A private action for securities fraud must be brought within two years of the discovery of the violation or five years after the violation, whichever is earlier [Section 804].

V.   REGULATION OF INVESTMENT COMPANIES

The SEC regulates investment companies and mutual funds under the Investment Company Act of 1940, the Investment Company Act Amendments of 1970, the Securities Act Amendments of 1975, and later amendments.

A. WHAT AN INVESTMENT COMPANY IS

Any entity that (1) is engaged primarily "in the business of investing, reinvesting, or trading in securities" or (2) is engaged in such business and has more than 40 percent of the company's assets in investment securities. (Does not include banks, finance companies, and others).

B. WHAT AN INVESTMENT COMPANY MUST DO

Register with the SEC by filing a notification of registration and, each year, file reports with the SEC. All securities must be in the custody of a bank or stock-exchange member.

C. WHAT AN INVESTMENT COMPANY CANNOT DO

No dividends may be paid from any source other than accumulated, undistributed net income. There are restrictions on investment activities.

VI.   STATE SECURITIES LAWS

Each state regulates the offer and sale of securities within its borders. Exemptions from federal law are not exemptions from state laws, which have their own exemptions. Under the National Market Securities Improvement Act of 1996, the SEC regulates most national securities activities. The National Conference of Commissioners on Uniform State Laws recommends that the states adopt the revised Uniform Securities Act, which is designed to coordinate state and federal securities regulation and enforcement efforts.

VII.   ONLINE SECURITIES OFFERINGS AND DISCLOSURES

Federal and state laws set out the requirements for online initial public offerings. Under SEC interpretations, there is no difference in the disclosure requirements, only in the medium of disclosure, for which there may be new avenues of liability. Also, an online prospectus may not qualify for a Regulation D exemption.

VIII.   ONLINE SECURITIES FRAUD

Issues include the use of chat rooms to affect the price of securities, fictitious press releases, and illegal offerings. The First Amendment protects the use of chat rooms. Also, there is a distinction between statements of fact and opinion.

TRUE-FALSE QUESTIONS

(Answers at the Back of the Book)

____ 1. A security that does not qualify for an exemption must be registered before it is offered to the public.

____ 2. Before a security can be sold to the public, prospective investors must be provided with a prospectus.

____ 3. Stock splits are exempt from the registration requirements of the Securities Act of 1933, if no commission is paid.

____ 4. Sales of securities may not occur until twenty days after registration.

____ 5. Private offerings of securities in unlimited amounts that are not generally solicited or advertised must be registered before they can be sold.

_____ **6.** A proxy statement must fully and accurately disclose all of the facts that are pertinent to the matter on which shareholders are being asked to vote.

_____ **7.** All states have disclosure requirements and antifraud provisions that cover securities.

_____ **8.** *Scienter* is not a requirement for liability under Section 10(b) of the Securities Exchange Act of 1934.

_____ **9.** No one who receives inside information as a result of another's breach of his or her fiduciary duty can be liable under SEC Rule 10b-5.

_____ **10.** No security can be resold without registration.

FILL-IN QUESTIONS

(Answers at the Back of the Book)

The SEC can award "bounty" payments to persons providing information leading to the _____ (conviction/prosecution) of insider-trading violations. Civil penalties include _____ (double/triple) the profits gained or the loss avoided. Criminal penalties include maximum jail terms of _____ (five/ ten) years. Individuals and corporations _____ (may/may not) also be subject to million dollar fines.

MULTIPLE-CHOICE QUESTIONS

(Answers at the Back of the Book)

_____ **1.** Beth, a director of Alpha Company, learns that an Alpha engineer has developed a new, improved product. Over the next six months, Beth buys and sells Alpha stock for a profit. Of Beth's profit, Alpha may recapture

a. all.
b. half.
c. 10 percent.
d. none.

_____ **2.** Frank, an officer of Gamma, Inc., learns that Gamma has developed a new source of energy. Frank tells Gail, an outsider. They each buy Gamma stock. When the development is announced, the stock price increases, and they each immediately sell their stock. Subject to liability for insider trading is

a. Frank and Gail.
b. Frank only.
c. Gail only
d. neither Frank nor Gail.

_____ **3.** Huron, Inc., makes a $6 million private offering to twenty accredited investors and less than thirty unaccredited investors. Huron advertises the offering and believes that the unaccredited investors are sophisticated enough to evaluate the investment. Huron gives material information about itself, its business, and the securities to all investors. Concerning registration, this offering is

a. exempt because of the low amount of the issue.
b. exempt because it was advertised.
c. exempt because the issuer believed that the unaccredited investors were sophisticated enough to evaluate the investment.
d. not exempt.

____ 4. Superior, Inc., is a private, noninvestment company. In one year, Superior advertises a $300,000 offering. Concerning registration, this offering is

a. exempt because of the low amount of the issue.
b. exempt because it was advertised.
c. exempt because the issuer is a private company.
d. not exempt.

____ 5. Ontario, Inc., in one year, advertises two $2.25 million offerings. Buying the stock are twelve accredited investors. Concerning registration, this offering is

a. exempt because of the low amount of the issue.
b. exempt because it was advertised.
c. exempt from registration because only accredited investors bought stock.
d. not exempt from registration.

____ 6. Omega Corporation's registration statement must include

a. a description of the accounting firm that audits Omega.
b. a description of the security being offered for sale.
c. a financial forecast for Omega's nest five years.
d. all of the above.

____ 7. Central Brokerage Associates sells securities, which include investment contracts. The definition of an investment contract does *not* include, as an element,

a. an investment.
b. a common enterprise.
c. a reasonable expectation of profits.
d. profits derived entirely from the efforts of the investor.

____ 8. Under the Securities Exchange Act of 1934, the Securities and Exchange Commission is responsible for all of the following activities EXCEPT

a. investigating securities fraud.
b. prosecuting criminal violations of federal securities laws.
c. regulating the activities of securities brokers.
d. requiring disclosure of facts concerning offerings of securities listed on national securities exchanges.

____ 9. National Sales, Inc., wants to make an offering of securities to the public. The offer is not exempt from registration. Before National sells these securities, it must provide *investors* with

a. a prospectus.
b. a registration statement.
c. a tombstone ad.
d. all of the above.

____ 10. Great Lakes Company is a private, noninvestment company. Last year, as part of a $250,000 advertised offering, Great Lakes sold stock to John, a private investor. John would now like to sell the shares. Concerning registration, this resale is

a. exempt because of the low amount of the original issue.
b. exempt because the offering was advertised.
c. exempt because all resales are exempt.
d. not exempt.

SHORT ESSAY QUESTIONS

1. What is the process by which a company sells securities to the public?

2. How is insider trading regulated by Section 10(b), SEC Rule 10b-5, and Section 16(b)?

ISSUE SPOTTERS

(Answers at the Back of the Book)

1. When a corporation wants to issue certain securities, it must provide sufficient information for an unsophisticated investor to evaluate the financial risk involved. Specifically, the law imposes liability for making a false statement or omission that is "material." What sort of information would an investor consider material?

2. Lee is an officer of Macro Oil, Inc. Lee knows that a Macro geologist has just discovered a new deposit of oil. Can Lee take advantage of this information to buy and sell Macro stock?

3. The Securities Act of 1933, the Securities Exchange Act of 1934, and other securities regulation is federal law. In-State Corporation incorporated in one state, does business exclusively in that state, and offers its securities for sale only in that state. Are there securities laws to regulate this offering?

CUMULATIVE HYPOTHETICAL PROBLEM
FOR UNIT FIVE—INCLUDING CHAPTERS 16–21

(Answers at the Back of the Book)

Beta Chemical Corporation makes and sells chemical products to industrial customers and individual consumers.

____ 1. Beta advertises its products with slogans that consist of vague generalities. Because of this advertising, the Federal Trade Commission may

a. issue a cease-and-desist order only.
b. require counteradvertising only.
c. issue a cease-and-desist order or require counteradvertising.
d. none of the above.

____ 2. To determine whether Beta is violating regulations issued by the Environmental Protection Agency (EPA), the EPA may NOT

a. arbitrarily order Beta to shut its manufacturing site down.
b. conduct an on-site inspection of Beta's manufacturing site.
c. test Beta's products on its manufacturing site.
d. none of the above.

____ 3. Beta's manufacturing process generates hazardous waste that is transported to Gamma Company's disposal site by Omega Trucking, Inc. If the EPA cleans up Gamma's site, liability for the cost may be assessed against

a. Beta or Gamma only.
b. Gamma or Omega only.
c. Beta or Omega only.
d. Beta, Gamma, or Omega.

____ **4.** Beta charges National Refining, Inc., less per item than Beta charges International Export Corporation for the same product. The two industrial buyers are competitors. This pricing difference violates anti-trust law

   a. if both buyers' customers pay the same price for the buyers' products.
   b. if National and International know what each other pays.
   c. if the pricing substantially lessens competition.
   d. under no circumstances.

____ **5.** The Beta board of directors decides to issue additional stock in the firm. The registration statement must include

   a. a copy of the corporation's most recent proxy statement.
   b. the names of prospective accredited investors.
   c. the names of the current shareholders.
   d. the principal purposes for which the proceeds from the offering will be used.

Chapter 22:
The Regulation of International Transactions

WHAT THIS CHAPTER IS ABOUT

This chapter outlines some of the principles of international law, some of the ways in which international business is conducted, and some of the ways in which that business is regulated.

CHAPTER OUTLINE

I. INTERNATIONAL PRINCIPLES AND DOCTRINES
The following are based on courtesy and respect and are applied in the interest of maintaining harmony among nations.

A. THE PRINCIPLE OF COMITY
One nation defers and gives effect to the laws and judicial decrees of another country, so long as those laws and judicial decrees are consistent with the law and public policy of the accommodating nation.

B. THE ACT OF STATE DOCTRINE
A judicially created doctrine under which the judicial branch of one country will not examine the validity of public acts committed by a recognized foreign government within its own territory. Often used in cases involving—

1. **Expropriation**
   This occurs when a government seizes a privately owned business or goods for a proper public purpose and pays just compensation.

2. **Confiscation**
   This occurs when a government seizes private property for an illegal purpose or without just compensation.

C. THE DOCTRINE OF SOVEREIGN IMMUNITY
Immunizes foreign nations from the jurisdiction of domestic courts. In the United States, the Foreign Sovereign Immunities Act (FSIA) of 1976 exclusively governs the circumstances in which an action may be brought against a foreign nation.

1. **When Is a Foreign State Subject to U.S. Jurisdiction?**
   When the state has waived its immunity expressly or impliedly, or when the action is based on commercial activity in the United States by the foreign state [Section 1605].

2. **What Entities Fall within the Category of Foreign State?**
   A political subdivision and an instrumentality (an agency or entity acting for the state) [Section 1603].

3. **What Is Commercial Activity?**
   The FSIA leaves it to the courts to decide whether an activity is governmental or commercial.

II. DOING BUSINESS INTERNATIONALLY

A. EXPORTING

The simplest way to do business internationally is to export to foreign markets. Direct exporting: signing a sales contract with a foreign buyer. Indirect exporting: selling directly to consumers through a foreign agent or foreign distributor.

B. MANUFACTURING ABROAD

A domestic firm can establish a manufacturing plant abroad by—

1. Licensing

A domestic firm may license its intellectual property to a foreign manufacturer. The foreign firm agrees to keep the technology secret and to pay royalties for its use. Franchising is a form of licensing.

2. Investing in a Wholly Owned Subsidiary or a Joint Venture

When a wholly owned subsidiary is established, the domestic firm retains ownership of the foreign facilities and control over the entire operation. In a joint venture, a domestic firm and one or more foreign firms share ownership, responsibilities, profits, and liabilities.

III. COMMERCIAL CONTRACTS IN AN INTERNATIONAL SETTING

To avoid problems in international commercial contracts, special provisions are available.

A. CONTRACT CLAUSES

1. Choice of Language

This clause designates the official language by which a contract will be interpreted in the event of disagreement. Clauses may also provide for translations and arbitration in certain languages.

2. Choice of Forum

This clause designates the jurisdiction, including the court, in which a dispute will be litigated. The forum may be anywhere (it does not have to be in the nations of the contracting parties).

3. Choice of Law

This clause designates what law will apply in a dispute. There is no limit on the parties' choice. If no law is specified, the governing law is that of the country in which the seller's place of business is located.

4. *Force Majeure* ("Impossible or Irresistible Force")

This clause stipulates that acts of God and other eventualities (government orders or regulations, embargoes, or shortages of materials) may excuse a party from liability for nonperformance.

B. CIVIL DISPUTE RESOLUTION

1. Arbitration

Arbitration clauses (see Chapter 3) are often in international contracts. The arbitrator may be a neutral entity, a panel of individuals representing both parties' interests, or another group. The United Nations Convention on the Recognition and Enforcement of Foreign Arbitral Awards assists in the enforcement of arbitration clauses, as do provisions in specific treaties between nations.

2. Litigation

Litigation may be subject to forum-selection and choice-of-law clauses. If no forum and law are specified, litigation may be complex and uncertain (held simultaneously in two countries, for example, without regard of one for the other; a judgment may not be enforced).

IV. MAKING PAYMENT ON INTERNATIONAL TRANSACTIONS

A. MONETARY SYSTEMS
Doing business abroad requires dealing with different currencies. Problems arising from this situation can be reduced by—

1. Foreign Exchange Markets
Foreign exchange markets are a global system for converting (buying and selling) foreign currencies. The exchange rate is the price of a unit of one country's currency in terms of another.

2. Correspondent Banking
Correspondent banking is a means of transferring funds internationally. A domestic bank with correspondent banks in other countries can transfer funds, etc., through those banks.

B. LETTERS OF CREDIT

1. Principal Parties
The issuer (a bank) agrees to issue a letter of credit and to ascertain whether the beneficiary (seller) does certain acts. The account party (buyer) promises to reimburse the issuer for payment to the beneficiary.

2. Other Banks
An advising bank sends information; a paying bank expedites payment.

3. Issuer's Obligation
The issuer is bound to pay the beneficiary when the beneficiary has complied with the terms of the letter of credit (by presenting the required documents—typically a bill of lading).

4. The Value of a Letter of Credit
Payment is made against documents, not against what those documents represent. The issuer does not police the contract; this reduces costs.

5. Compliance with a Letter of Credit
Some courts require strict compliance with the terms of a letter; others require reasonable compliance. If the beneficiary complies as required, but the issuer refuses to pay, the beneficiary can sue to enforce payment.

V. REGULATION OF SPECIFIC BUSINESS ACTIVITIES

A. INVESTING
When a government confiscates property without just compensation, few remedies are available. Many countries guarantee compensation to foreign investors in their constitutions, statutes, or treaties. Some countries provide insurance for their citizens' investments abroad.

B. EXPORT CONTROLS

1. Restricting Exports
Under the U.S. Constitution, Congress cannot tax exports, but may set export quotas. Under the Export Administration Act of 1979, restrictions can be imposed on the flow of technologically advanced products and technical data.

2. Stimulating Exports
Devices to stimulate exports include export incentives and subsidies.

C. IMPORT CONTROLS
Laws prohibit, for example, importing illegal drugs and agricultural products that pose dangers to domestic crops or animals.

1. **Quotas and Tariffs**
    Quotas limit how much can be imported. Tariffs are taxes on imports (usually a percentage of the value, but can be a flat rate per unit).

2. **Dumping**
    A tariff may be assessed on imports to prevent *dumping* (sales of imported goods at "less than fair value," usually determined by prices in the exporting country).

3. **Minimizing Trade Barriers**

    a. **World Trade Organization (WTO)**
        This the principal instrument for regulating international trade. Each member country agrees to grant *most-favored-nation status* to other members (the most favorable treatment with regard to trade).

    b. **European Union (EU)**
        A regional trade association that minimizes trade barriers among European member nations.

    c. **North American Free Trade Agreement (NAFTA)**
        NAFTA created a regional trading unit consisting of Mexico, the United States, and Canada. The goal is to eliminate tariffs among them on substantially all goods over a period of fifteen to twenty years.

    d. **Central American-Dominican Republic Free Trade Agreement (CAFTA-DR)**
        CAFTA-DR aims to reduce tariffs and improve market access among Costa Rica, Dominican Republic, El Salvador, Guatemala, Honduras, Nicaragua, and the United States.

D. **BRIBING FOREIGN OFFICIALS**
    To reduce bribery of foreign officials by U.S. corporations, Congress enacted the Foreign Corrupt Practices Act (FCPA) in 1977 (see Chapter 2).

VI. U.S. LAWS IN A GLOBAL CONTEXT

A. **ANTITRUST LAWS**
    For U.S. courts to exercise jurisdiction over a foreign entity under U.S. antitrust laws, a violation must (1) have a substantial effect on U.S. commerce or (2) constitute a *per se* violation (see Chapter 20). Foreign governments and persons can also sue U.S. firms and persons for antitrust violations.

B. **DISCRIMINATION LAWS**
    U.S. employers must abide by U.S. employment discrimination laws (see Chapter 14) unless to do so would violate the laws of the country in which their workplace is located.

TRUE-FALSE QUESTIONS

(Answers at the Back of the Book)

____   1.   All nations must give effect to the laws of all other nations.

____   2.   Under the act of state doctrine, foreign nations are subject to the jurisdiction of U.S. courts.

____   3.   Under the doctrine of sovereign immunity, foreign nations are subject to the jurisdiction of U.S. courts.

____   4.   The Foreign Sovereign Immunities Act states the circumstances in which the United States can be sued in foreign courts.

____   5.   A member of the World Trade Organization must usually grant other members most-favored nation status with regard to trade.

_____ 6. The Foreign Corrupt Practices Act is an attempt to stop the bribery of foreign officials by U.S. corporations.

_____ 7. U.S. courts cannot exercise jurisdiction over foreign entities under U.S. antitrust laws.

_____ 8. U.S. employers with workplaces abroad must generally comply with U.S. discrimination laws.

_____ 9. When a seller complies with the terms of a letter of credit, the issuing bank is obliged to pay.

_____ 10. Under a *force majeure* clause, a party may be excused from liability for nonperformance.

FILL-IN QUESTIONS
(Answers at the Back of the Book)

_____ (A confiscation/An expropriation) occurs when a national government seizes a privately owned business or privately owned goods for a proper public purpose. _____ (A confiscation/An expropriation) occurs when the taking is made for an illegal purpose. When _____ (a confiscation/an expropriation) occurs, the government pays just compensation. When _____ (a confiscation/an expropriation) occurs, the government does not pay just compensation.

MULTIPLE-CHOICE QUESTIONS
(Answers at the Back of the Book)

_____ 1. A group of foreign manufacturers organize to control the price for digital cameras in the United States. FotoQuik Company, a U.S. firm, joins the group. If their actions have a substantial effect on U.S. commerce, a suit for violation of U.S. antitrust laws may be brought against

a. FotoQuik and the foreign manufacturers.
b. neither FotoQuik nor the foreign manufacturers.
c. only FotoQuik.
d. only the foreign manufacturers.

_____ 2. To obtain a contract in Russia, Standard Company bribes a government official whose signature is needed on the contract. This may violate

a. the act of state doctrine.
b. the doctrine of sovereign immunity.
c. the Foreign Corrupt Practices Act.
d. the principle of comity.

_____ 3. El Salvador issues bonds to finance the construction of an international airport. Fred, in the United States, buys some of the bonds. A terrorist group destroys the airport, and El Salvador refuses to pay interest or principal on the bonds. Fred files suit in a U.S court. The court will hear the suit

a. if El Salvador's acts constitute a confiscation.
b. if El Salvador's acts constitute an expropriation.
c. if El Salvador's selling bonds is a "commercial activity."
d. under no circumstances.

____ 4. To obtain new computers, Liberia accepts bids from U.S. firms, including Macro Corporation and Micro, Inc. Macro wins the contract. Alleging impropriety in the awarding of the contract, Micro files a suit in a U.S. court against Liberia and Macro. The court may decline to hear the suit under

a. the act of state doctrine.
b. the doctrine of sovereign immunity.
c. the Foreign Corrupt Practices Act.
d. the World Trade Organization.

____ 5. A South African seller and a U.S. buyer form a contract that the buyer breaches. The seller sues in a South African court and wins damages, but the buyer's assets are in the United States. If a U.S. court enforces the judgment, it will be because of

a. the act of state doctrine.
b. the doctrine of sovereign immunity.
c. the principle of comity.
d. the World Trade Organization.

____ 6. Global, Inc., is a U.S. firm. Holly, a U.S. citizen, works for Global in a country outside the United States. Ilsa, a citizen of a foreign country, also works for Global outside the United States. Holly and Ilsa believe that they are being harassed on the job, in violation of U.S. discrimination laws. Those laws protect

a. Holly and Ilsa.
b. Holly only.
c. Ilsa only.
d. neither Holly nor Ilsa.

____ 7. A contract between Delta, Inc., a U.S. firm, and Electronique, S.A., a French company, provides that disputes between the parties will be adjudicated in a specific British court. This clause is

a. a choice-of-forum clause.
b. a choice-of-law clause.
c. a *force majeure* clause.
d. an arbitration clause.

____ 8. Alpha, Inc., a U.S. firm, signs a contract with Beta, Ltd., a Russian company, to give Beta the right to sell Alpha's products in Russia. This is

a. a distribution agreement.
b. a joint venture.
c. direct exporting.
d. licensing.

____ 9. Digital, Inc., makes supercomputers that feature advanced technology. To inhibit Digital's export of its products to other countries, Congress can

a. confiscate all profits on exported supercomputers.
b. expropriate all profits on exported supercomputers.
c. set quotas on exported supercomputers.
d. tax exported supercomputers.

____   10.   Auto Corporation makes cars in the United States. To boost the sales of Auto Corporation and other domestic car makers, Congress can

a.   neither set quotas nor tax imports.
b.   only set quotas on imports.
c.   only tax imports.
d.   set quotas and tax imports.

SHORT ESSAY QUESTIONS

1.   In what ways may a company conduct international business?

2.   How does the Foreign Sovereign Immunities Act affect commercial activities by foreign governments?

ISSUE SPOTTERS

(Answers at the Back of the Book)

1.   Cafe Rojo, Ltd., a Colombian firm, agrees to sell coffee beans to A.B. Coffee Company, a U.S. firm. A.B. accepts the beans, but refuses to pay. Cafe Rojo sues A.B. in a Colombian court and is awarded damages, but A.B.'s assets are in the United States. Under what circumstances would a U.S. court enforce the Colombian court's judgment?

2.   Hi-Cola Corporation, a U.S. firm, markets a popular soft drink. The formula is secret, but with careful chemical analysis, its ingredients could be discovered. What can Hi-Cola do to prevent its product from being pirated abroad?

3.   Gems International, Ltd., is a foreign firm that has a 12-percent share of the U.S. market for diamonds. To capture a larger share, Gems offers its products at a below-cost discount to U.S. buyers (and inflates the prices in its own country to make up the difference). How can this attempt to undersell U.S. businesses be defeated?

CUMULATIVE HYPOTHETICAL PROBLEM FOR UNIT SIX—INCLUDING CHAPTER 22

(Answers at the Back of the Book)

Eagle, Inc., is a U.S. firm, doing business in the United States and in other nations, including China.

____   1.   Eagle contracts with Fong, Ltd., a Hong Kong firm, allowing Fong to use and profit from Eagle's patented products. This is

a.   a distribution agreement.
b.   a joint venture.
c.   direct exporting.
d.   licensing.

____   2.   A dispute arises between Eagle and Fong, and Eagle obtains a judgment in a U.S. court against Fong. Whether the U.S. court's judgment will be enforced by a court in China depends on the Chinese court's application of

a.   the act of state doctrine.
b.   the doctrine of sovereign immunity.
c.   the principle of comity.
d.   the World Trade Organization.

____ 3. China, which governs Hong Kong, seizes the property of Eagle, without paying the owners just compensation. This is

a. a confiscation.
b. a dumping.
c. a licensing.
d. an expropriation.

____ 4. Eagle files a suit in a U.S. court against China to recover for China's seizure of Eagle's property. Eagle's recovery may be prevented by

a. the act of state doctrine.
b. the doctrine of sovereign immunity.
c. the Foreign Corrupt Practices Act.
d. the principle of comity.

____ 5. As a conciliatory gesture, China hires Eagle to perform certain services but fails to pay. Eagle files a suit in a U.S. court against China on this basis. China may be exempt from the court's jurisdiction under

a. the act of state doctrine.
b. the doctrine of sovereign immunity.
c. the Foreign Corrupt Practices Act.
d. the principle of comity.

Answers

Chapter 1

True-False Questions

1. T
2. F. Legal positivists believe that there can be no higher law that a nation's positive law (the law created by a particular society at a particular point in time). The belief that law should reflect universal moral and ethical principles that are part of human nature is part of the natural law tradition.
3. T
4. T
5. T
6. F. Each state's constitution is supreme within each state's borders, so long as it does not conflict with the U.S. Constitution.
7. F. The National Conference of Commissioners on Uniform State Laws drafted the Uniform Commercial Code (and other uniform laws and model codes) and proposed it for adoption by the states.
8. F. This is the definition of civil law. Criminal law relates to wrongs against society as a whole and for which society has established sanctions.
9. T
10. F. A citation may contain the names of the parties, the year in which the case was decided, and the volume and page numbers of a reporter in which the opinion may be found, but it does not include the name of the judge who decided the case.

Fill-in Questions

with similar facts; precedent; permits a predictable

Multiple-Choice Questions

1. D. Legal positivists believe that there can be no higher law than the written law of a given society at a particular time. They do not believe in "natural rights."
2. B. The use of precedent—the doctrine of *stare decisis*—permits a predictable, relatively quick, and fair resolution of cases. Under this doctrine, a court must adhere to principles of law established by higher courts.
3. D. Equity and law provide different remedies, and at one time, most courts could grant only one type. Today, most states do not maintain separate courts of law and equity, and a judge may grant either or both forms of relief. Equitable relief is generally granted, however, only if damages (the legal remedy) is inadequate.
4. C. The U.S. Constitution is the supreme law of the land. Any state or federal law or court decision in conflict with the Constitution is unenforceable and

will be struck. Similarly, provisions in a state constitution take precedence over the state's statutes, rules, and court decisions.

5. D. The doctrine of *stare decisis* attempts to harmonize the results in cases with similar facts. When the facts are sufficiently similar, the same rule is applied. Cases with identical facts could serve as binding authority, but it is more practical to expect to find cases with facts that are not identical but similar—as similar as possible.

6. A. An order to do or refrain from a certain act is an injunction. An order to perform as promised is a decree for specific performance. These remedies, as well as rescission, are equitable remedies. An award of damages is a remedy at law.

7. C. In establishing case law, or common law, the courts interpret and apply state and federal constitutions, rules, and statutes. Case law applies in areas that statutes or rules do not cover. Federal law applies to all states, and preempts state law in many areas.

8. A. Law that defines, describes, regulates, or creates rights or duties is substantive la w. Law that establishes methods for enforcing rights established by substantive law is procedural law. Criminal law governs wrongs committed against society for which society demands redress.

9. D. International law comes from a variety of sources, and represents attempts to reconcile desires for national authority and profitable commerce. Enforcement of international law can only be accomplished by cooperation, persuasion, or coercion.

10. C. A concurring opinion makes or emphasizes a point different from those made or emphasized in the majority's opinion. An opinion written for the entire court is a unanimous opinion. An opinion that outlines only the majority's views is a majority opinion. A separate opinion that does not agree with the majority's decision is a dissenting opinion.

Issue Spotters

1. Case law includes courts' interpretations of statutes, as well as constitutional provisions and administrative rules. Statutes often codify common law rules. For these reasons, a judge might rely on the common law as a guide to the intent and purpose of a statute.

2. No. The U.S. Constitution is the supreme law of the land, and applies to all jurisdictions. A law in violation of the Constitution (in this question, the First Amendment to the Constitution) will be declared unconstitutional.

3. Yes. Administrative rulemaking starts with the publication of a notice of the rulemaking in the *Federal Register*. A public hearing is held at which proponents and opponents can offer evidence and question witnesses. After the hearing, the agency considers what was presented at the hearing and drafts the final rule.

Chapter 2

True-False Questions

1. T

2. T

3. F. According to utilitarianism, it is the consequences of an act that determine how ethical the act is. Applying this theory requires determining who will be affected by an act, assessing the positive and negatives effects of alternatives, and choosing the alternative that will provide the greatest benefit for the most people. Utilitarianism is premised on acting so as to do the greatest good for the greatest number of people. An act that affects a minority negatively may still be morally acceptable.

4. T

5. F. The legality of a particular action may be unclear, in part because it can be difficult to predict how a court may rule on a particular issue. The best course is to act responsibly and in good faith. Similarly, in situations involving *ethical* decisions, a balance must sometimes be struck between equally good or equally poor courses of action, and sometimes one group—employees or shareholders for example—may be adversely affected.

6. T

7. F. Simply obeying the law will not meet all ethical obligations. The law does not cover all ethical requirements. An act may be unethical but not illegal. In fact, compliance with the law is at best a moral minimum. Furthermore, there is an ethical aspect to almost every decision that a business firm makes.

8. T

9. F. Compliance with GAAP and GAAS may be required, but it is no guarantee of freedom from liability. Also, there may be a higher standard of conduct under a state statute or judicial decision.

10. F. Bribery is also a legal issue, regulated in the United States by the Foreign Corrupt Practices Act. Internationally, a treaty signed by the members of the Organization for Economic Cooperation and Development makes bribery of public officials a serious crime. Each member nation is expected to enact legislation implementing the treaty.

Fill-in Questions

Religious standards; Kantian ethics; the principle of rights

Multiple-Choice Questions

1. C. Business ethics focus on the application of moral principles in a business context. Different standards are not required. Business ethics is a subset of ethics that relates specifically to what constitutes right and wrong in situations that arise in business.

2. B. Traditionally, ethical reasoning relating to business has been characterized by two fundamental approaches—duty-based ethics and utilitarianism, or outcome-based ethics. Duty-based ethics derive from religious sources or philosophical principles. These standards may be absolute, which means that an act may not be undertaken, whatever the consequences.

3. A. Under religious ethical standards, it is the nature of an act that determines how ethical the act is, not its consequences. This is considered an *absolute* standard. But this standard is tempered by an element of compassion (the "Golden Rule").

4. A. In contrast to duty-based ethics, outcome-based ethics (utilitarianism) involves a consideration of the consequences of an action. Utilitarianism is premised on acting so as to do the greatest good for the greatest number of people.

5. C. Utilitarianism requires determining who will be affected by an action, assessing the positive and negatives effects of alternatives, and choosing the alternative that will provide the greatest benefit for the most people. This approach has been criticized as tending to reduce the welfare of human beings to plus and minus signs on a cost-benefit worksheet.

6. A. In part because it is impossible to be entirely aware of what the law requires and prohibits, the best course for a business firm is to act responsibly and in good faith. This course may provide the best defense if a transgression is discovered. Striking a balance between what is profitable and what is legal and ethical can be difficult, however. A failure to act legally or ethically can result in a reduction in profits, but a failure to act in the profitable interest of the firm can also cause profits to suffer. *Optimum* profits are the maximum profits that a firm can realize while staying within legal and ethical limits.

7. C. Under the Securities Act of 1933, an accountant may be liable for any false statement of material fact or omission of a material fact in a registration statement. An accountant is required to exercise due diligence in preparing financial statements, which means that "using" due diligence would not result in liability for losses based on those statements. Also, financial statements should include all essential information concerning the issuance of stock, which means that if the statements contain that information, liability would not result on that basis.

8. D. In this problem, the attorney failed to exercise reasonable care and professional judgment, thereby breaching the duty of care owed to clients. If a statute of limitations runs out, a client can no longer file a suit and loses a potential award of damages.

9. D. The principle of rights theory of ethics follows the belief that persons have fundamental rights. This belief is implied by duty-based ethical standards and Kantian ethics. The rights are implied by the duty that forms the basis for the standard (for example, the duty not to kill implies that persons have a right to live), or

by the personal dignity implicit in the Kantian belief about the fundamental nature of human beings. Not to respect these rights would, under the principle of rights theory, be morally wrong.

10. C. The Foreign Corrupt Practices Act prohibits any U.S. firm from bribing foreign officials to influence official acts to provide the firm with business opportunities. Such payments are allowed, however, if they would be lawful in the foreign country. Thus, to avoid violating the law, the firm in this problem should determine whether such payments are legal in the minister's country.

Issue Spotters

1. The answer depends on which system of ethics is used. Under a duty-based ethical standard, it may not be the consequences of an act that determine how ethical the act is; it may be the nature of the act itself. Stealing would be unethical regardless of whether the fruits of the crime are given to the poor. In contrast, utilitarianism is premised on acting so as to do the greatest good for the greatest number of people. It is the consequences of an act that determine how ethical the act is.

2. Maybe. On the one hand, it is not the company's "fault" when a product is misused. Also, keeping the product on the market is not a violation of the law, and stopping sales would hurt profits. On the other hand, suspending sales could reduce suffering and could stop potential negative publicity if sales continued.

3. When a corporation decides to respond to what it sees as a moral obligation to correct for past discrimination by adjusting pay differences among its employees, an ethical conflict is raised between the firm and its employees and between the firm and its shareholders. This dilemma arises directly out of the effect such a decision has on the firm's profits. If satisfying this obligation increases profitability, then the dilemma is easily resolved in favor of "doing the right thing." In any case, there will likely be a conflict among the various interest groups, however, which may require a decision as to which group will receive priority.

Chapter 3

True-False Questions

1. T

2. T

3. F. The decisions of a state's highest court on all questions of state law are final. The United States Supreme Court can overrule only those state court decisions that involve questions of federal law.

4. T

5. T
6. T
7. F. A losing party may appeal an adverse judgment to a higher court, but the party in whose favor the judgment was issued may also appeal if, for example, he or she is awarded less than sought in the suit.
8. F. Most lawsuits—as many as 95 percent—are dismissed or settled before they go to trial. Courts encourage alternative dispute resolution (ADR) and sometimes order parties to submit to ADR, particularly mediation, before allowing their suits to come to trial.
9. F. In mediation, a mediator assists the parties in reaching an agreement, but not by deciding the dispute. The mediator emphasizes points of agreement, helps the parties evaluate their positions, and proposes solutions.
10. F. If an arbitration agreement covers the subject matter of a dispute, a party to the agreement can be compelled to arbitrate the dispute. A court would order the arbitration without ruling on the basic controversy.

Fill-in Questions

to dismiss; for judgment on the pleadings; summary judgment

Multiple-Choice Questions

1. A. On a "sliding scale" test, a court's exercise of personal jurisdiction depends on the amount of business that an individual or firm transacts over the Internet. Jurisdiction is most likely proper when there is substantial business, most likely improper when a Web site is no more than an ad, and may or may not be appropriate when there is some interactivity. "Any" interactivity with "any resident" of a state would likely not be enough, however.
2. A. This is part of discovery. Discovery saves time, and the trend is toward more, not less, discovery. Discovery is limited, however, to relevant materials. A party cannot obtain access to such data as another's trade secrets or, in testimony, an admission concerning unrelated matters. A party is not entitled to any privileged material either.
3. C. In the suit in this question, the court can exercise *in rem* jurisdiction. A court can exercise jurisdiction over property located within its boundaries. A corporation is also subject to the jurisdiction of the courts in any state in which it is incorporated, in which it has its main office, or in which it does business.
4. A. As noted above, a corporation is subject to the jurisdiction of the courts in any state in which it is incorporated, in which it has its main office, or in which it does business. The court may be able to exercise

personal jurisdiction or *in rem* jurisdiction, or the court may reach a defendant corporation with a long arm statute. In the right circumstances, this firm might also be involved in a suit in a federal court, if the requirements for federal jurisdiction are met: a federal question is involved, or there is diversity of citizenship and the amount in controversy is $75,000 or more.
5. D. An appeals court examines the record of a case, looking mostly at questions of law for errors by the court below. If it determines that a retrial is necessary, the case is sent back to the lower court. For this reason, an appellant's best ground for an appeal focuses on the law that applied to the issues in the case, not questions concerning the credibility of the evidence or other findings of fact.
6. D. The United States Supreme Court is not required to hear any case. The Court has jurisdiction over any case decided by any of the federal courts of appeals and appellate authority over cases decided by the states' highest courts if the latter involve questions of federal law. But the Court's exercise of its jurisdiction is discretionary, not mandatory.
7. C. If a defendant's motion to dismiss is denied, the defendant must then file an answer, or another appropriate response, or a default judgment will be entered against him or her. Of course, the defendant is given more time to file this response. If the motion is granted, the plaintiff is given more time to file an amended complaint.
8. D. Negotiation is an informal means of dispute resolution. Generally, unlike mediation and arbitration, no third party is involved in resolving the dispute. In those two forms, a third party may render a binding or nonbinding decision. Arbitration is a more formal process than mediation or negotiation. Litigation involves a third party—a judge—who renders a legally binding decision.
9. C. In a summary jury trial, the jury's verdict is advisory, not binding as it would otherwise be in a court trial. In a mini-trial, the attorneys argue a case and a third party renders an opinion, but the opinion discusses how a court would decide the dispute. Early neutral case negotiation is what its name suggests, involving a third party who evaluates the disputing parties' positions.
10. C. Online dispute resolution (ODR) is a new type of alternative dispute resolution. Most ODR forums resolve disputers informally and come to nonbonding resolutions. Any party to a dispute being considered in ODR may discontinue the process and appeal to a court at any time.

Issue Spotters

1. Yes. Submission of the dispute to mediation or nonbinding arbitration is mandatory, but compliance with a decision of the mediator or arbitrator is voluntary.

2. Tom could file a motion for a directed verdict. This motion asks the judge to direct a verdict for Tom on the ground that Sue presented no evidence that would justify granting Jan relief. The judge grants the motion if there is insufficient evidence to raise an issue of fact.

3. Either a plaintiff or a defendant, or both, can appeal a judgment to a higher court. An appellate court can affirm, reverse, or remand a case, or take any of these actions in combination. To appeal successfully, it is best to appeal on the basis of an error of law, because appellate courts do not usually reverse on findings of fact.

Cumulative Hypothetical Problem for Unit One—Including Chapters 1–3

1. C. The power of judicial review is the power of any state or federal court to review a statute and declare it unconstitutional. Courts can also review the actions of the executive branch, which includes administrative agencies, to determine their constitutionality. A statute or rule that is declared unconstitutional is void. The power of judicial review is not expressly stated in the Constitution but is implied.

2. A. Mediation involves the a third party, a mediator. The mediator does not decide the dispute but only assists the parties to resolve it themselves. Although the mediator does not render a legally binding decision, any agreement the parties reach may be legally binding.

3. D. These state and federal courts would all have jurisdiction over the defendant. The customer's state could exercise jurisdiction over the firm through its long arm statute. The firm's state would have jurisdiction over it as a resident. A federal court could hear the case under its diversity jurisdiction: the parties are residents of different states and the amount in controversy is at least $75,000.

4. A. Damages, or money damages, is a remedy at law. Remedies in equity include injunctions, specific performance, and rescission. The distinction arose because the law courts in England could not always grant suitable remedies, and so equity courts were created to grant other types of relief. The U.S. legal system derives from the English system.

5. D. Ethics is the study of what constitutes right or wrong behavior. It focuses on the application of moral principles to conduct. In a business context, ethics involves the application of moral principles to business conduct. Legal liability is a separate question and may, or may not, indicate unethical behavior. Profitability is also a separate issue. *Optimum* profitability is the *maximum* profitability a business may attain within the limits of the law *and* ethics.

Chapter 4

True-False Questions

1. F. A federal form of government is one in which separate states form a union and divide sovereign power between themselves and a central authority. The United States has a federal form of government.

2. F. The president does not have this power. Under the doctrine of judicial review, however, the courts can hold acts of Congress and of the executive branch unconstitutional.

3. T

4. T

5. F. Under the supremacy clause, when there is a direct conflict between a federal law and a state law, the federal law takes precedence over the state law, and the state law is rendered invalid.

6. T

7. F. The protections in the Bill of Rights limit the power of the federal government. Most of these protections also apply to the states through the due process clause of the Fourteenth Amendment.

8. F. Commercial speech (advertising) can be restricted as long as the restriction (1) seeks to implement a substantial government interest, (2) directly advances that interest, and (3) goes no further than necessary to accomplish its objective.

9. F. Due process relates to the limits that the law places on the liberty of *everyone*. Equal protection relates to the limits that the law places on only *some people*.

10. T

Fill-in Questions

states; states; state

Multiple-Choice Questions

1. D. Under Articles I, II, and III of the U.S. Constitution, the legislative branch makes the law, the judicial branch interprets the law, and the executive branch enforces the law. There is no separate "administrative branch."

2. A. Under the commerce clause, Congress has the power to regulate every commercial enterprise in the United States. Recently, the United States Supreme Court has struck down federal laws, to limit this power somewhat, in areas that have "nothing to do with commerce," including non-economic, criminal conduct.

3. A. State statutes that impinge on interstate commerce are not always struck down, nor are they always upheld. A court will balance a state's interest in regulating a certain matter against the burden that the statute places on interstate commerce. If the statute does not substantially interfere, it will not be held in violation of the commerce clause.

4. A. The First Amendment provides corporations and other business entities with significant protection of their political speech. As another example, a law that forbids a corporation from using inserts in its bills to its customers to express its views on controversial issues would also violate the First Amendment.

5. B. Commercial speech does not have as much protection under the First Amendment as noncommercial speech. Commercial speech that is misleading may be restricted, however, if the restriction (1) seeks to advance a substantial government interest, (2) directly advances that interest, and (3) goes no further than necessary.

6. B. Aspects of the Fifth and Fourteenth Amendments that cover procedural due process concern the procedures used to make any government decision to take life, liberty, or property. These procedures must be fair, which generally mean that they give an opportunity to object.

7. C. Substantive due process focuses on the content (substance) of a law under the Fifth and Fourteenth Amendments. Depending on which rights a law regulates, it must either promote a compelling or overriding government interest or be rationally related to a legitimate governmental end.

8. A. Equal protection means that the government must treat similarly situated individuals in a similar manner. The equal protection clause of the Fourteenth Amendment applies to state and local governments, and the due process clause of the Fifth Amendment guarantees equal protection by the federal government. Generally, a law regulating an economic matter is considered valid if there is a "rational basis" on which the law relates to a legitimate government interest.

9. D. A federal law takes precedence over a state law on the same subject. Also under the supremacy clause, if Congress chooses to act exclusively in an area in which the states have concurrent power, Congress is said to preempt the area.

10. C. Dissemination of obscene materials is a crime. Speech that harms the good reputation of another, or defamatory speech, is not protected under the First Amendment. "Fighting words," which are words that are likely to incite others to respond with violence, are not constitutionally protected. Other unprotected speech includes other speech that violates criminal laws, such as threats.

Issue Spotters

1. No. Even if commercial speech is not related to illegal activities nor misleading, it may be restricted if a state has a substantial interest that cannot be achieved by less restrictive means. In this case, the interest in energy conservation is substantial, but it

could be achieved by less restrictive means. That would be the utilities' defense against the enforcement of this state law.

2. Yes, the law would violate both types of due process. The law would be unconstitutional on substantive due process grounds, because it abridges freedom of speech. The law would be unconstitutional on procedural due process grounds, because it imposes a penalty without giving an accused a chance to defend his or her actions.

3. Yes. The tax would limit the liberty of some persons (out of state businesses), so it is subject to a review under the equal protection clause. Protecting local businesses from out-of-state competition is not a legitimate government objective. Thus, such a tax would violate the equal protection clause.

Chapter 5

True-False Questions

1. T

2. F. Puffery is seller's talk—the seller's *opinion* that his or her goods are, for example, the "best." For fraud to occur, there must be a misrepresentation of a *fact*.

3. T

4. F. To establish negligence, the courts apply a *reasonable person* standard to determine whether certain conduct resulted in a breach of a duty of care.

5. T

6. F. This is not misconduct, in terms of a wrongful interference tort. Bona fide competitive behavior is permissible, whether or not it results in the breaking of a contract or other business relation. In fact, it is a defense to charges of wrongful interference.

7. F. In an action based on strict liability, a plaintiff does not have to prove that there was a failure to exercise due care. That distinguishes an action based on strict liability from an action based on negligence, which requires proof of a lack of due care. A plaintiff must show, however, that (1) a product was defective, (2) the defendant was in the business of distributing the product, (3) the product was unreasonably dangerous due to the defect, (4) the plaintiff suffered harm, (5) the defect was the proximate cause of the harm, and (6) the goods were not substantially changed from the time they were sold.

8. T

9. F. There is no duty to warn about such risks. Warnings about such risks do not add to the safety of products and could make other warnings seem less significant. In fact, a plaintiff's action in the face of such a risk can be raised as a defense in a product liability suit.

10. T

Fill-in Questions

1. negligence
2. assumption of risk
3. comparative

Multiple-Choice Questions

1. A. To delay a customer suspected of shoplifting, a merchant must have probable cause (which requires more than a mere suspicion). A customer's concealing merchandise in his or her bag and leaving the store without paying for it would constitute probable cause. Even with probable cause, a merchant may delay a suspected shoplifter only for a reasonable time, however.

2. A. The standard of a business that invites persons onto its premises is a duty to exercise reasonable care. Whether conduct is unreasonable depends on a number of factors, including how easily the injury could have been guarded against. A landowner has a duty to discover and remove hidden dangers, but obvious dangers do not need warnings.

3. C. To commit negligence, a breach of a duty of care must cause harm. If an injury was foreseeable, there is causation in fact. This can usually be determined by the but-for test: but for the wrongful act, the injury would not have occurred. Thus, an actor is not necessarily liable to all who are injured. Insurance coverage and business dealings are not factors.

4. D. Advertising is bona fide competitive behavior, which is not a tort even if it results in the breaking of a contract. Obtaining more customers is one of the goals of effective advertising. Taking unethical steps to interfere with others' contracts or business relations could constitute a tort, however.

5. D. Under the Communications Decency Act, an Internet service provider (ISP) may not be held liable for defamatory statements made by its customers online. Congress provided this immunity as an incentive to ISPs to "self-police" the Internet for offensive material.

6. D. This is a statement of opinion (puffing). Puffing creates no warranty. If the salesperson had said something factual about the vehicle (its miles per gallon, its total mileage, whether it had been in an accident, etc.), it would be more than puffing and could qualify as an express warranty.

7. A. Assumption of risk is a defense in an action based on product liability if the plaintiff knew and appreciated the risk created by the defect and voluntarily undertook the risk, even though it was unreasonable to do so.

8. A. A manufacturer may be held liable if its product is unsafe as a result of negligence in the manufacture or if the design makes it unreasonably dangerous for the use for which it is made. A manufacturer also has a duty to warn and to anticipate reasonably foreseeable misuses. An injury must not have been due to a change in the product after it was sold, but there is no requirement of privity. There is no liability, however, with respect to injuries caused by commonly known dangers, even if the manufacturer does not warn against them.

9. D. In a product liability action based on strict liability, the plaintiff does not need to prove that anyone was at fault. Privity of contract is also not an element of an action in strict liability. A plaintiff does have to show, however, in a suit against a seller, that the seller was a merchant engaged in the business of selling the product on which the suit is based. Note that recovery is possible against sellers who are processors, assemblers, packagers, bottlers, wholesalers, distributors, retailers, or lessors, as well as against manufacturers.

10. C. All courts extend the doctrine of strict liability to injured bystanders. A defendant does not have to prove that the manufacturer or seller failed to use due care, nor is there a requirement of privity (or "intent" with regard to entering into privity). The defense of assumption of risk does not apply, because one cannot assume a risk that one does not know about.

Issue Spotters

1. Yes. Trespass to personal property occurs when an individual unlawfully harms another's personal property or otherwise interferes with the owner's right to exclusive possession and enjoyment.

2. No. As long as competitive behavior is bona fide, it is not tortious even if it results in the breaking of a contract. The public policy that favors free competition in advertising outweighs any instability that bona fide competitive activity causes in contractual or business relations. To constitute wrongful interference with a contractual relationship, there must be (1) a valid, enforceable contract between two parties; (2) the knowledge of a third party that this contract exists; and (3) the third party's intentionally causing the breach of the contract (and damages) to advance the third party's interest.

3. Yes. Under the doctrine of strict liability, persons may be liable for the results of their acts regardless of their intentions or their exercise of reasonable care (that is, regardless of fault). There is no requirement of privity.

Chapter 6

True-False Questions

1. T
2. F. Felonies are crimes punishable by imprisonment of a year or more (in a state or federal prison). Crimes punishable by imprisonment for lesser periods (in a local facility) are classified as misdemeanors.

3. F. These are elements of the crime of robbery. (Robbery also involves the use of force or fear.) Burglary requires breaking and entering a building with the intent to commit a crime. (At one time, burglary was defined to cover only breaking and entering the dwelling of another at night to commit a crime.)

4. F. This is an element of larceny. The crime of embezzlement occurs when a person entrusted with another's property fraudulently appropriates it. Also, unlike robbery, embezzlement does not require the use of force or fear.

5. T.

6. F. The crime of bribery occurs when a bribe is offered. Accepting a bribe is a separate crime. In either case, the recipient does not need to perform the act for which the bribe is offered for the crime to exist. Note, too, that a bribe can consist of something other then money.

7. F. The recipient of the goods only needs to know that the goods are stolen. The recipient does not need to know the identity of the thief or of the true owner to commit this crime. Thus, not knowing these individuals' identities is not a defense.

8. T

9. T

10. T

Fill-in Questions

unreasonable; probable; due process of law; jeopardy; trial; trial by; witnesses; bail and fines

Multiple-Choice Questions

1. D. A person who wrongfully or fraudulently takes and carries away another's personal property commits larceny. Unlike burglary, larceny does not involve breaking and entering. Unlike embezzlement, larceny requires that property be taken and carried away from the owner's possession. Unlike forgery, larceny does not require the making or altering of a writing. Unlike robbery, larceny does not involve force or fear.

2. C. The elements of most crimes include the performance of a prohibited act and a specified state of mind or intent on the part of the actor.

3. C. Fraudulently making or altering a writing in a way that changes another's legal rights is forgery. Forgery also includes changing trademarks, counterfeiting, falsifying public documents, and altering other legal documents.

4. B. Embezzlement involves the fraudulent appropriation of another's property, including money, by a person entrusted with it. Unlike larceny, embezzlement does not require that property be taken from its owner.

5. B. The standard to find a criminal defendant guilty is beyond a reasonable doubt. This means that each juror must be convinced, beyond a reasonable

doubt, of the defendant's guilt. The standard of proof in most civil cases is a preponderance of the evidence.

6. C. The federal crime of mail fraud has two elements: a scheme to defraud by false pretenses, and mailing, or causing someone else to mail, a writing for the purpose of executing the scheme. It would also be a crime to execute the scheme by wire, radio, or television transmissions.

7. B. In considering the defense of entrapment, the important question is whether a person who committed a crime was pressured by the police to do so. Entrapment occurs when a government agent suggests that a crime be committed and pressure an individual, who is not predisposed to its commitment, to do it.

8. C. A person in police custody who is to be interrogated must be informed that he or she has the right to remain silent; anything said can and will be used against him or her in court; and he or she has the right to consult with an attorney. The person also must be told that if he or she is indigent, a lawyer will be appointed. These rights may be waived if the waiver is knowing and voluntary.

9. C. If, for example, a confession is obtained after an illegal arrest, the confession is normally excluded. Under the exclusionary rule, all evidence obtained in violation of the constitutional rights spelled out in the Fourth, Fifth, and Sixth Amendments normally is excluded, as well as all evidence derived from the illegally obtained evidence. The purpose of the rule is to deter police misconduct.

10. B. A formal charge issued by a grand jury is an indictment. A charge issued by a government prosecutor is called an information. In either case, there must be sufficient evidence to justify bringing a suspect to trial. The arraignment occurs when the suspect is brought before the trial court, informed of the charges, and asked to enter a plea.

Issue Spotters

1. No. A mistake of fact, as opposed to a mistake of law, will constitute a defense if it negates the mental state required for the crime. The mental state required for theft involves the knowledge that the property is another's and the intent to deprive the owner of it.

2. Yes. With respect to the gas station, she has obtained goods by false pretenses. She might also be charged with larceny and forgery, and most states have special statutes covering illegal use of credit cards.

3. Yes. The National Information Infrastructure Protection Act of 1996 amended the Counterfeit Access Device and Computer Fraud and Abuse Act of 1984. The statute provides that a person who accesses a computer online, without permission, to obtain classified data (such as consumer credit files in a credit agency's database) is subject to criminal prosecution. The crime has two elements: accessing the computer without permission and taking data. It is a felony if done for private financial gain. Penalties include fines and imprisonment for up to twenty years. The victim of the theft can also bring a civil suit against the criminal to obtain damages and other relief.

Cumulative Hypothetical Problem for Unit Two—Including Chapters 4–6

1. B. Of these choices, the firm most likely violated tort law, which includes negligence and strict liability, both as distinct torts and as a part of product liability. Negligence requires proof of intent. Strict liability does not. These firms may also have breached their contracts and their warranties, topics that are discussed in the next Unit.
2. B. A corporation can be compelled to produce its business records, even when those records incriminate its officers or other persons affiliated with the corporation. A partnership is subject to the same requirement. Only individuals can refuse, under the Fifth Amendment to the U.S. Constitution, to provide incriminating testimony, including business records.
3. A. A corporation can be held liable for the crimes of its employees, officers, or directors. Imprisonment is not possible, in a practical sense, as a punishment for a corporation. A business firm can be fined or denied certain privileges, however.
4. C. Use of another's computer, computer information system, or data without permission is larceny, which of course is a type of theft. Robbery involves the forceful taking of property, usually by intimidating another with a weapon. Embezzlement requires that a person appropriating property had been entrusted with it. Wire fraud requires a scheme to defraud.
5. C. If a law affects only some persons (for example, when only some persons are prohibited from doing something), it may raise an equal protection issue. If all persons are affected, there may be a question of substantive due process. Under the Fifth Amendment, the federal government must treat all similarly situated persons in a similar manner.

Chapter 7

True-False Questions

1. T
2. F. A copyright is granted automatically when a qualifying work is created, although a work can be registered with the U.S. Copyright Office.
3. T
4. T
5. F. Anything that makes an individual company unique and would have value to a competitor is a trade secret. This includes a list of customers, a formula for a chemical compound, and other confidential data.

6. F. Trade names cannot be registered with the federal government. They are protected, however, under the common law (when used as trademarks or service marks) by the same principles that protect trademarks.
7. F. A copy does not have to be the same as an original to constitute copyright infringement. A copyright is infringed if a substantial part of a work is copied without the copyright holder's permission.
8. F. A trademark may be infringed by an intentional or unintentional use of a mark in its entirety, or a copy of the mark to a substantial degree. In other words, a mark can be infringed if its use is intended or not, and whether the copy is identical or similar. Also, the owner of the mark and its unauthorized user need not be in direct competition.
9. T
10. F. Proof of a likelihood of confusion is not required in a trademark dilution action. The products involved do not even have to be similar, and the owner and the unauthorized user of a mark do not have to be competitors. Proof of likely confusion is required in a suit for trademark *infringement*, however.

Fill-in Questions

70; 95; 120; 70

Multiple-Choice Questions

1. B. A firm that makes, uses, or sells another's patented design, product, or process without the owner's permission commits patent infringement. It is not required that an invention be copied in its entirety. Also, the object that is copied does not need to be trademarked or copyrighted, in addition to being patented.
2. A. The user of a trademark can register it with the U.S. Patent and Trademark Office, but registration is not necessary to obtain protection from trademark infringement. A trademark receives protection to the degree that it is distinctive. A fanciful symbol is the most distinctive mark.
3. B. Ten years is the period for later renewals of a trademark's registration. The life of a creator plus seventy years is a period for copyright protection. No intellectual work is protected forever, at least not without renewal. To obtain a patent, an applicant must satisfy the U.S. Patent and Trademark Office that the invention or design is genuine, novel, useful, and not obvious in light of contemporary technology. A patent is granted to the first person to create whatever is to be patented, rather than the first person to file for a patent.
4. A. Copyright protects a specific list of creative works, including literary works, musical works, sound recordings, and pictorial, graphic, and sculptural works. Although there are exceptions for "fair use," a work need not be copied in its entirety to be infringed. Also, to make a case for infringement, proof of con-

sumers' confusion is not required, and the owner and unauthorized user need not be direct competitors.

5. D. A process used to conduct business on the Web may be patented in some circumstances. Other business processes and information that cannot be patented, copyrighted, or trademarked are protected against appropriation as trade secrets. These processes and information include production techniques, as well as a product's idea and its expression.

6. C. Trademark law protects a distinctive symbol that its owner stamps, prints, or otherwise affixes to goods to distinguish them from the goods of others. Use of this mark by another party without the owner's permission is trademark infringement.

7. B. A certification mark certifies the region, materials, method of manufacture, quality, or accuracy of goods or services. A collective mark is a certification mark used by members of a cooperative, association, or other organization (a union, in this problem). A service mark distinguishes the services of one person or company from those of another. A trade name indicates all or part of a business's name.

8. D. This is not copyright infringement or patent infringement because no copyright or patent is involved. Trademark dilution occurs when a trademark is used, without the owner's permission, in a way that diminishes the distinctive quality of the mark. That has not happened here. Also, this is not cybersquatting because no one is offering to sell a domain name to a trademark owner. It is further unlikely that this violates the Anticybersquatting Consumer Protection Act because there is no indication of "bad faith intent."

9. C. The Berne Convention provides some copyright protection, but its coverage and enforcement were not as complete or as universal as that of the TRIPS (Trade-Related Aspects of Intellectual Property Rights) Agreement. The Paris Convention allows parties in one signatory country to file for patent and trademark protection in other signatory countries.

10. A. Publishers cannot put the contents of their periodicals into online databases and other electronic resources, including CD-ROMs, without securing the permission of the writers whose contributions are included.

Issue Spotters

1. The owner of the customer list can sue its competitor for the theft of trade secrets. Trade secrets include customer lists. Liability extends to those who misappropriate trade secrets by any means, including modems.

2. This is patent infringement. A software maker in this situation might best protect its product, save litigation costs, and profit from its patent by the use of a license. In the context of this problem, a license would grant permission to sell a patented item. (A license can

be limited to certain purposes and to the licensee only.)

3. Yes. This may be an instance of trademark dilution. Dilution occurs when a trademark is used, without permission, in a way that diminishes the distinctive quality of the mark. Dilution does not require proof that consumers are likely to be confused by a connection between the unauthorized use and the mark. The products involved do not have to be similar. Dilution does require, however, that a mark be famous when the dilution occurs.

Chapter 8

True-False Questions

1. F. All contracts involve promises, but all promises do not establish contracts. (A contract is an agreement that can be enforced in court.) Contract law reflects which promises society believes should be legally enforced, and assures parties to private contracts that the agreements they make will be enforceable.

2. T

3. F. A contract right cannot be assigned if (1) a statute expressly prohibits its assignment; (2) a contract stipulates that it cannot be assigned; (3) it is under a contract that is uniquely personal; or (4) assignment would materially increase or alter the risk of the obligor.

4. F. One of the elements for a valid offer is that the terms be definite enough to be enforced by a court. This is so a court can determine if a breach had occurred and, if so, what the appropriate remedy would be. The term "a fair share" is too indefinite to constitute an enforceable term. An offer that invites, and receives, a specifically worded acceptance can create sufficiently definite terms.

5. T

6. T

7. T

8. T

9. F. The Statute of Frauds requires that contracts for all transfers of interests in land be in writing to be enforceable. Included are sales, mortgages, leases, and other transfers. Other contracts that must be in writing to be enforceable under the Statute of Frauds include contracts that cannot be performed within one year of formation, collateral promises, promises made in consideration of marriage, and contracts for sale of goods priced at $500 or more.

10. T

Fill-in Questions

objective; objective; did; circumstances surrounding; in a particular transaction

Multiple-Choice Questions

1. D. To constitute consideration, the value of whatever is exchanged for the promise must be legally sufficient. Its economic value (its "adequacy") is rarely the basis for a court's refusal to enforce a contract.

2. B. According to the objective theory of contracts, a party's intent to enter into a contract is judged by outward, objective facts as a reasonable person would interpret them, rather than by the party's own subjective intentions. A reasonable person in the position of a party receiving an offer can know what is in the offer only from what is offered. A court might consider the circumstances surrounding a transaction, and the statements of the parties and the way they acted when they made their contract.

3. C. In general, ads (which include catalogs, price lists, and circulars, or flyers) are treated as invitations to negotiate, not offers.

4. B. This statement makes a second offer without rejecting the first offer. An offeree may make an offer without rejecting the original offer, in which case two offers exist, each capable of acceptance.

5. A. Generally, a unilateral mistake—a mistake on the part of only one of the parties—does not give the mistaken party any right to relief. There are two exceptions. One of the exceptions is that the rule does not apply if the other party knew or should have known that a mistake was made.

6. A. Consideration must be bargained for. Performance or a promise is bargained for if, as in this problem, the promisor seeks it in exchange for his or her promise and the promisee gives it in exchange for that promise.

7. A. In considering an implied-in-fact contract, a court looks at the parties' actions leading up to what happened. If, for example, a plaintiff furnished services, expecting to be paid, which the defendant should have known, and the defendant had a chance to reject the services and did not, the court would hold that the parties had an enforceable implied-in-fact contract.

8. D. To disaffirm a contract, a minor must return whatever he or she received under it. In a state in which there is also an obligation to return the other party to the position he or she was in before the contract, the minor must also pay for any damage to the goods.

9. C. Under the Statute of Frauds, a contract for the sale of an interest in land must be in writing to be enforceable. A party to an oral contract involving an interest in land cannot force the other party to buy or sell the property. There is an exception to this rule. If a buyer pays part of the price, takes possession, and makes permanent improvements, and the parties cannot be returned to their pre-contract status quo, a court may grant specific performance of an oral contract for the transfer of an interest in land.

10. C. A right cannot normally be assigned if the assignment would materially increase or alter the risk of the obligor (the different circumstances represented by different persons with different property alter the risk in this problem). A right under a personal service contract cannot normally be assigned, but this is not a personal service contract, which requires a service unique to the person rendering it (an insurance policy is unlikely to qualify).

Issue Spotters

1. Under the objective theory of contracts, if a reasonable person would have thought that the offeree accepted the offeror's offer when the offeree signed and returned the letter, a contract was made, and the offeree is bound. This depends in part on what was said in the letter (was it a valid offer?) and what was said in response (was it a valid acceptance?). Under any circumstances, the issue is not whether either party subjectively believed that they did, or did not, have a contract.

2. The acceptance is effective on dispatch (when the offeree sends the fax). Traditional rules of contract apply to new forms of communication. Under the mailbox rule, using a mode of communication impliedly authorized by the offeror makes an acceptance effective when sent. Here, the offeror did not specify a certain mode, so the mode the offeror used to make the offer was a reasonable means of acceptance.

3. Yes. Under the doctrine of detrimental reliance, or promissory estoppel, the promisee is entitled to payment of $5,000 from the promisor on graduation. There was a promise, on which the promisee relied, the reliance was substantial and definite (the promisee went to college for the full term, incurring considerable expenses, and will likely graduate), and it would only be fair to enforce the promise.

Chapter 9

True-False Questions

1. T

2. F. A material breach of contract (which occurs when performance is not at least substantial) excuses the nonbreaching party from performance of his or her contractual duties and gives the party a cause of action to sue for damages caused by the breach. A *minor* breach of contract does not excuse the nonbreaching party's duty to perform, however, although it may affect the extent of his or her performance and, like any contract breach, allows the nonbreaching party to sue for damages.

3. F. An executory contract can be rescinded. If it is executory on both sides, it can be rescinded solely by agreement. In any case, the parties must make a new agreement, and this agreement must qualify as a contract. (The parties' promises not to perform are consideration for the new contract.)

4.   T

5.   F. There can be no enforceable contract if the doctrine of quasi contract is to be applied. Under this doctrine, to prevent unjust enrichment, the law implies a promise to pay the reasonable value for benefits received in the absence of an enforceable contract. This recovery is useful when one party has partially performed under a contract that is unenforceable.

6.   T

7.   F. Liquidated damages are certain amounts of money estimated in advance of, and payable on, a breach of contract. *Liquidated* means determined, settled, or fixed.

8.   T

9.   T

10.   F. Damages is the usual on breach of contracts for sales of goods. To obtain specific performance, damages must *not* be an adequate remedy. If goods are unique, or a contract involves a sale of land, damages would not adequately compensate an innocent party for a breach of contract, so specific performance is available.

Fill-in Questions

Rescission; Novation; Substitution of a new contract; An accord; accord

Multiple-Choice Questions

1.   D. Accord and satisfaction, agreement, and operation of law are valid bases on which contracts are discharged, but most contracts are discharged by the parties' doing what they promised to do. A contract is fully discharged by performance when the contracting parties have fully performed what they agreed to do (exchange services for payment, for example).

2.   A. A breach of contract entitles the nonbreaching party to damages, but only a material breach discharges the nonbreaching party from his or her duty to perform under the contract. In this problem, the builder has a claim for the amount due on the contract, but the buyer is entitled to have set off the difference in the value of the building as constructed (that is, to subtract the expense to finish the construction).

3.   D. Contracts that have not been fully performed on either side can be rescinded. The parties must make another agreement (which must satisfy the legal requirements for a contract). The parties' promises not to perform are consideration for the new agreement. A contract that has been fully performed on one side can be rescinded only if the party who has performed receives additional consideration to call off the deal.

4.   B. This contract would thus be discharged by objective impossibility of performance. On this basis, a contract may be discharged if, for example, after it is made, performance becomes objectively impossible because of a change in the law that renders that performance illegal. This is also the result if one of the parties dies or becomes incapacitated, or the subject matter of the contract is destroyed.

5.   C. A novation substitutes a new party for an original party, by agreement of all the parties. The requirements are a previous valid obligation, an agreement of all the parties to a new contract, extinguishment of the old obligation, and a new contract (which must meet the requirements for a valid contract, including consideration).

6.   C. A breach of contract by failing to perform entitles the nonbreaching party to rescind the contract, and the parties must make restitution by returning whatever benefit they conferred on each other, particularly when the breaching party would otherwise be unjustly enriched.

7.   C. Under a contract for a sale of goods, the usual measure of compensatory damages is the difference between the contract price and the market price, plus incidental damages. On a seller's breach, the measure includes the difference between what the seller would have been owed if he or she had performed and what the buyer paid elsewhere for the goods.

8.   B. On the seller's breach of a contract, the buyer is entitled to be compensated for the loss of the bargain. Here, the buyer will receive what was contracted for, but it will be late. When, as in this problem, a seller knew that the buyer would lose business if the goods were not delivered on time, the loss of the bargain is the consequential damages (the amount lost as a foreseeable consequence of the breach).

9.   C. Specific performance is an award of the act promised in a contract. This remedy is granted when the legal remedy (damages) is inadequate. Damages are generally inadequate for a buyer on the breach of a contract for a sale of land, because every piece of land is considered unique. If specific performance is not available, however, as when the land cannot be sold by the contracting seller, damages are possible, and their measure is the benefit of the buyer's bargain (the difference between the contract price and the market price of the land at the time of the breach).

10.   D. If the clause is determined to be a penalty clause, it will be unenforceable. To determine whether a clause is a liquidated damages clause or a penalty clause, consider first whether, when the contract was made, damages would clearly be difficult to estimate in the event of a breach. Second, consider whether the amount set as damages is a reasonable estimate. Two "yeses" mean the clause is enforceable. One "no" means the provision is an unenforceable penalty.

Issue Spotters

1.   No. The builder has substantially performed its duties under the contract. Assuming this performance was in good faith, the builder could thus successfully sue for the value of the work performed. For the sake of justice and fairness, the buyer will be held to the duty to pay, less damages for the deviation from the contract deadline.

2. No. To recover damages that flow from the consequences of a breach but that are caused by circumstances beyond the contract (consequential damages), the breaching party must know, or have reason to know, that special circumstances will cause the non-breaching party to suffer the additional loss. That was not the circumstance in this problem.

3. This clause is known as an exculpatory clause. In many cases, such clauses are not enforced, but to be effective in any case, all contracting parties must have consented to it. A clause excluding liability for negligence may be enforced if the contract was made by parties in roughly equal bargaining positions, as two large corporations would be.

Chapter 10

True-False Questions

1. T
2. F. If a transaction involves only a service, the common law usually applies (one exception is the serving of food or drink, which is governed by the UCC). When goods and services are combined, courts have disagreed over whether a particular transaction involves a sale of goods or a rendering of service. Usually, a court will apply the law that applies to whichever feature is dominant. Article 2 does not cover sales of real estate, although sales of goods associated with real estate, including crops, may be covered. A contract for a sale of minerals, for example, is considered a contract for a sale of goods if the severance is to be made by the seller.
3. F. A contract will be enforceable, and a writing will be sufficient under the UCC's Statute of Frauds, if it indicates that a contract was intended, if it includes a quantity term, and—except for transactions between merchants—if it is signed by the party against whom enforcement is sought. Most terms can be proved by oral testimony or be supplied by the UCC's open term provisions (for example, price, delivery, and payment terms). A contract is not enforceable beyond the quantity of goods shown in the writing, however, except for output and requirements contracts.
4. F. A seller can accept an offer to buy goods for current or prompt shipment by promptly *shipping* the goods or by promptly *promising* to ship the goods. Of course, under the mirror image rule, an offer must be accepted in its entirety without modification, or there is no contract. Under the UCC, additional terms may become part of the contract if both parties are merchants (though not if at least one party is a nonmerchant).

5. T
6. F. If the parties do not agree otherwise, the buyer or lessee must pay for the goods at the time and place of their receipt (subject, in most cases, to the buyer or lessee's right to inspect). When a sale is on credit, a buyer must pay according to credit terms, not when the goods are received. Credit terms may provide for payment within thirty days, for example. A credit period usually begins on the date of shipment.
7. T
8. T
9. F. Warranties are not exclusive. A contract can include an implied warranty of merchantability, an implied warranty of fitness for a particular purpose, and any number of express warranties.
10. F. Courts usually do enforce click-on agreements. The reasoning is that the click-on terms constitute an offer, proposed by a seller and accepted by a buyer after the buyer had an opportunity to review the terms by an act of active consent (unlike a situation involving browse-wrap terms, which sellers argue are binding without the buyer's active consent).

Fill-in Questions

conforming; and; buyer; receipt; unless

Multiple-Choice Questions

1. A. Under the UCC, a sales contract will not fail for indefiniteness even if one or more terms are left open, as long as the parties intended to make a contract and there is a reasonably certain basis for the court to grant an appropriate remedy. If the price term is left open, for example, and the parties cannot later agree on a price, a court will set the price according to what is reasonable at the time for delivery. If one of the parties is to set the price, it must be set in good faith. If it is not fixed, the other party can set the price or treat the contract as canceled.
2. D. In a transaction between merchants, additional terms in the acceptance of an offer become part of a contract *unless* they qualify as one of these exceptions.
3. C. A firm offer can only be made by a merchant in a signed writing. The other party does not need to be a merchant. Consideration is not necessary, and no definite period need be specified. This question and answer are based on a question that appeared in the CPA exam in November 1995.
4. C. A buyer (or lessee) can sue for damages when a seller (or lessor) repudiates the contract or fails to deliver the goods, or when the buyer has rightfully rejected or revoked acceptance of the goods. The place for determining the price is the place at which the seller was to deliver the goods. The buyer may also recover incidental and consequential damages, less expenses saved due to the breach.
5. A. If, before the time of performance, a party to a contract informs the other party that he or she will not

perform, the nonbreaching party can treat the repudiation as a final breach and seek a remedy or wait, for a commercially reasonable time, hoping that the breaching party will decide to honor the contract. In either case, the nonbreaching party can suspend his or her performance.

6.   C. The parties to a contract can stipulate the time, place, and manner of delivery. In the absence of specified details, however, tender of delivery must be at a reasonable hour and in a reasonable manner. The buyer must be notified, and the goods must be kept available for a reasonable time.

7.   C. Depending on the circumstances, when a seller or lessor delivers nonconforming goods, the buyer or lessee can reject the part of the goods that does not conform (and rescind the contract or obtain cover). The buyer or lessee may instead revoke acceptance, or he or she may recover damages, for accepted goods.

8.   C. If a lessee (or buyer) wrongfully refuses to accept, the lessor (or seller) can recover the difference between the contract price and the market price (at the time and place of tender), plus incidental damages. If the market price is less than the contract price, the lessor (or seller) can recover lost profits.

9.   A. This phrase, or similar language, will generally disclaim most implied warranties. To specifically disclaim an implied warranty of fitness for a particular purpose, a writing must be conspicuous, but the word *fitness* does not have to be used. A specific disclaimer of the implied warranty of merchantability must mention *merchantability*. Note that warranties of title can be disclaimed only by specific language (for example, a seller states that it is transferring only such rights as it has in the goods), or by circumstances that indicate no warranties of title are made.

10.   D. To fall under the UETA, the parties to a contract must agree to conduct their transaction electronically. The UETA then applies in the absence of an agreement between the parties to the contrary, although they can waive or vary any or all of its provisions. Whether the contract involves computer information is irrelevant under the UETA.

Starbucks Coffee Co. International Sales Contract Applications

1.   B. As stated in the "Breach or Default of Contract" clause on the second page, this contract is subject to Article 2 of the UCC. If the parties to a sales contract do not express some of the terms in writing, including the price term, the contract is still enforceable. A sales contract that must be in writing is only enforceable, however, to the extent of the quantity stated in writing. If these parties did not state the amount of product ordered, the contract may not be enforced because if a quantity term were left out, a court would have no basis for determining a remedy.

2.   B. When a seller, as a party to a sales contract, states or otherwise expresses what the goods will be, then the goods must be that. The goods must at least conform to the seller's description of them, wherever that descriptions is, whether in the contract, in promotional materials, on labels, by salespersons, by comparison to a sample, etc. A seller's subjective belief is not the standard. The buyer's subjective belief may be the standard if the contract specifies that the goods must personally satisfy the buyer.

3.   C. This clause states the terms for payment under this sales contract and indicates that the buyer has two days after the day of tender in which to pay for the goods or will be considered in breach. The "BREACH OR DEFAULT OF CONTRACT" clause sets out what happens "if either party hereto fails to perform." These are all incentives for the buyer to pay on time.

4.   A. This clause allows the buyer to reject nonconforming product, although this is limited to a specific number of days. (Note that the buyer' right to reject does not need to be stated in a contract for the buyer to have that right.) This clause details the procedures that the parties may follow if the product does not meet its description. These are incentives for the seller to deliver conforming goods.

5.   D. This is a destination contract, as indicated by the "ARRIVAL," "DELIVERY," "INSURANCE," and "FREIGHT" clauses. This means that the seller bears the risk of loss until the coffee is delivered to its destination (a "Bonded Public Warehouse" in Laredo, Texas).

Issue Spotters

1.   A shipment of nonconforming goods constitutes an acceptance and a breach, unless the seller seasonably notifies the buyer that the nonconforming shipment does not constitute an acceptance and is offered only as an accommodation. Without the notification, the shipment is an acceptance and a breach. Thus, here, the shipment was both an acceptance and a breach.

2.   The buyer can recover the difference between the market price—at the time that the buyer learned of the breach, at the place for tender—and the contract price, plus incidental damages (reasonable expenses incident to the breach) and consequential damages (of which the seller knew at the time of the breach), less any expenses saved by the breach. Thus, in this problem, the buyer can recover $2,000 ($10,000 x $.20), plus incidental damages and consequential damages (for the halt to the buyer's operation), less any expenses saved by the breach.

3.   No, at least not on this ground. Merchantable food means food that is fit to eat. Food containing cholesterol is merchantable—that is, it is fit to eat—if it is similar to all other food of the kind on the market.

Chapter 11

True-False Questions

1. F. A sole proprietorship is the simplest form of business organization. In a sole proprietorship, the owner and the business are the same. Anyone who creates a business without designating a specific form for its organization is doing business as a sole proprietorship.

2. T

3. F. A franchisor can exercise greater control in this area than in some other areas of the business, because the *franchisor* has a legitimate interest in maintaining the quality of the product or service to protect its name and reputation.

4. F. One of the chief advantages of a limited liability company (LLC) is that it offers the limited liability of a corporation. Because an LLC also offers the tax advantages of a partnership, many businesses are using this form of organization.

5. F. A corporation formed in a country other than the United States, but that does business in the United States, is an alien corporation. A foreign corporation is a corporation formed in one state, but doing business in another state.

6. F. An S corporation has tax imposed only at the shareholder level. Other corporations are subject to double taxation, however, which was one of the reasons for the enactment of the S corporation statute. Only corporations with seventy-five or fewer shareholders can qualify for S-corporation status, although in some circumstances, a corporation can be an S-corporation shareholder.

7. F. Any damages recovered in a shareholder's derivative suit are normally paid to the corporation on whose behalf the shareholder or shareholders exercised the derivative right.

8. T

9. F. Officers and directors owe the same fiduciary duties to the corporations for which they work. They both owe a duty of loyalty. This duty requires them to subordinate their personal interests to the welfare of the corporation.

10. F. The business judgment rule immunizes directors (and officers) from liability for poor business decisions and other honest mistakes that cause a corporation to suffer a loss. Directors are not immunized from losses that do not fit this category, however.

Fill-in Questions

but ownership is not; can; recorded as the owner in the corporation's books

Multiple-Choice Questions

1. D. There are no limits on the liability of the owner of a sole proprietorship for the debts and obligations of the firm. A sole proprietorship has greater organizational flexibility, however, than other forms of business organization.

2. B. A partnership arises from an agreement between two or more persons to carry on a business for profit. No formal declaration is necessary. A proprietorship can have only a single owner. A corporation can be formed only through compliance with specific formalities.

3. C. A franchisee may have some protection under the Franchise Rule of the Federal Trade Commission with respect to what the franchisor must disclose, and how and when the disclosure must be made, before the franchisee invests in a franchise. A franchisee may have additional protection under federal law, depending on the nature of the products or services being sold. State protection, while similar to federal law, may include more protection under deceptive practices acts or Article 2 of the UCC.

4. B. A limited liability company (LLC) can be taxed as a partnership, a sole proprietorship (if there is only one member), or a corporation, but when there is more than on member, electing to be taxed as a partnership is generally preferable. The income can be passed through to its members without being taxed at the company level. Generally, there is no particular advantage to being taxed as a corporation. In fact, avoiding the double corporate tax is one reason for forming an LLC.

5. A. Dividends may be paid from a limited number of sources and once declared, a dividend becomes a debt enforceable at law like any other debt. Generally, state law allows dividends to be paid as long as a corporation can pay its other debts as they come due and the amount of the dividend is not more than the net worth of the corporation. But shareholders are not entitled to the payment of dividends. Their payment is at the discretion of the board of directors, who may choose not to order a dividend.

6. A. Officers and other executive employees are hired by a corporation's board of directors. The rights of the officers and other high-level managers are defined by their employment contracts with the corporation.

7. D. The other choices do not represent proper purposes for which a shareholders' derivative suit may be filed. A shareholder's derivative suit is a claim filed on behalf of the corporation. Such a suit may allege, for example, that officers or directors misused corporate assets. Of course, any damages that are awarded must be paid to the corporation.

8. C. Cumulative voting can often be used in the election of directors to enhance the power of minority shareholders in electing a representative. In calculating a shareholder's votes under the cumulative voting method, in this problem, Mary's number of shares is multiplied by the number of directors to be elected.

9.   A. The board of directors hires the company's officers and other managerial employees, and determines their compensation. Ultimate responsibility for all policy decisions necessary to the management of corporate affairs also rests with the directors.

10   A. Other factors that a court may use to pierce the corporate veil include that a party is tricked or misled into dealing with the firm rather than the individual, that the firm is too thinly capitalized (not overcapitalized), and that the firm holds too few (not too many) shareholders' meetings.

Issue Spotters

1.   Too much control may result in the franchisor's liability for torts of a franchisee's employees. For example, if the employee performs in a manner that is attributed to the control of the franchisor, and this performance results in an injury to another, the franchisor may be held liable.

2.   Under these circumstances, a minority shareholder can petition a court to appoint and receiver and liquidate the assets of the corporation.

3.   Yes. A shareholder can bring a derivative suit on behalf of a corporation, if some wrong is done to the corporation. Normally, any damages recovered go into the corporate treasury.

Chapter 12

True-False Questions

1.   F. A mechanic's lien involves real property. An artisan's lien or an innkeeper's lien involves personal property.

2.   F. This is prohibited under federal law. Garnishment of an employee's wages for any one indebtedness cannot be a ground for dismissal of an employee.

3.   T

4.   T

5.   F. This is the most important concept in suretyship: a surety can use any defenses available to a debtor (except personal defenses) to avoid liability on the obligation to the creditor. Note, though, that a debtor does need not to have defaulted on the underlying obligation before a surety can be required to answer for the debt. Before a *guarantor* can be required to answer for the debt of a debtor, the debtor must have defaulted on the underlying obligation, however.

6.   T

7.   F. Any individual can be a debtor under Chapter 7, and any debtor who is liable on a claim held by a creditor may file for bankruptcy under Chapter 7. A debtor does not have to be insolvent.

8.   T

9.   F. Under Chapter 11, the creditors and the debtor formulate a plan under which the debtor pays some of the debts, the other debts are discharged, and the debtor is then allowed to continue the operation of his or her business.

10.   F. Some small businesses—those who do not own or manage real estate and do not have debts of more than $2 million—can choose to avoid creditors' committees under Chapter 11. Those who choose to do so, however, are subject to shorter deadlines with respect to filing a reorganization plan.

Fill-in Questions

contract of suretyship; surety; surety; guaranty contract; guarantor

Multiple-Choice Questions

1.   B. The creditor in this problem can use prejudgment attachment. Attachment occurs at the time of or immediately after commencement of a suit but before entry of a final judgment. The court issues a writ of attachment, directing the sheriff or other officer to seize property belonging to the debtor. If the creditor prevails at trial, the property can be sold to satisfy the judgment. (A writ of execution can be used after all of the conditions represented by the answer choices in this problem have been met.)

2.   D. The creditor can use garnishment, a collection remedy directed at a debtor's property or rights held by a third person. A garnishment order can be served on the employer so that part of debtor's paycheck will be paid to the creditor.

3.   C. The debt is $200,000. The amount of the homestead exemption ($50,000) is subtracted from the sale price of the house ($150,000), and the remainder ($100,000) is applied against the debt. Proceeds from the sale of any nonexempt personal property could also be applied against the debt. The debtor gets the amount of the homestead exemption, of course.

4.   B. A guarantor is secondarily liable (that is, the principal must first default). Also, in this problem, if the officer were, for example, the borrower's only salaried employee, the guaranty would not have to be in writing under the main-purpose exception to the Statute of Frauds. A surety is primarily liable (that is, the creditor can look to the surety for payment as soon as the debt is due, whether or not the principal debtor has defaulted). Usually, also, in the case of a guarantor, a creditor must have attempted to collect from the principal, because usually a debtor would not otherwise be declared in default.

5.   C. A guarantor has the right of subrogation when he or she pays the debt owed to the creditor. This means that any right the creditor had against the debtor becomes the right of the guarantor. A guaran-

tor also has the right of contribution, when there are one or more other guarantors. This means that if he or she pays more than his or her proportionate share on a debtor's default, the guarantor is entitled to recover from the others the amount paid above the guarantor's obligation. This problem illustrates how these principles work.

6. D. Under Chapter 11, creditors and debtor plan for the debtor to pay some debts, be discharged of the rest, and continue in business. Under Chapter 13, with an appropriate plan, a small business debtor can also pay some (or all) debts, be discharged of the rest, and continue in business. A petition for a discharge in bankruptcy under Chapter 11 may be filed by a sole proprietor, a partnership, or a corporation; a petition for a discharge under Chapter 13, however, may be filed only by a sole proprietor, among these business entities, subject to certain debt maximums.

7. D. Claims that are not dischargeable in bankruptcy include the claims listed in the other answer choices: claims for back taxes accruing within three years before the bankruptcy, claims for domestic support, and claims for most student loans (unless their payment would result in undue hardship to the debtor, as stated in the correct answer choice). There are many other debts that are not dischargeable in bankruptcy.

8. A. Other grounds on which a discharge may be denied include concealing property with the intent to defraud a creditor, fraudulently destroying financial records, and refusing to obey a lawful court order. Having obtained a discharge in bankruptcy within the eight previous years is also a ground for denial. The other choices represent individual debts that are not dischargeable in bankruptcy, but they are not grounds for denying a discharge altogether.

9. C. The first unsecured debts to be paid are domestic support obligations, subject to certain administrative costs, and then other administrative expenses of the bankruptcy proceeding. Among the debts listed in this problem, the order of priority is unpaid wages, consumer deposits, and taxes. Each class of creditors is fully paid before the next class is entitled to anything.

10. D. Most corporations can file for bankruptcy under Chapter 7 or 11. The same principles that govern liquidation cases generally govern reorganizations as well. Corporate debtors most commonly file petitions for bankruptcy under Chapter 11. One important difference between the two chapters is that in a Chapter 11 proceeding, the debtor can continue in business.

Issue Spotters

1. Larry and Midwest can place a mechanic's lien on Joe's property. If Joe does not pay what he owes, the property can be sold to satisfy the debt. The only requirements are that the lien be filed within a specific time from the time of the work, depending on the state statute, and notice of the foreclosure and sale must be given to Joe in advance.

2. Yes. In this problem, the party who assured the lender of payment on behalf of the debtor is a surety. A surety has a right of reimbursement from the debtor for all outlays the surety makes, as here, on behalf of the suretyship arrangement.

3. Yes. A debtor's payment to a creditor made for a preexisting debt, within ninety days (one year in the case of an insider or fraud) of a bankruptcy filing, can be recovered if it gives a creditor more than he or she would have received in the bankruptcy proceedings. A trustee can recover this preference using his or her specific avoidance powers.

Cumulative Hypothetical Problem for Unit Three—Including Chapters 7–12

1. B. Intellectual property law protects such intangible rights as copyrights, trademarks, and patents, which include the rights that an individual or business firm has in the products it produces. Protection for software comes from patent law and from copyright law. Protection for the distinguishing trademarks on the software comes from, of course, trademark law.

2. D. An offeror can revoke an offer for a bilateral contract, which is what this offer is, any time before it is accepted. This may be after the offeree is aware of the offer.

3. C. The modification would not be considered a rejection. Under UCC 2–207, a merchant can add an additional term to a contract, with his or her acceptance, as part of the contract, unless the offeror expressly states otherwise.

4. B. Only a debtor can file a plan under Chapter 11, but for the court to confirm it, the secured creditors must accept it. There is another condition that the plan must meet. It must provide that the creditors retain their liens and the value of the property to be distributed to them is not less than the secured portion of their claims, or the debtor must surrender to the creditors the property securing those claims.

5. A. A Chapter 11 plan must provide for the full payment of all claims entitled to priority and the same treatment of each claim within a particular class. After the payments are completed, all debts provided for by the plan are discharged.

Chapter 13

True-False Questions

1. T
2. T
3. T
4. F. An agent is liable for his or her own torts, but a principal may also be liable under the doctrine of *re-*

spondeat superior. The key is whether the tort is committed within the scope of employment. One of the important factors is whether the act that constituted the tort was authorized by the principal.

5.   T

6.   T

7.   F. The Electronic Communications Privacy Act prohibits the interception of telephone (and other electronic) communications. Some courts recognize an exception for employers monitoring employee business-related calls, but monitoring personal conversations is not permitted.

8.   F. These laws do not cover all employees. Although statutes vary in their coverage from state to state, they often exclude domestic workers (such as maids), agricultural workers, temporary employees, and employees of common carriers (such as trucking companies).

9.   T

10. F. Under the Fair Labor Standards Act, minors (persons under the age of eighteen) cannot work in hazardous occupations.

Fill-in Questions

performance; notification; loyalty; obedience; accounting

Multiple-Choice Questions

1.   A. There is a long list of factors that courts can consider in determining whether an individual is an employee or an independent contractor, and all of the choices in this question are among those factors. The most important factor, however, is the degree of control that the employer has over the details of the work.

2.   A. An agent's duties to a principal include a duty to act solely in the principal's interest in matters concerning the principal's business. This is the duty of loyalty. The agent must act solely in the principal's interest and not in the interest of the agent, or some other party. It is also a breach of the duty of loyalty to use a principal's trade secrets or other confidential information (but not acquired skills) even after the agency has terminated.

3.   C. When an agent acts within the scope of his or her authority to enter into a valid contract on behalf of an undisclosed principal, the principal is liable on the contract. Ratification is not necessary. The agent may also be liable on the contract.

4.   A. Apparent authority exists when a principal causes a third party reasonably to believe that an agent has the authority to act, even if the agent does not otherwise have the authority to do so. If the third party changes positions in reliance on the principal's representation, the principal may be estopped from denying the authority. Thus, here, the principal could not hold the customers liable for failing to pay.

5.   C. An agent (or employee) is liable for his or her own torts, whether or not they were committed within the scope of a principal's employment. The principal is also liable under the doctrine of *respondeat superior* when a tort is within the scope of the employment. One of the important factors in determining liability is whether the agent was on the principal's business or on a "frolic of his or her own."

6.   A. Child-labor, minimum-wage, and maximum-hour provisions are included in the Fair Labor Standards Act (also known as the Wage-Hour Law), covering virtually all employees. The employer may also be subject to the other laws given as choices in this problem, but those laws concern other rights and duties of employees and employers.

7.   B. Intentionally inflicted injuries are not covered by workers' compensation. Many states cover problems arising out of preexisting conditions, but that is not part of the test for coverage. To collect benefits, an employee must notify the employer of an injury and file a claim with the appropriate state agency.

8.   C. The Federal Unemployment Tax Act of 1935 concerns the system that provides unemployment compensation. The Employee Retirement Income Security Act (ERISA) of 1974 concerns the regulation of private pension plans. There is no "Employee Payments Act" that covers any of these subjects.

9.   B. The Employment Retirement Income Security Act (ERISA) covers such employers. The Labor Management Services Administration of the U.S. Department of Labor enforces ERISA. Most of the other laws mentioned in the choices in this problem regulate other areas of retirement and security income. There is no "Employer Payments Act" that covers any of these subjects.

10. B. Under the Family and Medical Leave Act (FMLA) of 1993, employees can take up to twelve weeks of family or medical leave during any twelve-month period and are entitled to continued health insurance coverage during the leave. Employees are also guaranteed the same, or a comparable, job on returning to work.

Issue Spotters

1.   Yes. A principal has a duty to indemnify an agent for liabilities incurred because of authorized and lawful acts and transactions and for losses suffered because of the principal's failure to perform his or her duties.

2.   No. An agent is prohibited from taking advantage of the agency relationship to obtain property that the principal wants to purchase. This is the duty of loyalty that arises with every agency relationship.

3.   No. Generally, the right to recover under workers' compensation laws is determined without regard to negligence or fault. Unlike the potential for recovery in a lawsuit based on negligence or fault, however,

recovery under a workers' compensation statute is limited to the specific amount designated in the statute for the employee's injury.

Chapter 14

True-False Questions

1. T
2. F. An employer may be liable even though an employee did the harassing, if the employer knew, or should have known, and failed to take corrective action, or if the employee was in a supervisory position.
3. F. Just as an employer may be liable for an employee's misconduct, the employer may be liable for harassment by a nonemployee, if the employer knew, or should have known, and failed to take corrective action.
4. T
5. T
6. T
7. F. If the Equal Employment Opportunity Commission (EEOC) decides not pursue a claim, the victim can file a suit against alleged violator. The EEOC can pursue a claim in federal district court, however, in its own name against alleged violators. The EEOC can also intervene in a suit filed by a private party.
8. F. Title VII covers only employers with fifteen or more employees, labor unions with fifteen or more members, labor unions that operate hiring halls, employment agencies, and federal, state, and local agencies.
9. T
10. T

Fill-In Questions

can; may sue if a settlement between the parties is not reached; reinstatement, back pay, and retroactive promotions

Multiple-Choice Questions

1. A. Before filing a lawsuit, the best step for a person who believes that they may be a victim of discrimination is to contact a state or federal agency to see whether their claim is justified. The appropriate federal agency is the Equal Employment Opportunity Commission. Most states have similar agencies that evaluate claims under state law.
2. A. Sexual harassment occurs when, in a workplace, an employee is subject to comments or contact that is perceived as sexually offensive. An employer may be liable even though an employee did the harassing. If the employee was in a supervisory position, as in this problem, for an employer to be held liable, a tangible employment action may need to be proved. Here, the employee's pay was cut.
3. A. The other choices would not subject the employer to liability under the Age Discrimination in Employment Act (ADEA). Discrimination is prohibited against persons forty years of age or older, even if the discrimination is unintentional. Mandatory retirement may be instituted, but not on account of an employee's age, and an employee may be discharged for cause at any age.
4. C. The employer's best defense in this problem would be that being able to pass the tests is a business necessity—it is a necessary requirement for the job. Discrimination may be illegal even if it is not intentional, and whether or not all men pass the tests is not relevant to whether there is discrimination against women. If the employer hires some women for the job, it could not argue successfully that gender is a BFOQ for the job.
5. C. An employer who is subject to the Americans with Disabilities Act cannot exclude arbitrarily a person who, with reasonable accommodation, could do what is required of a job. A disabled individual is not required to reasonably accommodate an employer. Also, the standard is not "significant additional costs," to either the employer or the disabled individual.
6. C. Title VII prohibits employment discrimination on the basis of race. This includes discriminating against members of a minority with darker skin than other members of the same minority. Title VII also prohibits using physical characteristics that are typical of some races to distinguish applicants or employees.
7. C. Title VII prohibits showing a preference for members of one minority over members of another. Title VII also prohibits making distinctions according to the race of a person's spouse, friends, or other contacts. The other laws mentioned in the answer choices prohibit discrimination on the basis of age and disability, respectively, as suggested by their titles.
8. C. The Equal Pay Act of 1963 prohibits gender-based discrimination in wages for equal work. Different wages are acceptable because of any factor but gender, including seniority and merit.
9. C. Here, the employer would seem to have a valid business necessity defense. It appears reasonable that administrative assistants be able to type. An employer can insist that, to be hired, a job applicant possess the actual skills required for a job. Except for an applicant's willingness or unwillingness to acquire certain skills, the other answer choices might be legitimate defenses in other circumstances.
10. A. The Age Discrimination in Employment Act (ADEA) of 1967 requires, for the establishment of a *prima facie* case, that at the time of the alleged discrimination, the plaintiff was forty or older, was qualified for the job, and was discharged or otherwise rejected in circumstances that imply discrimination. The difference between a *prima facie* case under the ADEA

and under Title VII is that the ADEA does not require a plaintiff to show that someone who is not a member of a protected class filled the position at the center of the claim.

Issue Spotters

1. Yes, if he is a member of a protected class. These circumstances would then include all of the elements of a *prima facie* under Title VII of the Civil Rights Act of 1964: (1) the applicant is a member of a protected class, (2) he applied and was qualified for an open position, (3) he was rejected, and (4) the employer continued to seek applicants or filled the position with a person who is not in a protected class. The employer would then have to offer a legitimate reason for its action, and the applicant would have to show that this is a pretext, that discriminatory intent was the motivation.

2. Yes. One type of sexual harassment occurs when a request for sexual favors is a condition of employment, and the person making the request is a supervisor or acts with the authority of the employer. A tangible employment action, such as continued employment, may also lead to the employer's liability for the supervisor's conduct. That the injured employee is a male and the supervisor a female, instead of the other way around, would not affect the outcome. Same-gender harassment is also actionable.

3. Yes, if she can show that she was not hired solely because of her disability. The other elements for a discrimination suit based on a disability are that the plaintiff (1) has a disability and (2) is otherwise qualified for the job. Both of these elements appear to be satisfied in this problem.

Chapter 15

True-False Questions

1. F. Secondary boycotts, including hot-cargo agreements, which are described in the question, are illegal.
2. F. It is the central legal right of a *union* to serve as the bargaining representative of employees in negotiations with management, not the other way around, as set out in this question.
3. T
4. F. Employees' right to engage in collective bargaining through elected representatives, like their right to organize and their right to engage in concerted activities for those and other purposes, was established in the National Labor Relations Act.
5. T
6. T
7. T

8. F. A lockout is a shut down to prevent employees from working. An employer cannot use this tactic to break a union or to pressure employees into decertifying it.
9. T
10. T

Fill-in Questions

Norris-LaGuardia; National Labor Relations; Relations; allows; prohibits

Multiple-Choice Questions

1. D. It is not a violation of any of these laws *not* to pay workers for time spent on union activities (going to meetings, soliciting support, canvassing co-workers, and so on). In fact, paying workers for participating in union activities is an unfair labor practice because it is considered to be giving support to the union.
2. B. The National Labor Relations Act protects employees who engage in union activity and prohibits employers from refusing to bargain with employees' designated representative. Firing workers for supporting or joining a union is an unfair labor practice, as is refusing to recognize and bargain with the union.
3. C. It is an unfair labor practice to ask employees to declare their views on a union without anonymity. An employer can poll its employees during a unionization campaign, or any time, only if their identities are protected.
4. D. An employer cannot refuse to negotiate in good faith, during collective bargaining, over either of these terms and conditions of employment. They are mandatory subjects for collective bargaining. Because an employer must agree to talk about these subjects does not mean that the employer must accept the union's position on the topics, however.
5. A. Management is not required to bargain with a union over a decision to close a facility—although an employer may bargain over this topic if it chooses to do so. (Economic consequences of the decision must be bargained over, however.) On the other hand, the procedure for employee grievances is an appropriate subject for the bargaining table.
6. C. Denying nonunion workers access to a plant is illegal, whether or not the occasion is a strike and regardless of whether the nonunion workers are replacement workers for the strikers, regular company employees, supervisors, or managers.
7. D. It is not an unfair labor practice to do either of the activities described in this problem. The picketers cannot keep others who wish to enter the workplace from going in, however, nor can they use violence or threats of violence. Also, striking workers cannot picket the worksite of a secondary employer.
8. D. This question may seem difficult because it is phrased in the negative, but none of these choices represent unfair labor practices. Campaigning against a

union during a union election campaign is not an unfair labor practice. Furthermore, an employer can campaign against a union without giving the union any opportunity for rebuttal. An employer can also make an election speech within twenty-four hours of an election if the employees are not required to listen but can attend voluntarily on their own time.

9.   D. It is an unfair labor practice for an employer to threaten employees with the loss of their jobs if a union wins a scheduled union election. What can be difficult is determining what constitutes a threat. Explicit statements, such as "if the union wins, you're all fired," are obvious violations. Less clear is whether such a statement as "if the union wins, we will lose business to our competitors" is a violation. The point, however, is that an employer cannot require rejection of a union as a condition of employment. The other choices are, of course, not unfair labor practices.

10.   D. An employer can hire permanent replacement workers during an economic strike. After the strike, the replacement workers do not have to be fired to make way for the strikers. Temporary replacement workers may be hired during any strike.

Issue Spotters

1.   No. A closed shop (a company that requires union membership as a condition of employment) is illegal. A union shop (a company that does not require union membership as a condition of employment but requires workers to join the union after a certain time on the job) is illegal in a state with a right-to-work law, which makes it illegal to require union membership for continued employment.

2.   Yes. If the employee complains, the employer can be required to show that it did not have an unlawful discriminatory motive. Factors to be considered in determining motive include whether the employer applied its rules inconsistently and, in particular, more strictly against union advocates.

3.   Yes. An action by a single employee is protected concerted activity if it is taken for the benefit of other employees, if the employee discussed the action with other approving workers, and if the employer is aware that it is concerted activity taken with the assent of other workers.

Cumulative Hypothetical Problem for Unit Four—Including Chapters 13–15

1.   B. The requirements for recovery under state workers' compensation laws include the existence of an employment relationship and an accidental injury that occurs on the job or within the scope of employment. Accepting benefits precludes an employee from suing his or her employer, but it does not bar the employee from suing a third party for causing the injury.

2.   D. The Social Security Act of 1935 provides payments for persons who are retired or disabled. The Social Security Administration is a federal agency that also administers the Medicare program. Unemployment benefits, however, are part of a state system created by the Federal Unemployment Tax Act of 1935.

3.   D. One of the agent's fiduciary duties to the principal is the duty of loyalty. This means that the agent must not engage in conflicts of interest, and the agent cannot compete with the principal without informing the principal of the conflict of interest and obtaining the principal's consent.

4.   A. Title VII of the Civil Rights Act of 1964 covers many forms of discrimination, including discrimination based on gender, race, religion, color, and national origin. But Title VII does not prohibit discrimination based on age, which is the subject of the Age Discrimination in Employment Act of 1967.

5.   B. The Age Discrimination in Employment Act of 1967 prohibits discrimination against persons aged forty or more. This includes mandatory retirement of such individuals. In most circumstances, however, an employer can discharge an employee for cause, regardless of his or her age, without running afoul of this, or any other, federal anti-discrimination law.

Chapter 16

True-False Questions

1.   T

2.   T

3.   T

4.   F. Agencies formulate and issue their rules under the authority of Congress. These rules are as legally binding as the laws enacted by Congress. It is for this reason, in part, that rulemaking procedures generally include opportunities for public comment, that the rules are subject to review by the courts, and that agencies are subject to other controls by the three branches of government.

5.   F. Appeal is not mandatory, although either side may appeal, to the agency commission or ultimately to a federal court. If there is no appeal, the initial order becomes final.

6.   F. Congress can influence agency policy in several ways. These include that Congress can create or abolish an agency, or influence policy by the appropriation of funds for certain purposes. Congress can also revise the functions of an agency.

7.   T

8.   T

9.   F. State and federal agency actions often parallel each other. When there is a conflict, the supremacy clause of the Constitution requires that the federal agency's operation prevail over an inconsistent state agency's action.

10. F. In most circumstances, a warrant is required for a search. Warrants are not required, however, to conduct searches in businesses in highly regulated industries, in certain hazardous operations, and in emergencies.

Fill-in Questions

Federal Register; anyone; must; *Federal Register*

Multiple-Choice Questions

1. D. Agency powers include functions associated with the legislature (rulemaking), executive branch (investigation), and courts (adjudication). Under Article I of the U.S. Constitution and the delegation doctrine, Congress has the power to establish administrative agencies and delegate any or all of these powers to those agencies.

2. C. Agencies may obtain information through subpoenas or searches. A subpoena may compel the appearance of a witness (a subpoena *ad testificandum*) or the provision of certain documents and records (a subpoena *duces tecum*). In some cases, particularly searches of businesses involved in highly regulated industries, searches may be conducted without warrants.

3. C. Procedures vary widely among agencies, even within agencies, but under the Administrative Procedure Act, rulemaking typically includes these steps: notice, opportunity for comment, and publication in the *Federal Register* of a final draft of the rule.

4. C. An agency has the authority to issue subpoenas. There are limits on agency demands for information, however. An investigation must have a legitimate purpose. The information that is sought must be relevant. The party from whom the information is sought must not be unduly burdened by the request. And the demand must be specific.

5. D. The president's veto is a method by which the authority of an agency can be checked or curtailed. The limits listed in the other responses in this question are choices available to Congress to limit the authority of administrative agencies.

6. B. The Government-in-the-Sunshine Act requires "every portion of every meeting of an agency" that is headed by a "collegial body" to be open to "public observation." The Freedom of Information Act requires the federal government to disclose certain records to persons on request, with some exceptions. The Regulatory Flexibility Act requires, among other things, analyses of new regulations in certain circumstances. The Small Business Regulatory Enforcement Fairness Act covers several matters important to businesses, including the federal courts' authority to en-

force the Regulatory Flexibility Act, but it does not cover the opening of agency meetings to the public.

7. C. The Administrative Procedure Act provides for court review of most agency actions, but first a party must exhaust all other means of resolving a controversy with an agency. Also, under the ripeness doctrine, the agency action must be ripe for review: the action must be reviewable (which agency actions presumably are), the party must have standing, and an actual controversy must be at issue.

8. A. This is the "arbitrary and capricious" test under which acts committed willfully, unreasonable, and without considering the facts can be overturned. (The other choices are not legitimate grounds for judicial review.) A court may also consider whether the agency has exceeded its authority or violated any constitutional provisions. Depending on the circumstances, when a court reviews an act of an administrative agency, the court may also determine whether the agency has properly interpreted laws applicable to the action under review, acted in accord with procedural requirements, or reached conclusions that are not supported by substantial evidence.

9. B. After an agency publishes notice of a proposed rule, any interested parties can express their views in writing, or orally if a hearing is held. The agency must respond to all significant comments by modifying the final rule or explaining, in the statement accompanying the final rule, why it did not modify the rule in response to the comments.

10. B. An administrative law judge (ALJ) presides over hearings when cases are brought to the agency. Like other judges, an ALJ has the power to administer oaths, take testimony, rule on questions of evidence, and make determinations of fact. It is important to note that an ALJ works for the agency but must not be biased in the agency's favor. There are provisions in the Administrative Procedure Act to prevent the bias, and to otherwise promote the fairness, of the ALJs, for example by prohibiting *ex parte* comments to the ALJ from any party to the proceeding.

Issue Spotters

1. Checks against the arbitrary use of agency power include the courts' power to review agency actions. Congress also has considerable power over agencies. Among other things, Congress can create, restrict, or abolish an agency. Congress can also limit the funds that it appropriates to an agency. The president can exercise control over a federal agency through the appointment of its officers.

2. Under the Administrative Procedure Act (APA), the ALJ must be separate from the agency's investigative and prosecutorial staff. *Ex parte* communications between the ALJ and a party to a proceeding are prohibited. Under the APA, an ALJ is exempt from agency discipline except on a showing of good cause.

3. A formal adjudicatory hearing resembles a trial in that, in both types of proceedings, the parties can undertake extensive discovery (involving depositions, interrogatories, and so on), and during the hearing they may give testimony, present other evidence, and cross-examine witnesses. An administrative proceeding differs from a trial in that in the former, more information, including hearsay, can be introduced as evidence.

Chapter 17

True-False Questions

1. T
2. T
3. F. Under certain circumstances, consumers have a right to rescind their contracts. This is particularly true when a creditor has not made all required disclosures. A contract entered into as part of a door-to-door sale may be rescinded within three days, regardless of the reason.
4. T
5. F. A consumer can also include a note in his or her credit file to explain any misinformation in the file. Under the Fair Credit Reporting Act, consumers are entitled to have deleted from their files any misinformation that leads to a denial of credit, employment, or insurance. Consumers are also entitled to receive information about the source of the misinformation and about anyone who was given the misinformation.
6. T
7. F. The Fair Debt Collection Practices Act applies only to debt collectors that attempt to collect debts on another party's behalf. Typically, the collector is paid a commission—a percentage of the amount owed or collected—for a successful collection effort.
8. F. The Federal Trade Commission (FTC), the Federal Reserve Board of Governors (Fed), and other federal agencies regulate the terms and conditions of sales. For example, the FTC issues regulations covering warranties and labels, and the Fed regulates credit provisions in sales contracts.
9. F. One who leases consumer goods in the ordinary course of their business must disclose *all* material terms in writing—clearly and conspicuously—if the goods are priced at $25,000 or less and the lease term exceeds four months. The Consumer Leasing Act of 1988 requires this.
10. T

Fill-in Questions

$50; before; prohibits; from billing; if

Multiple-Choice Questions

1. D. The FTC has the power to issue a cease-and-desist order, but in some cases, such an order is not enough to stop the harm. With counteradvertising (also known as corrective advertising), an advertiser attempts to correct earlier misinformation by admitting that prior claims about a product were untrue.
2. B. A regular-size box of laundry soap, for example, cannot be labeled "super-size" to exaggerate the amount of product in the box. Labels on consumer goods must identify the product, the manufacturer, the distributor, the net quantity of the contents, and the quantity of each serving (if the number of servings is given). Other information may also be required.
3. B. In a door-to-door sale, a consumer generally has at least a three-day cooling-off period within which to rescind the transaction. Salespersons are required to give consumers written notice of this right. If a sales presentation is to a consumer who speaks only Spanish, the notice must be in Spanish, too.
4. C. Under the Fair Debt Collection Practices Act, once a debtor has refused to pay a debt, a collection agency can contact the debtor *only* to advise him or her of further action to be taken. None of the rest of these choices would be legitimate possibilities.
5. B. This is required under Regulation Z (which was issued by the Federal Reserve Board under the Truth in Lending Act) and applies to any creditor who, in the ordinary course of business, lends money or sells goods on credit to consumers, or arranges for credit for consumers. The information that must be disclosed includes: the specific dollar amount being financed; the annual percentage rate of interest; any financing charges, premiums or points; the number, amounts, and due dates of payments; and any penalties imposed on delinquent payments or prepayment.
6. D. When contracting parties are subject to the Truth-in-Lending Act (TILA), Regulation Z applies to any transaction involving an installment sales contract in which payment is to be made in more than four installments. Normally, such loans as those described in this problem require more than four installments to repay. In any transaction subject to Regulation Z, the lender must disclose all of the credit terms clearly and conspicuously.
7. C. The Fair Packaging and Labeling Act requires that products include a variety of information on their labels. Besides the information specified in the answer to this problem, manufactures must identify themselves and the packager or distributor or the product, as well as nutrition details, including how much and what type of fat a product contains.
8. B. Under the Smokeless Tobacco Health Education Act of 1986, packages of smokeless tobacco products must include warnings about the health hazards associated with the use of smokeless tobacco similar to warnings contained on cigarette packages.

9. A. The Consumer Product Safety Commission (CPSC) has sufficiently broad authority to remove from store shelves any product that it believes is imminently hazardous and to require manufacturers to report on products already sold. Additionally, the CPSC can ban the make and sale of any product that the CPSC deems to be potentially hazardous. The CPSC also administers other product safety legislation.

10. D. The Truth-in-Lending Act includes rules covering credit cards. There is a provision that limits the liability of a cardholder to $50 per card for unauthorized charges made before the creditor is notified, and exempts a consumer from liability if the card was not properly issued. When a card is not solicited, it is not "properly issued," however, and thus a consumer, in whose name unauthorized charges are made, is not liable for those charges in any amount.

Issue Spotters

1. Yes. The FTC has issued rules to govern advertising techniques, including rules designed to prevent bait-and-switch advertising. Under the FTC guidelines, bait-and-switch advertising occurs if the seller refuses to show the advertised item, fails to have in stock a reasonable quantity of the item, fails to promise to deliver the advertised item within a reasonable time, or discourages employees from selling the item.

2. Under the Truth-in-Lending Act, a buyer who wishes to withhold payment for a faulty product purchased with a credit card must follow specific procedures to settle the dispute. The credit card issuer then must intervene and attempt to settle the dispute.

3. Under an extensive set of procedures established by the FDA, which administers the Federal, Food, Drug and Cosmetic Act, drugs must be shown to be effective as well as safe before they may be marketed to the public. In general, manufacturers are responsible for ensuring that the drugs they offer for sale are free of any substances that could injure consumers.

Chapter 18

True-False Questions

1. F. Common law doctrines that were applied against polluters centuries ago may be applicable today. These include nuisance and negligence doctrines.

2. T

3. F. There are different standards for different pollutants and for different polluters. There are even different standards for the same pollutants and polluters in different locations. The standards cover the amount of emissions, the technology to control them, the notice that must be given to the public, and the penalties that may be imposed for noncompliance.

4. F. The Toxic Substances Control Act of 1976 regulates substances that the production and labeling of substances of that potentially pose an imminent hazard or an unreasonable risk of injury to health or the environment. The Comprehensive Environmental Response, Compensation, and Liability Act (CERCLA) of 1980 regulates the clean up of leaking hazardous waste disposal sites.

5. T

6. T

7. F. To penalize those for whom a violation is cost-effective, the EPA can obtain a penalty equal to a violator's economic benefits from noncompliance. Other penalties include criminal fines. Private citizens can also sue polluters. It is generally more economically beneficial for a business to comply with the Clean Air Act.

8. T

9. F. Under CERCLA, a party who transports waste to a hazardous waste site may be held liable for any and all of the cost to clean up the site. There is a variety of "potentially responsible parties" who may also be held liable, including the party who generated the waste, and current and past owners and operators of the site. A party assessed with these costs can bring a contribution action against the others, however, to recoup the amount of their proportion.

10. T

Fill-in Questions

federal; federal; environmental impact that an action will have; environment; an action might cause to the environment; and reasons

Multiple-Choice Questions

1. A. An environmental impact statement (EIS) must be prepared when a major federal action significantly affects the quality of the environment. An action that affects the quality of the environment is "major" if it involves a substantial commitment of resources and "federal" if a federal agency has the power to control it.

2. C. Under the 1990 amendments to the Clean Air Act, different standards apply to existing sources and major new sources. Major new sources must use the maximum achievable control technology (MACT) to reduce emissions from the combustion of fossil fuels. Other factories and businesses must reduce emissions of hazardous air pollutants with the best available technology.

3. D. Sport utility vehicles are now subject to the same standards for polluting emissions as automobiles. If new motor vehicles do not meet the emission standards of regulations issued under the Clean Air Act, the EPA can order a recall of the vehicles and a repair or replacement of pollution-control devices.

4. C. A polluter can be ordered to clean up the pollution or to pay for the clean-up costs, and other penalties may be imposed. For example, fines may be assessed and imprisonment ordered.
5. B. Under the Resource Conservation and Recovery Act, producers of hazardous waste must properly label and package waste to be transported. Under the Comprehensive Environmental Response, Compensation, and Liability Act, the party who generated the waste disposed of at a site can be held liable for clean-up costs.
6. B. Under the Resource Conservation and Recovery Act of 1976, the EPA monitors and controls the disposal of hazardous waste. Under the Comprehensive Environmental Response, Compensation, and Liability Act, the EPA regulates the clean up of hazardous waste sites when a release occurs.
7. B. An action that affects the quality of the environment is "major" if it involves a substantial commitment of resources. Minor landscaping does not qualify because it does not involve such a commitment. The landscaping in this problem is "federal," however, because a federal agency controls it, and any landscaping can affect the quality of the environment.
8. C. Under the 1990 amendments to the Clean Air Act, different standards apply to existing sources and major new sources. Major new sources must use the maximum achievable control technology to reduce emissions from the combustion of fossil fuels. Other factories and businesses must reduce emissions of hazardous air pollutants with the best available technology.
9. B. One of the goals of the Clean Water Act is to protect fish and wildlife. In part, this goal is met by protecting their habitats, such as swamps and other wetlands. Protecting these areas can also protect navigable waters into which wetlands drain and other surrounding resources. Before dredging and filling wetlands, a permit must be obtained from the Army Corps of Engineers.
10. B. Any potentially responsible party can be charged with the entire cost to clean up a hazardous waste disposal site. Potentially responsible parties include former owners and may, under certain circumstances, include a lender to the owner. Of course, a party held responsible for the entire cost may be able to recoup some of it in a contribution action against other potentially responsible parties.

Issue Spotters

1. The Comprehensive Environmental Response, Compensation, and Liability Act of 1980 regulates the clean-up of hazardous waste disposal sites. Any potentially responsible party can be charged with the entire cost to clean up a hazardous waste disposal site. Potentially responsible parties include the person who generated the waste (ChemCorp) the person who

transported the waste to the site (Central), the person who owned or operated the site at the time of the disposal (Intrastate Disposal), and the current owner or operator of the site (ABC). A party held responsible for the entire cost may be able to recoup some of it in a lawsuit against other potentially responsible parties.
2. Yes. On the ground that the hardships to be imposed on the polluter and on the community are greater than the hardships suffered by the residents, the court might deny an injunction—if the plant is the core of a local economy, for instance, the residents may be awarded only damages.
3. The Environmental Protection Agency (EPA) was established to administer most federal environmental policies and statutes. Although not identified in the text, other federal agencies with authority to regulate specific environmental matters include the U.S. Departments of the Interior, Defense, and Labor, the Food and Drug Administration, and the Nuclear Regulatory Commission.

Chapter 19

True-False Questions

1. T
2. F. The owner of a life estate has the same rights as a fee simple owner except that the value of the property must be kept intact for the holder of the future interest.
3. F. An easement merely allows a person to use land without taking anything from it, while a profit allows a person to take something from the land.
4. T
5. F. Under the Fifth Amendment to the U.S. Constitution, when taking private property, the government is required to pay the owner just compensation.
6. F. The government has the power to take private property, but the purposes for which such property may be taken must be *public*.
7. T
8. T
9. T
10. F. To be entitled to a variance, a landowner must show that a granting of the variance would *not* substantially alter the essential character of the zoned area.

Fill-in Questions

warranty; quitclaim

Multiple-Choice Questions

1. C. A *profit* is the right to go onto land in possession of another and take away some part of the land itself or some product of the land. In contrast, an easement is a right to make limited use of another person's land without taking anything from the property. A license is a revocable right to come onto another person's land.

2. A. What the local authorities have done is to have effectively confiscated the developer's property. In this developer's case, it does not matter that the surrounding undeveloped property was zoned for use as a nature preserve only. If the developer sues the county, the regulation will likely be held unconstitutional and void unless the county pays for its effective confiscation of the developer's land.

3. C. This situation meets all the requirements for acquiring property by adverse possession: the possession was (1) actual and exclusive; (2) open, visible, and notorious; (3) continuous and peaceful for the statutory period; and (4) hostile, against the whole world, including the original owner.

4. B. An easement is a right to make limited use of another's real property without taking anything from it. In this problem, it is an easement by necessity—the owner needs access to his property. The right to take something from the property is a profit. A revocable right to come onto the property is a license.

5. C. A general development plan provides information about growth in a community. This plan may be supplemented by specific area plans that indicate special requirements. Zoning ordinances relate to particular land uses and include building and use restrictions and requirements. Other sources of relevant local policy and law include growth-management ordinances.

6. C. As a parcel of land is developed, it needs such public services as streets and sewers. When the land is developed for residential use, new schools and other public facilities, such as parks, must often be built. To meet these needs, subdivision development typically takes shape in a process of give and take between a developer and local authorities. Sometimes, a developer is asked to dedicate land to public use, or to otherwise contribute to the cost of public facilities.

7. A. A lease that does not specify how long it is to last but does specify that rent is to be paid at certain intervals creates a periodic tenancy. The tenancy is automatically renewed for each rental period unless it has been properly terminated.

8. A. The federal government can take private property for public use (a "taking"), but it cannot do so, under the Fifth Amendment to the Constitution, without paying the property owner just compensation. In some cases, to obtain title, a condemnation proceeding is brought before the property is taken. In a separate proceeding, a court determines the property's fair value (usually market value) to be paid to the owner.

9. C. The rights that accompany ownership in fee simple include the right to sell the land or give it away, as well as the right to use the land for whatever

purpose the owner sees fit, subject, of course, to the law's limitations.

10. C. Warranty deeds include a number of promises, including a covenant of quiet enjoyment, which guarantees that the buyer will not be disturbed in his or her possession of the land by the seller or any third persons. If this covenant is breached, the buyer can recover from the seller the purchase price and any damages for the eviction.

Issue Spotters

1. Yes. An owner of a fee simple has the most rights possible—he or she can give the property away, sell it, transfer it by will, use it for almost any purpose, possess it to the exclusion of all the world, or as in this case, transfer possession for any period of time. The party to whom possession is transferred can also transfer his or her interest (usually only with the owner's permission) for any lesser period of time.

2. Probably not. A zoning ordinance is considered discriminatory if it affects one parcel of land in a way unlike surrounding parcels if there is no rational basis for the difference. The facts as stated in the problem do not indicate any basis for zoning this land differently.

3. One important ground, unrelated to a specific property owner, on which the zoning authorities could limit the issuance of this, and other, permits is to prevent population growth from racing ahead of the local community's ability to provide public services (water and sewer, trash removal, streets, schools, and so on).

Chapter 20

True-False Questions

1. F. This is a vertical restraint.

2. F. This is a horizontal restraint.

3. T

4. F. Exclusive dealing contracts are those under which a seller forbids a buyer from purchasing products from the seller's competitors.

5. F. Price discrimination occurs when sellers charge competitive buyers different prices for identical goods.

6. F. This is a *vertical* merger. A horizontal merger is a merger between firms that compete with each other in the same market.

7. F. This is a *horizontal* merger. A vertical merger occurs when a company at one stage of production acquires another company at a higher or lower stage in the chain of production and distribution.

8. T

9. T

10. T

Fill-in Questions

A restraint of trade; Monopoly power; monopoly power

Multiple-Choice Questions

1. A. An agreement to set prices in the manner described in the problem is a price-fixing agreement, which is a restraint of trade and a *per se* violation of Section 1 of the Sherman Act.
2. C. Conduct that is blatantly anticompetitive is a *per se* violation of antitrust law. Such conduct typically includes price-fixing agreements, group boycotts, and horizontal market divisions.
3. D. Territorial or customer restrictions, like the restriction described in the problem, are judged under a rule of reason. The rule of reason involves a weighing of competitive benefits against anticompetitive harms. Here, the manufacturer's restriction on its dealers would likely be considered lawful because, although it reduces *intra*brand competition, it promotes *inter*brand competition.
4. D. In applying the rule of reason, courts consider the purpose of the conduct, the effect of the conduct on trade, the power of the parties to accomplish what they intend, and in some cases, whether there are less restrictive alternatives to achieve the same goals.
5. C. The elements of the offense of monopolization include monopoly power and its willful acquisition. Market domination that results from legitimate competitive behavior (such as foresight, innovation, skill, and good management) is not a violation.
6. D. Price discrimination occurs when a seller charges different buyers different prices for identical goods. To violate the Clayton Act, among other requirements, the effect of the price discrimination must be to substantially lessen competition or otherwise create a competitive injury.
7. A. Conduct subject to the rule of reason is unlawful if its anticompetitive harms outweigh its competitive benefits. Conduct typically subject to a rule of reason analysis includes trade association activities, joint ventures, territorial or customer restrictions, refusal to deal, price discrimination, and exclusive-dealing contracts.
8. B. Similar exemptions from the antitrust laws include cooperative research among small business firms, cooperation among U.S. exporters to compete with comparable foreign associations, and joint efforts by businesspersons to obtain legislative, judicial, or executive action.
9. D. The U.S. Department of Justice can prosecute violations of the Sherman Act as criminal or civil violations, but can enforce the Clayton Act only through civil proceedings. The Federal Trade Commission can also enforce the Clayton Act (and has sole authority to enforce the Federal Trade Commission Act). A private party can sue under the Clayton Act if he or she is injured by a violation of *any* antitrust law.
10. A. An important consideration in determining whether a merger substantially lessens competition and hence violates the Clayton Act is market concentration (the market chares among the firms in the market). If a merger creates an entity with more than a small percentage market share, it is presumed illegal.

Issue Spotters

1. A unilateral refusal to deal violates antitrust law if it involves offenses proscribed under Section 2 of the Sherman Act. This occurs if the firm refusing to deal has, or is likely to acquire, monopoly power and the refusal is likely to have an anticompetitive effect on a particular market.
2. Size alone does not determine whether a firm is a monopoly—size in relation to the market is what matters. A small store in a small, isolated town is a monopolist if it is the only store serving that market. Monopoly involves the power to affect prices and output. If a firm has sufficient market power to control prices and exclude competition, that firm has monopoly power. Monopoly power in itself is not a violation of Section 2 of the Sherman Act. The offense also requires an intent to acquire or maintain that power through anticompetitive means.
3. This agreement is a tying arrangement. The legality of a tying arrangement depends the purpose of the agreement, the agreement's likely effect on competition in the relevant markets (the market for the tying product and the market for the tied product), and other factors. Tying arrangements for commodities are subject to Section 3 of the Clayton Act. Tying arrangements for services can be agreements in restraint of trade in violation of Section 1 of the Sherman Act.

Chapter 21

True-False Questions

1. T
2. T
3. T
4. T
5. F. Rule 506, issued under the Securities Act of 1933, provides an exemption for these offerings, if certain other requirements are met. This is an important exemption, applying to private offerings to a limited number of sophisticated investors.
6. T
7. T
8. F. *Scienter* is not a requirement for liability under Section 16(b) of the Securities Exchange Act of 1934,

but it is required for liability under Section 10(b) and under Rule 10b-5.

9.   F. Anyone who receives inside information as a result of an insider's breach of his or her fiduciary duty can be liable under Rule 10b-5, which applies in virtually all cases involving the trading of securities. The key to liability is whether the otherwise undisclosed information is *material*.

10.   F. Most securities can be resold without registration. Also, under Rule 144 and 144A ("Safe harbor" provisions), there are specific exemptions for securities that might otherwise require registration with the SEC.

Fill-in Questions

prosecution; triple; ten; may

Multiple-Choice Questions

1.   A. This purchase and sale is a violation of Section 16(b) of the Securities Exchange Act of 1934. When a purchase and sale is within a six-month period, as in this problem, the corporation can recover all of the profit. Proof of *scienter* is not required.

2.   A. A corporate officer is a traditional inside trader. The outsider in this problem is a tippee who is liable because the tippee knew of the officer's misconduct. Liability here is based on the fact that the information was not public. Liability might be avoided if those who know the information wait for a reasonable time after its public disclosure before trading their stock.

3.   D. The amount of this offering is too high to exempt it from the registration requirements except possibly under Rule 506 or Section 4(6). This issuer advertised the offering, however, and Rule 506 prohibits general solicitation. Thus, without filing a registration statement, the issuer could not legally solicit *any* investors (whatever it may have believed about the unaccredited investors). This offering does not qualify under Section 4(6), because unaccredited investors participated.

4.   A. Because of the low amount of the issue, it qualifies as an exemption from registration under Rule 504. No specific disclosure document is required, and there is no prohibition on solicitation. If the amount had been higher than $1 million but lower than $5 million, this offer might have qualified for an exemption under Regulation A, which requires notice to the SEC and an offering circular for investors.

5.   D. This issue might qualify under Rule 505 or Section 4(6), except that again, the issuer advertised the offering, which it cannot do and remain exempt from registration. In other words, the amount of this offering disqualified the issuer from advertising it without filing a registration statement.

6.   B. A registration statement must supply enough information so that an unsophisticated investor can evaluate the financial risk involved. The statement must explain how the registrant intends to use the proceeds from the sale of the issue. Also, besides the description of management, there must be a disclosure of any of their material transactions with the firm. A certified financial statement must be included.

7.   D. Under the Securities Act of 1933, a security exists when a person invests in a common enterprise with the reasonable expectation of profits derived primarily or substantially from the managerial or entrepreneurial efforts of others (not from the investor's own efforts).

8.   B. Under the Securities Exchange Act of 1934, the Securities and Exchange Commission all of the other duties and more, including regulating national securities trading, supervising mutual funds, and recommending sanctions in cases involving violations of securities laws.

9.   A. Of course, the offering must be registered with the SEC before it can be sold, and this requires a registration statement. Investors must be given a prospectus that describes the security, the issuing corporation, and the risk of the security. A tombstone ad tells an investor how and where to obtain the prospectus.

10.   A. Most resales are exempt from registration if they are undertaken by persons other than issuers or underwriters. Resales of restricted securities acquired under Rule 504a, Rule 505, Rule 506, or Section 4(6) may trigger registration requirements, but the original sale in this problem came under Rule 504.

Issue Spotters

1.   The average investor is not concerned with minor inaccuracies but with facts that if disclosed would tend to deter or encourage him or her to buy or sell the securities. This would include facts that have an important bearing on the condition of the issuer and its business (liabilities, loans to officers and directors, customer delinquencies, and pending lawsuits).

2.   No. The Securities Exchange Act of 1934 extends liability to officers and directors in their personal transactions for taking advantage of inside information when they know it is unavailable to the persons with whom they are dealing.

3.   Yes. All states have their own corporate securities laws ("blue sky" laws).

Cumulative Hypothetical Problem for Unit Five—Including Chapters 16–21

1.   D. Advertising that consists of vague generalities is not illegal. This is also true of advertising that includes obvious exaggerations. Advertising that may lead to sanctions by the Federal Trade Commission is

deceptive advertising: advertising that misleads consumers.

2. A. An administrative agency has a number of options to determine whether a manufacturer is complying with the agency's rules, but the agency may not use its powers arbitrarily or capriciously or abuse its discretion. The options that an agency may choose include those in the other answer choices, as well as obtaining a search warrant to search the premises for a specific item and return it to the agency.

3. D. Under the Comprehensive Environmental Response, Compensation, and Liability Act of 1980, any "potentially responsible party" can be charged with the entire cost to clean up a hazardous waste disposal site. Potentially responsible parties include the party who generates the waste, the party who transports the waste to the site, and the party who owns or operates the site.

4. C. It is price discrimination when a seller charges different buyers different prices for identical products. Price discrimination is a violation of the Clayton Act if the effect of the pricing is to substantially lessen competition or otherwise create a competitive injury.

5. D. Other information that must be included in a registration statement, under the Securities Act of 1933, includes a description of the issuer's business, a description of the security, the capital structure of the business, the underwriting arrangements, and the certified financial statements.

Chapter 22

True-False Questions

1. F. According to the principle of comity, a nation will give effect to the laws of another nation if those laws are consistent with the law and public policy of the accommodating nation.

2. F. The act of state doctrine tends to immunize foreign nations from the jurisdiction of U.S. courts—that is, foreign nations are often exempt from U.S. jurisdiction under this doctrine.

3. F. As with the act of state doctrine, the doctrine of sovereign immunity tends to immunize foreign nations from the jurisdiction of U.S. courts.

4. F. The Foreign Sovereign Immunities Act sets forth the major exceptions to the immunity of foreign nations to U.S. jurisdiction.

5. T

6. T

7. F. U.S. courts can exercise jurisdiction over a foreign entity under U.S. antitrust laws when a violation has a substantial effect on U.S. commerce or is a *per se* violation of those laws.

8. T

9. T

10. T

Fill-in Questions

An expropriation; A confiscation; an expropriation; a confiscation

Multiple-Choice Questions

1. A. Of course, a U.S. firm is subject to the jurisdiction of a U.S. court. For a U.S. court to hear a case against a foreign entity under U.S. antitrust laws, the entity's alleged violation of the law must have a substantial effect on U.S. commerce (or be a *per se* violation). In other words, foreign and domestic firms may be sued for violations of U.S. antitrust laws.

2. C. The Foreign Corrupt Practices Act (FCPA) prohibits any U.S. firm from bribing foreign officials to influence official acts. Congress enacted the FCPA in 1977.

3. C. Under certain conditions, the doctrine of sovereign immunity prohibits U.S. courts from exercising jurisdiction over foreign nations. Under the Foreign Sovereign Immunities Act, a foreign state is not immune when the action is based on a commercial activity carried on in the United States by the foreign state.

4. A. Under the act of state doctrine, the judicial branch of one country will not examine the validity of public acts committed by a recognized foreign government within its own territory. The awarding of a government contract under the circumstances described in the problem meets this criterion.

5. C. U.S. courts give effect to the judicial decrees of another country under the principle of comity, if those decrees are consistent with the laws and public policies of the United States.

6. B. The Civil Rights Act of 1964 and other U.S. discrimination laws apply to U.S. firms employing U.S. citizens outside (and inside) the United States. U.S. employers everywhere must abide by U.S. employment discrimination laws, so long as those laws do not violate the laws of the countries in which their workplaces are located. But those laws protect only U.S. citizens, not citizens of foreign countries.

7. A. A choice-of-forum, or forum selection, clause can specify the forum in which the parties to a contract want their disputes to be heard and resolved. Choice-of-language clauses are often used in international contracts to declare an official language for the interpretation of a contract in the event of disagreement. Such a clause may also provide for translations in certain languages. A *force majeure* clause stipulates that acts of God and other events outside the parties' control may excuse liability for nonperformance under the contract. An arbitration clause can require the submission of a dispute to arbitration, according to certain procedures, before a suit is filed in a court.

8. A. A distribution agreement in this context is a contract between a seller and a distributor to distribute the seller's products in the distributor's country.

Such an agreement sets out the terms and conditions of the distributorship—price, currency of payment, availability of supplies, method of payment, and so on.

9. C. The U.S. Congress cannot tax exports, but it may establish export quotas. In particular, under the Export Administration Act of 1979, restrictions can be imposed on the export of technologically advanced products.

10. D. Unlike exports, imports can be taxed. A tax on an import is a tariff (generally set as a percent of the value). Imports can also be subject to quotas, which limit how much can be imported.

Issue Spotters

1. Under the principle of comity, a U.S court would defer and give effect to foreign laws and judicial decrees that are consistent with U.S. law and public policy.

2. A U.S. firm (or any domestic firm) can license its formula, product, or process to a foreign concern to avoid its theft. The foreign firm obtains the right to make and market the product according to the formula (or the right to use the process) and agrees to keep the necessary information secret and to pay royalties to the licensor.

3. The practice described in this problem is known as dumping. Seen as an unfair international trade practice, dumping is the sale of imported goods at "less than fair value." Based on the price of those goods in the exporting country, an extra tariff can be imposed on the imports. This is known as an antidumping duty.

Cumulative Hypothetical Problem for Unit Six—Including Chapter 22

1. D. Licensing is one party allowing another's use copyrighted, patented, or trademarked intellectual property or trade secrets. Licensing typically involves the payment of royalties and a promise not to reveal confidential information obtained as a result of the arrangement.

2. C. Under the principle of comity, one nation defers and gives effect to the laws and judicial decrees of another nation. The application of this principle is founded on courtesy and respect. The principle is most likely to be applied as long as the laws and decrees of the imposing nation are consistent with the law and public policy of the accommodating nation.

3. A. Generally observed legal principles of international law are violated by a confiscation. Expropriation, which is a taking of property for a proper public purpose and with the payment of just compensation, does not violate these principles.

4. A. The act of state doctrine is a judicially created doctrine that provides the judicial branch of one country will not examine the validity of public acts committed by a recognized foreign government within its own territory. Under this doctrine, and the Foreign Sovereign Immunities Act, there is little a firm can do when a foreign country confiscates (or expropriates) its property. The best protection might be to buy insurance to cover the risk.

5. B. The Foreign Sovereign Immunities Act governs the circumstances in which an action may be brought in the United States against a foreign nation. A foreign state is not immune from the jurisdiction of U.S. courts if the state has waived its immunity or if the action is based on a commercial activity carried on in the United States by the foreign state. That is not the situation in this question, however.

Notes

Notes

Notes

Notes

Notes

Notes

Notes

Notes

Notes

Notes

Notes

Notes

Notes

Notes